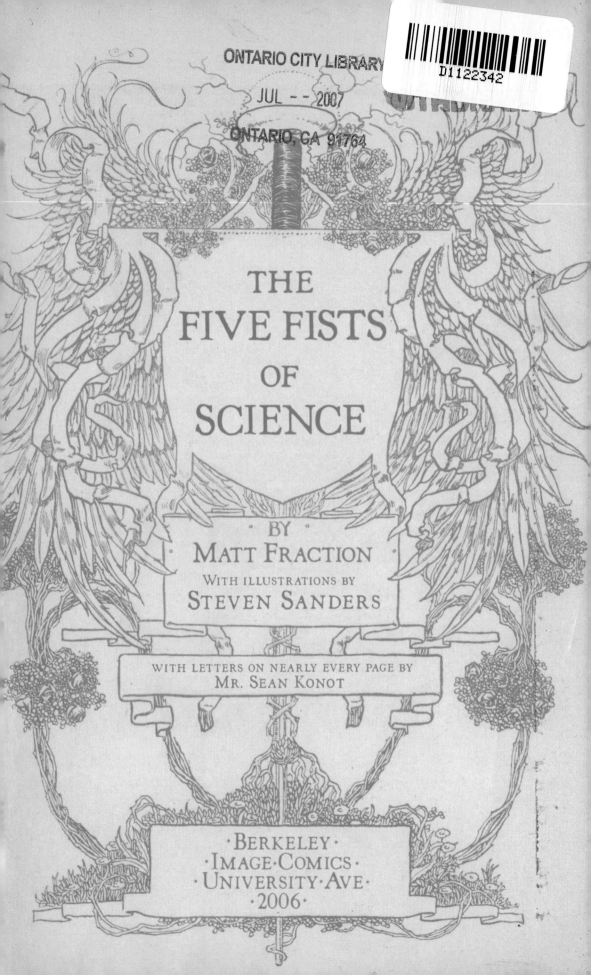

# THE
# FIVE FISTS
## OF
## SCIENCE

· BY ·
### MATT FRACTION

WITH ILLUSTRATIONS BY
### STEVEN SANDERS

WITH LETTERS ON NEARLY EVERY PAGE BY
### MR. SEAN KONOT

· BERKELEY ·
· IMAGE · COMICS ·
· UNIVERSITY · AVE ·
· 2006 ·

# ACKNOWLEDGEMENTS

THE AUTHORS WOULD LIKE TO THANK their wives, Dawn and Kelly Sue, and their parents, Mark and Marjeanne and Dennis and Karen, and their inspirations, Tesla and Twain.

THE AUTHORS WISH TO GIVE SHOUTS OUT to Maureen McTigue and Courtney Buckalew-Kramer for their editorial input and to give mad props to Harris Miller, Esq., for his staunch support of the work above and beyond.

THE AUTHORS WISH TO DEDICATE THE WORK to themselves. Because they are totally in love with one another.

\m/ RAWK! \m/

COVER DESIGN BY MAIKO KUZUNISHI @ DECOYLAB
WWW.DECOYLAB.COM

MATT FRACTION       STEVEN SANDERS
WWW.MATTFRACTION.COM       WWW.STUDIOSPUTNIK.COM

GET **THE FIVE FISTS OF SCIENCE**
FOR YOUR PHONE.
VISIT WWW.GOCOMICS.COM

## IMAGE COMICS, INC.

Erik Larsen · *Publisher*
Todd McFarlane · *President*
Marc Silvestri · *CEO*
Jim Valentino · *Vice-President*

Eric Stephenson · *Executive Director*
Mia MacHatton · *Accounts Manager*
Jim Demonakos · *PR & Marketing*
Traci Hui · *Administrative Assistant*
Laurenn McCubbin · *Designer*
Allen Hui · *Production Manager*
Joe Keatinge · *Traffic Manager*
Jonathan Chan · *Production Artist*
Drew Gill · *Production Artist*

WWW.IMAGECOMICS.COM

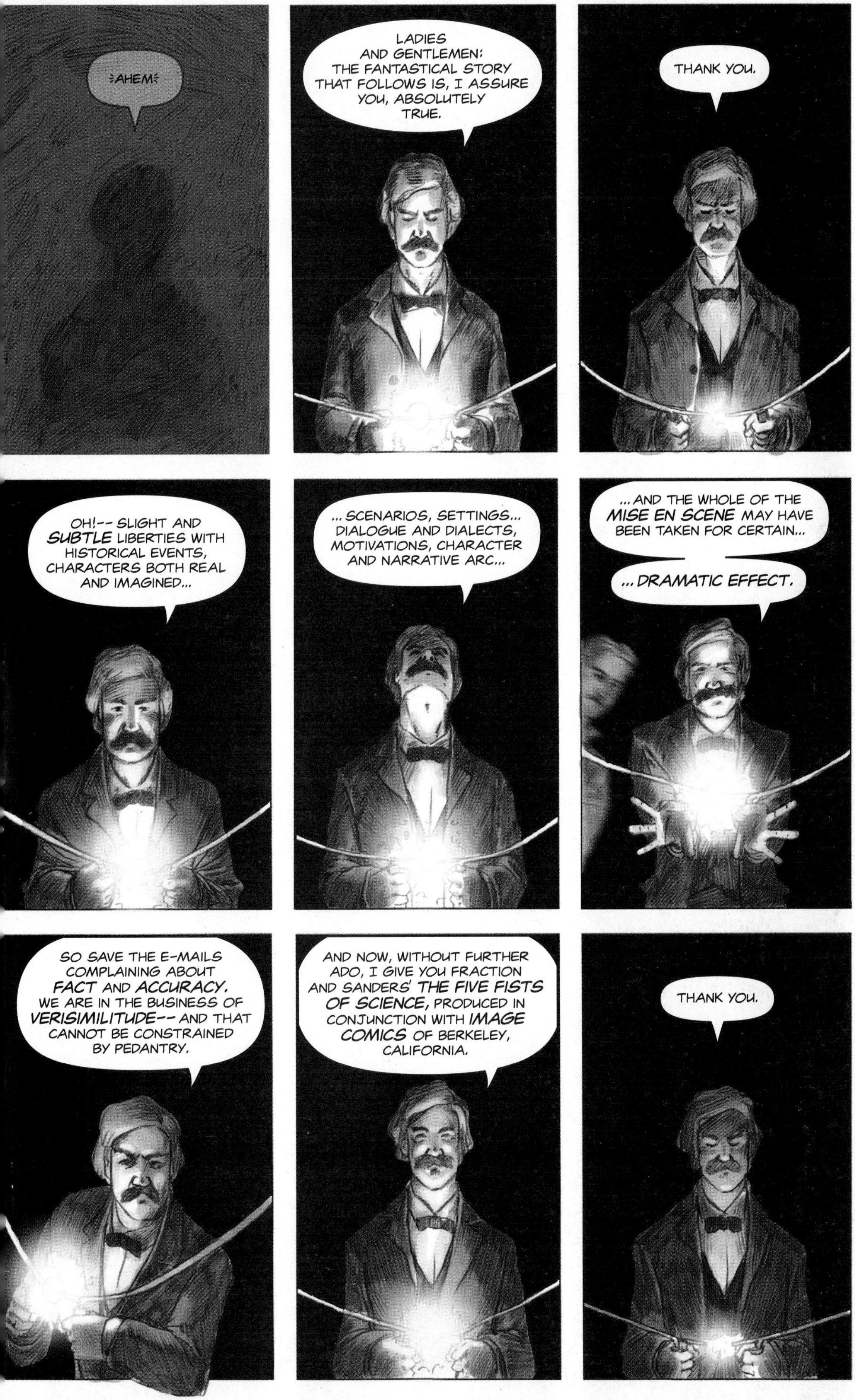

≷AHEM≶
LADIES AND GENTLEMEN: THE FANTASTICAL STORY THAT FOLLOWS IS, I ASSURE YOU, ABSOLUTELY TRUE.
THANK YOU.
OH!-- SLIGHT AND SUBTLE LIBERTIES WITH HISTORICAL EVENTS, CHARACTERS BOTH REAL AND IMAGINED...
... SCENARIOS, SETTINGS... DIALOGUE AND DIALECTS, MOTIVATIONS, CHARACTER AND NARRATIVE ARC...
... AND THE WHOLE OF THE MISE EN SCENE MAY HAVE BEEN TAKEN FOR CERTAIN...
... DRAMATIC EFFECT.
SO SAVE THE E-MAILS COMPLAINING ABOUT FACT AND ACCURACY. WE ARE IN THE BUSINESS OF VERISIMILITUDE-- AND THAT CANNOT BE CONSTRAINED BY PEDANTRY.
AND NOW, WITHOUT FURTHER ADO, I GIVE YOU FRACTION AND SANDERS' THE FIVE FISTS OF SCIENCE, PRODUCED IN CONJUNCTION WITH IMAGE COMICS OF BERKELEY, CALIFORNIA.
THANK YOU.

...Peace by compulsion. That seems a better idea than the other. Peace by persuasion has a pleasant sound, but I think we should not be able to work it. We should have to tame the human race first, and history seems to show that that cannot be done. Can't we reduce the armaments little by little · on a pro rata basis · by concert of the powers? Can't we get four great powers to agree to reduce their strength 10 percent a year and thrash the others into doing likewise? For, of course, we cannot expect all of the powers to be in their right minds at one time. It has been tried. We are not going to try to get all of them to go into the scheme peaceably, are we? In that case I must withdraw my influence; because, for business reasons, I must preserve the outward signs of sanity. Four is enough if they can be securely harnessed together. They can compel peace, and peace without compulsion would be against nature and not operative.

...Perpetual peace we cannot have on any terms, I suppose; but I hope we can gradually reduce the war strength of Europe till we get it down to where it ought to be... Then we can have all the peace that is worth while, and when we want a war anybody can afford it.

Mark Twain
January 9, 1899

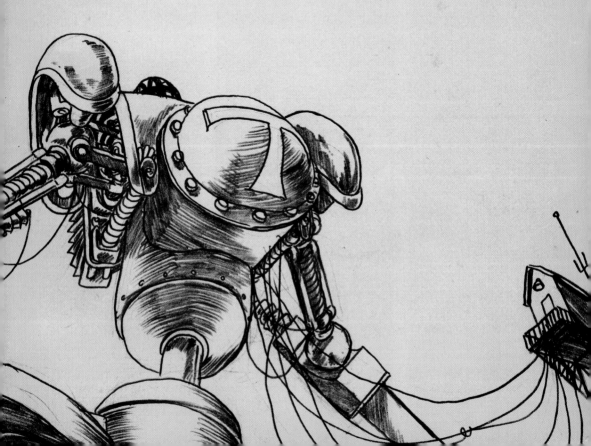

...(T)HE ART I HAVE EVOLVED DOES NOT CONTEMPLATE MERELY THE CHANGE OF DIRECTION OF A MOVING VESSEL; IT AFFORDS MEANS OF ABSOLUTELY CONTROLLING, IN EVERY RESPECT, ALL THE INNUMERABLE TRANSLATORY (SIC) MOVEMENTS, AS WELL AS THE OPERATIONS OF ALL THE INTERNAL ORGANS, NO MATTER HOW MANY, OF AN INDIVIDUALIZED AUTOMATON. CRITICISMS TO THE EFFECT THAT THE CONTROL OF THE AUTOMATON COULD BE INTER-FERED WITH WERE MADE BY PEOPLE WHO DO NOT EVEN DREAM OF THE WONDERFUL RESULTS WHICH CAN BE ACCOMPLISHED BY USE OF ELECTRICAL VIBRATIONS. THE WORLD MOVES SLOWLY, AND NEW TRUTHS ARE DIFFICULT TO SEE. CERTAINLY, BY THE USE OF THIS PRINCIPLE, AN ARM FOR ATTACK AS WELL AS DEFENSE MAY BE PRO-VIDED, OF A DESTRUCTIVENESS ALL THE GREATER AS THE PRIN-CIPLE IS APPLICABLE TO SUBMARINE AND AERIAL VESSELS. THERE IS VIRTUALLY NO RESTRICTION AS TO THE AMOUNT OF EXPLOSIVE IT CAN CARRY, OR AS TO THE DISTANCE AT WHICH IT CAN STRIKE, AND FAILURE IS ALMOST IMPOSSIBLE. BUT THE FORCE OF THIS NEW PRINCIPLE DOES NOT WHOLLY RESIDE IN ITS DESTRUCTIVE-NESS. ITS ADVENT INTRODUCES INTO WARFARE AN ELEMENT WHICH NEVER EXISTED BEFORE—A FIGHTING-MACHINE WITHOUT MEN AS A MEANS OF ATTACK AND DEFENSE. THE CONTINUOUS DE-VELOPMENT IN THIS DIRECTION MUST ULTIMATELY MAKE WAR A MERE CONTEST OF MACHINES WITHOUT MEN AND WITHOUT LOSS OF LIFE-- A CONDITION WHICH WOULD HAVE BEEN IMPOSSIBLE WITHOUT THIS NEW DEPARTURE, AND WHICH, IN MY OPINION, MUST BE REACHED AS PRELIMINARY TO PERMANENT PEACE. THE FUTURE WILL EITHER BEAR OUT OR DISPROVE THESE VIEWS. MY IDEAS ON THIS SUBJECT HAVE BEEN PUT FORTH WITH DEEP CON-VICTION, BUT IN A HUMBLE SPIRIT.

THE ESTABLISHMENT OF PERMANENT PEACEFUL RELATIONS BE-TWEEN NATIONS WOULD MOST EFFECTIVELY REDUCE THE FORCE RETARDING THE HUMAN MASS, AND WOULD BE THE BEST SOLU-TION OF THIS GREAT HUMAN PROBLEM. BUT WILL THE DREAM OF UNIVERSAL PEACE EVER BE REALIZED? LET US HOPE THAT IT WILL. WHEN ALL DARKNESS SHALL BE DISSIPATED BY THE LIGHT OF SCI-ENCE, WHEN ALL NATIONS SHALL BE MERGED INTO ONE, AND PA-TRIOTISM SHALL BE IDENTICAL WITH RELIGION, WHEN THERE SHALL BE ONE LANGUAGE, ONE COUNTRY, ONE END, THEN THE DREAM WILL HAVE BECOME REALITY.

FROM "THE PROBLEM OF INCREASING HUMAN ENERGY," BY NIKOLA TESLA

CENTURY ILLUSTRATED MAGAZINE, JANUARY, 1900.

# OUR CHARACTERS

MARK TWAIN (1835 - 1910): BORN DURING THE APPEARANCE OF HALLEY'S COMET AS SAMUEL LANGHORNE CLEMENS IN FLORIDA, MISSOURI, TWAIN WENT WEST TIN-PANNING FOR GOLD AND EVENTUALLY ENDED UP A WRITER IN SAN FRANCISCO. HE WROTE THE INNOCENTS ABROAD, THE ADVENTURES OF TOM SAWYER, AND THE BOOK HEMINGWAY SAID ALL AMERICAN LITERATURE CAME FROM, THE ADVENTURES OF HUCKLEBERRY FINN. TRULY THE FIRST AMERICAN CELEBRITY, TWAIN WINED AND DINED WITH EVERYONE WHO WAS ANYONE-- AND COUNTED AMONGST HIS FANS THE BRILLIANT YOUNG INVENTOR NIKOLA TESLA. BANKRUPTED BY DODGY INVESTMENTS, PLAGUED BY BAD BUSINESS DECISIONS, AND MOURNING THE DEATH OF HIS DAUGHTER, TWAIN AND HIS FAMILY LEFT FOR EUROPE IN 1898 UNDER "FINANCIAL EXILE." HE BECAME INVOLVED WITH THE ARMISTICE MOVEMENT WHILE IN VIENNA, WHERE HE WAS KNOWN AS "OUR FAMOUS GUEST."

NIKOLA TESLA (1856 - 1943): A SERBIAN SCIENTIST AND INVENTOR, TESLA INVENTED ALTERNATING CURRENT, THE SPARK PLUG, AND THE FIRST RADIO TRANSMITTER-- A FEAT THAT WOULD ONLY BE RECOGNIZED POSTHUMOUSLY BY THE SUPREME COURT. DEATHLY ILL IN HIS YOUTH, TESLA CLAIMED IT WAS READING THE WORKS OF MARK TWAIN (AND LAUGHING) THAT SAVED HIS LIFE. THOMAS EDISON HIRED TESLA AND LATER DEFRAUDED HIM-- SETTING THE STAGE FOR PERSONAL ANIMOSITY AND A "WAR OF THE CURRENTS" BETWEEN TESLA'S ALTERNATING CURRENT AND EDISON'S DIRECT CURRENT. TESLA'S FORTUNES ROSE AND FELL WILDLY THROUGHOUT HIS LIFE, BUT IN 1899, HE WAS LIVING IN NEW YORK CITY, WORKING IN HIS LAB AT 46-48 HOUSTON STREET, AND WAS THE TOAST OF MANHATTAN NIGHTLIFE. WE HAVE MADE UP NONE OF THE MAN'S PERSONAL QUIRKS, PHOBIAS, OR FOIBLES, EXCEPT FOR THE DRESSING UP AND FIGHTING CRIME BIT.

BERTHA SOPHIE FELICITAS FREIFRAU VON SUTTNER (BARONESS BERTHA VON SUTTNER) (1843 - 1914): AN AUSTRIAN WRITER DEEPLY INVOLVED IN THE ARMISTICE MOVEMENT STARTING WITH THE PUBLICATION OF HER NOVEL LAY DOWN YOUR ARMS! IN 1889. THAT SHE WAS ALFRED NOBEL'S HOUSEKEEPER AND SECRETARY ALLOWED HER A LONG CORRESPONDENCE WITH NOBEL; IT'S BELIEVED THAT THE NOTION OF A NOBEL "PEACE PRIZE" WAS, IN FACT, HERS-- AND SHE WON IT IN 1905. IN REAL LIFE, SHE WAS MARRIED, SECRETLY AT FIRST, TO AUTHOR AND ENGINEER BARON ARTHUR GUNDACCAR VON SUTTNER, BUT THIS IS A COMIC BOOK SO WE DON'T HAVE TO CONCERN OURSELVES WITH SUCH DETAILS. WE HAVE TAKEN GREAT LIBERTIES WITH THE BARONESS' AGE AND APPEARANCE WITHIN OUR PAGES AND FOR THIS WE SHOULD PROBABLY APOLOGIZE.

TIMOTHY BOONE (1884 - 1975): WHOLLY FICTIONAL. WHOOP-DEE-DO, WHOOP-DEE-DO.

# OUR CHARACTERS

JOHN PIERPONT MORGAN (1837 - 1913): A BANKER AND FINAN-
CIER THAT, IN 1895, FOUNDED J.P. MORGAN & CO. WITH ITS NUMER-
OUS INTERNATIONAL BANKING ASSOCIATIONS, J.P. MORGAN & CO.
BECAME STUNNINGLY POWERFUL- THEY FOUNDED THE FIRST BILLION
DOLLAR COMPANY, U.S. STEEL, AND FLOATED A $62 MILLION DOLLAR
LOAN TO THE U.S. TREASURY TO RAISE THE SURPLUS TO $100 MILLION.
A NOTED ART, BOOK, AND ANTIQUITIES COLLECTOR, MUCH OF
MORGAN'S COLLECTION TODAY POPULATES THE METROPOLITAN
MUSEUM OF ART. THESE TWO FACTS- THAT HE WAS RICHER THAN
GOD, AND HE WAS INTO ART, BOOKS, AND ANTIQUITIES, ALLOWED US TO
EXTRAPOLATE THE DEMENTED CHARACTER THAT APPEARS IN THESE
PAGES. IN REAL LIFE, MORGAN WAS NOT A BLACK MAGICIAN- HE WAS A
PROTESTANT.

THOMAS ALVA EDISON (1847 - 1931): "THE WIZARD OF MENLO
PARK" WAS A FAMED INVENTOR, INDUSTRIALIST, AND HOLDER OF 1,093
PATENTS. THOMAS EDISON STARTED THE EDISON ELECTRIC LIGHT
COMPANY WITH FINANCING PROVIDED BY J.P. MORGAN IN 1879. BY
1882, HIS PEARL STREET STATION UTILITY PROVIDED ELECTRICITY TO
THE 50-SOME CUSTOMERS LIVING AROUND THE STATION. HIS
MORGAN-BACKED DIRECT CURRENT SYSTEM WAS UNSAFE COMPARED
TO TESLA'S ALTERNATING CURRENT SYSTEM- YOU'D NEVER KNOW IT,
THOUGH, AS EDISON ENGAGED IN A DISINFORMATION CAMPAIGN
AGAINST AC THAT SAW THE INVENTION OF THE ELECTRIC CHAIR
AND THE ELECTROCUTION OF AN ELEPHANT NAMED "TOPSY"
AMONGST OTHER THINGS. EDISON FINANCED GUGLIELMO MARCONI'S
WORK DEVELOPING RADIO AND HOLDS THE PATENT FOR THE MOTION
PICTURE CAMERA. THE STORY GOES THAT HOLLYWOOD WAS STARTED
IN THE CALIFORNIA DESERT BECAUSE MOVIE PRODUCERS WANTED TO
BE AS FAR AWAY FROM EDISON AS POSSIBLE.

GUGLIELMO MARCONI (1874 - 1937): AN ENGINEER OF ITALIAN
DESCENT AND NOBEL PRIZE WINNER, MARCONI'S WIRELESS TELEGRA-
PHY SYSTEM- THE RADIO- WAS PRECEDED BY A SYSTEM FIRST THEORETI-
CALLY DEMONSTRATED BY NIKOLA TESLA THREE YEARS PRIOR. THIS WAS
EVENTUALLY RECOGNIZED BY THE SUPREME COURT IN 1943, EVEN
THOUGH MARCONI IS STILL KNOWN AS "THE FATHER OF RADIO." LATER
IN LIFE, HE AND TESLA MENDED FENCES, BUT STILL. MARCONI WAS A
MEMBER OF THE FASCIST GRAND COUNCIL IN ITALY- MUSSOLINI WAS
THE BEST MAN AT HIS WEDDING, EVEN. WE KNOW OF NO EVIDENCE
THAT PROVES HIM THE STRESS-EATER WE PRESENT IN THESE PAGES, BUT
IT WAS FUNNIER THAN MAKING HIM A FASCIST.

ANDREW CARNEGIE (1835 - 1919): A SCOT-
TISH BUSINESSMAN, FINANCIER, AND STEEL MAG-
NATE, CARNEGIE IS PROBABLY BEST KNOWN AS A
PHILANTHROPIST WHO GAVE AWAY ALMOST $400
MILLION DOLLARS BY THE TIME OF HIS DEATH. HE
WAS THE AUTHOR OF THE GOSPEL OF WEALTH, IN
WHICH HE ESPOUSED A PERSONAL PHILOSOPHY
THAT THE WEALTHY SHOULD HELP UPLIFT THEIR
FELLOW MAN. OUR RANCID CHARACTER ASSASSI-
NATION OF THIS MAN (AT LEAST BY ASSOCIATION) IS
PREDICATED SOLELY ON CARNEGIE SELLING HIS IN-
TERESTS IN CARNEGIE STEEL TO J.P. MORGAN IN
1901, PAVING THE WAY FOR THE INCEPTION OF U.S.
STEEL. REALLY, THOUGH, HE SEEMS TO HAVE BEEN
QUITE THE NICE GUY.

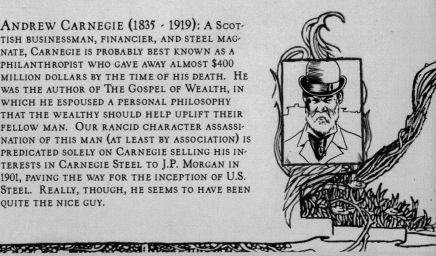

# INQUIRIES

CONCERNING

THE

# FIVE FISTS

OF

# SCIENCE

**EIGHTEENTH EDITION.**

LONDON:

JOHN MURRAY, ALBEMARLE STREET.

1899.

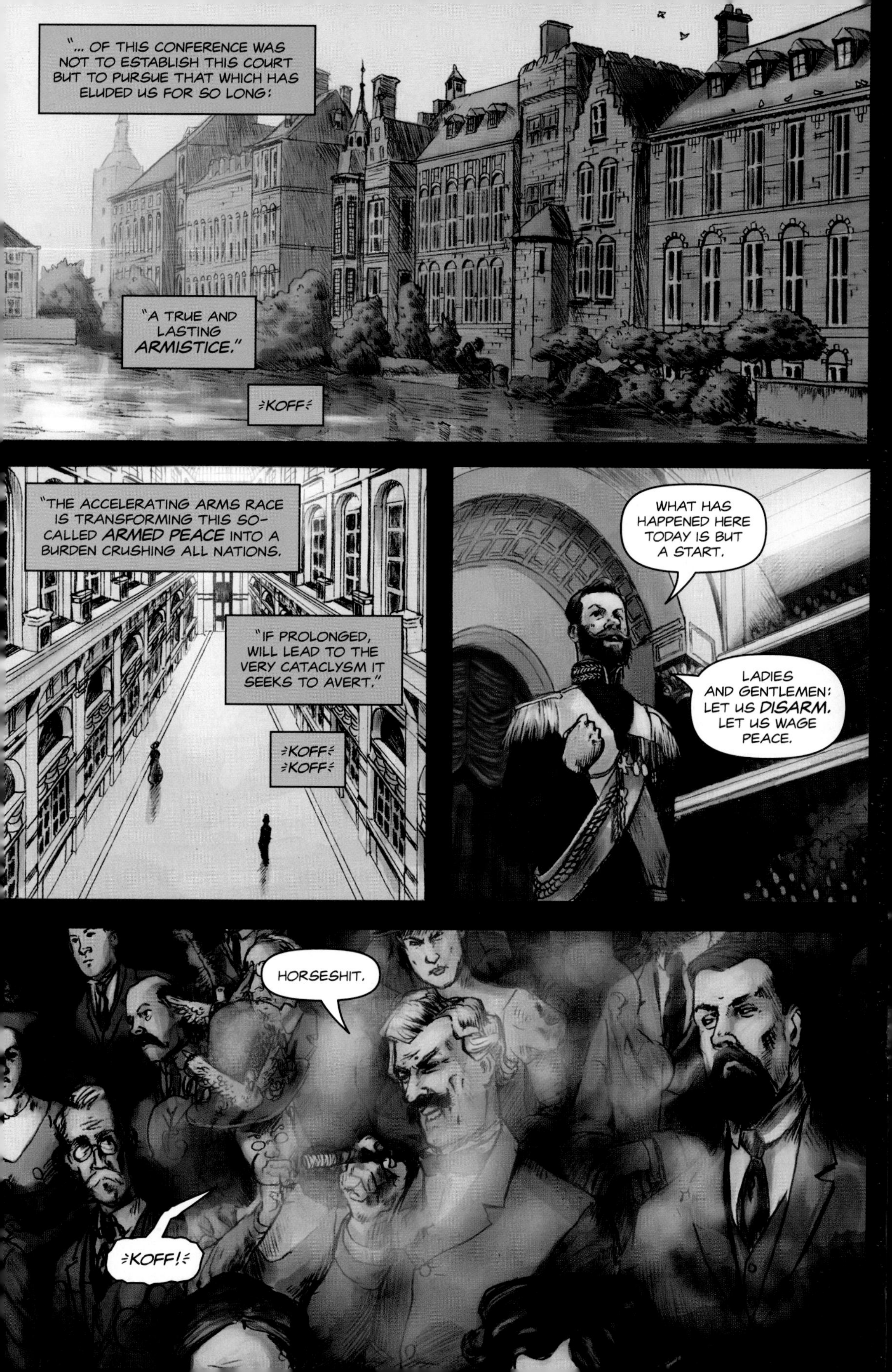
"... OF THIS CONFERENCE WAS NOT TO ESTABLISH THIS COURT BUT TO PURSUE THAT WHICH HAS ELUDED US FOR SO LONG:
"A TRUE AND LASTING ARMISTICE."
KOFF
"THE ACCELERATING ARMS RACE IS TRANSFORMING THIS SO-CALLED ARMED PEACE INTO A BURDEN CRUSHING ALL NATIONS.
"IF PROLONGED, WILL LEAD TO THE VERY CATACLYSM IT SEEKS TO AVERT."
KOFF KOFF
WHAT HAS HAPPENED HERE TODAY IS BUT A START.
LADIES AND GENTLEMEN: LET US DISARM. LET US WAGE PEACE.
HORSESHIT.
KOFF!

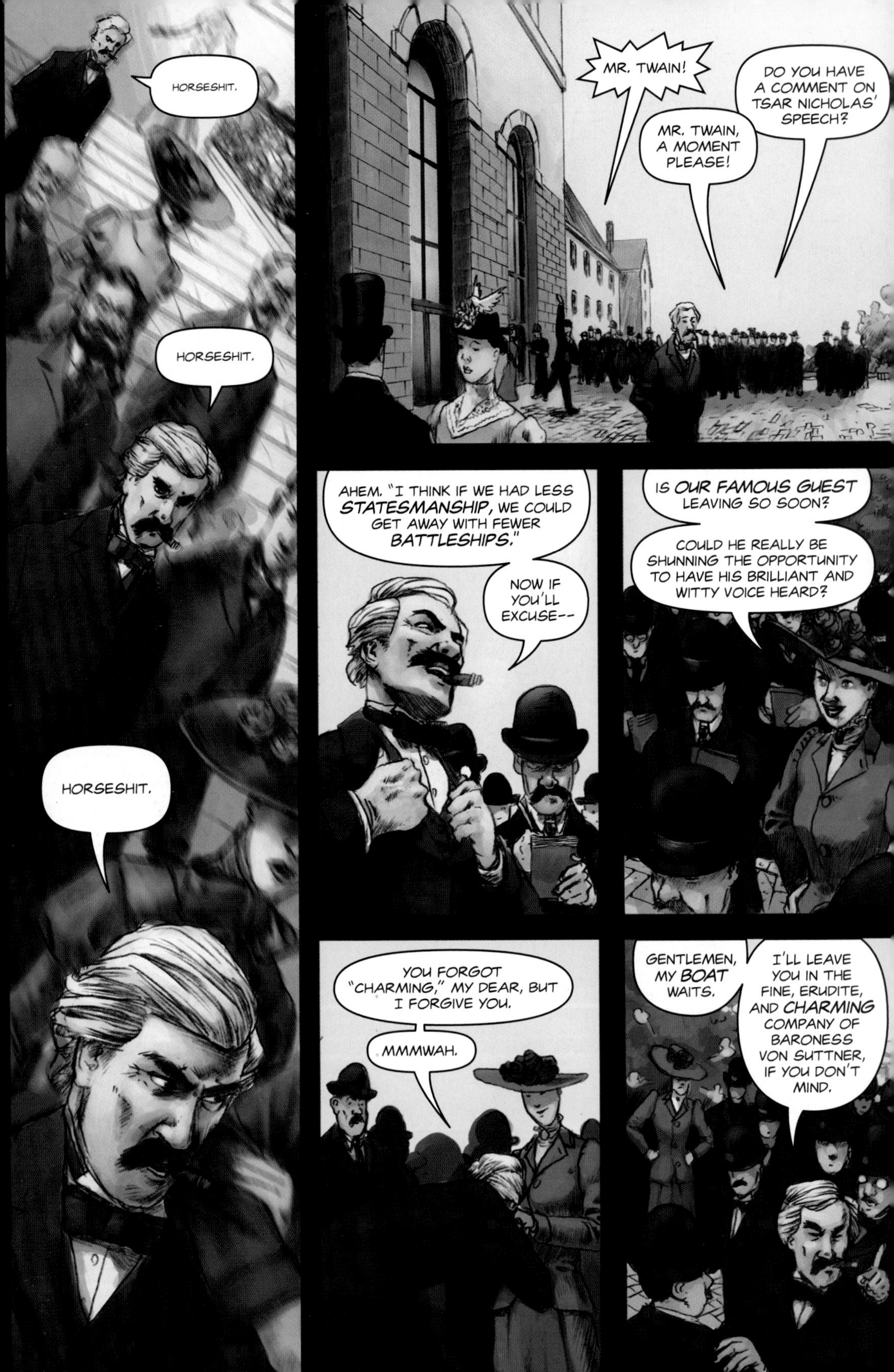
HORSESHIT.
HORSESHIT.
HORSESHIT.
MR. TWAIN!
DO YOU HAVE A COMMENT ON TSAR NICHOLAS' SPEECH?
MR. TWAIN, A MOMENT PLEASE!
AHEM. "I THINK IF WE HAD LESS STATESMANSHIP, WE COULD GET AWAY WITH FEWER BATTLESHIPS."
NOW IF YOU'LL EXCUSE--
IS OUR FAMOUS GUEST LEAVING SO SOON?
COULD HE REALLY BE SHUNNING THE OPPORTUNITY TO HAVE HIS BRILLIANT AND WITTY VOICE HEARD?
YOU FORGOT "CHARMING," MY DEAR, BUT I FORGIVE YOU.
MMMWAH.
GENTLEMEN, MY BOAT WAITS.
I'LL LEAVE YOU IN THE FINE, ERUDITE, AND CHARMING COMPANY OF BARONESS VON SUTTNER, IF YOU DON'T MIND.

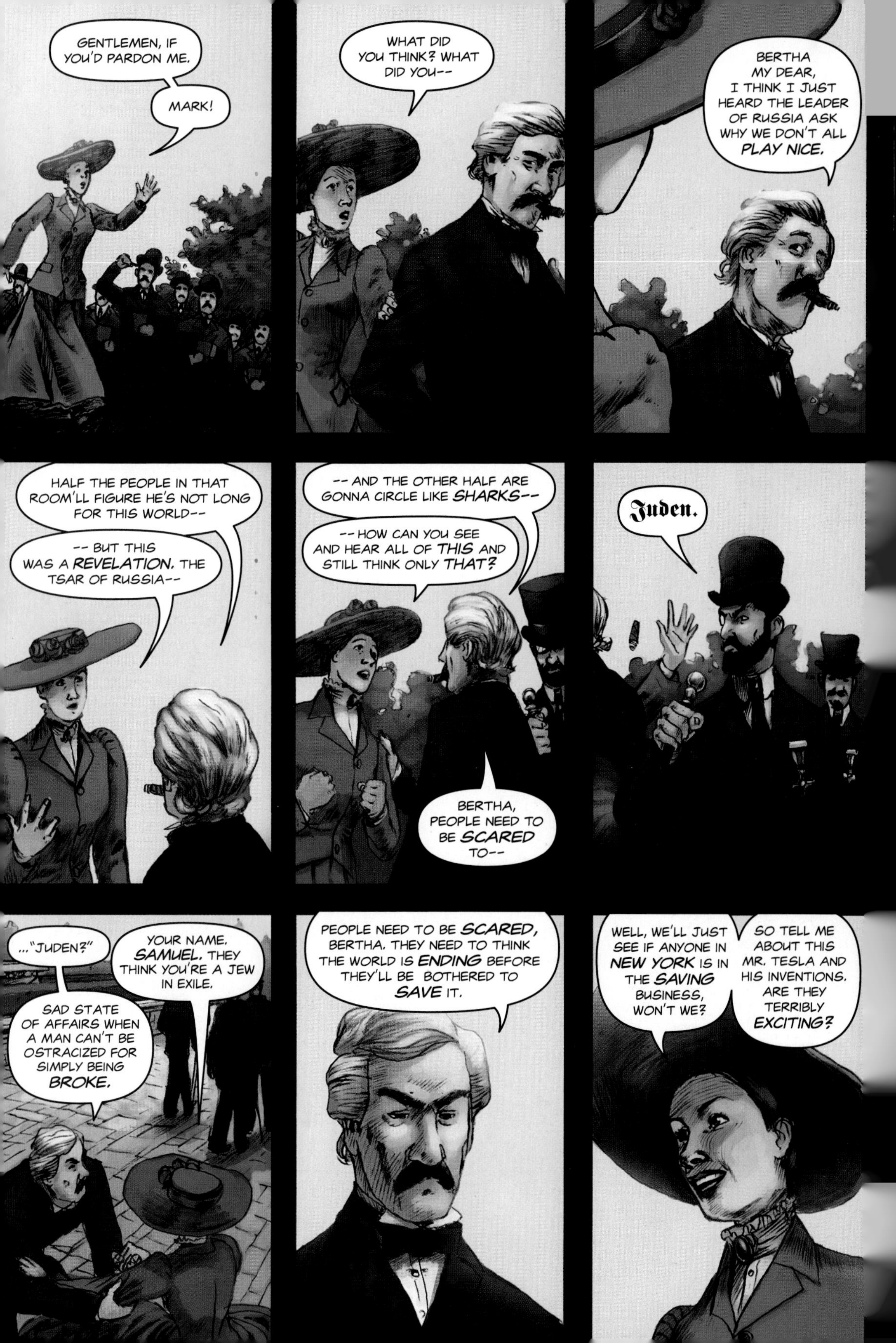
GENTLEMEN, IF YOU'D PARDON ME.
MARK!
WHAT DID YOU THINK? WHAT DID YOU--
BERTHA MY DEAR, I THINK I JUST HEARD THE LEADER OF RUSSIA ASK WHY WE DON'T ALL PLAY NICE.
HALF THE PEOPLE IN THAT ROOM'LL FIGURE HE'S NOT LONG FOR THIS WORLD--
-- BUT THIS WAS A REVELATION. THE TSAR OF RUSSIA--
-- AND THE OTHER HALF ARE GONNA CIRCLE LIKE SHARKS--
-- HOW CAN YOU SEE AND HEAR ALL OF THIS AND STILL THINK ONLY THAT?
BERTHA, PEOPLE NEED TO BE SCARED TO--
Juden.
..."JUDEN?"
YOUR NAME, SAMUEL. THEY THINK YOU'RE A JEW IN EXILE.
SAD STATE OF AFFAIRS WHEN A MAN CAN'T BE OSTRACIZED FOR SIMPLY BEING BROKE.
PEOPLE NEED TO BE SCARED, BERTHA. THEY NEED TO THINK THE WORLD IS ENDING BEFORE THEY'LL BE BOTHERED TO SAVE IT.
WELL, WE'LL JUST SEE IF ANYONE IN NEW YORK IS IN THE SAVING BUSINESS, WON'T WE?
SO TELL ME ABOUT THIS MR. TESLA AND HIS INVENTIONS. ARE THEY TERRIBLY EXCITING?

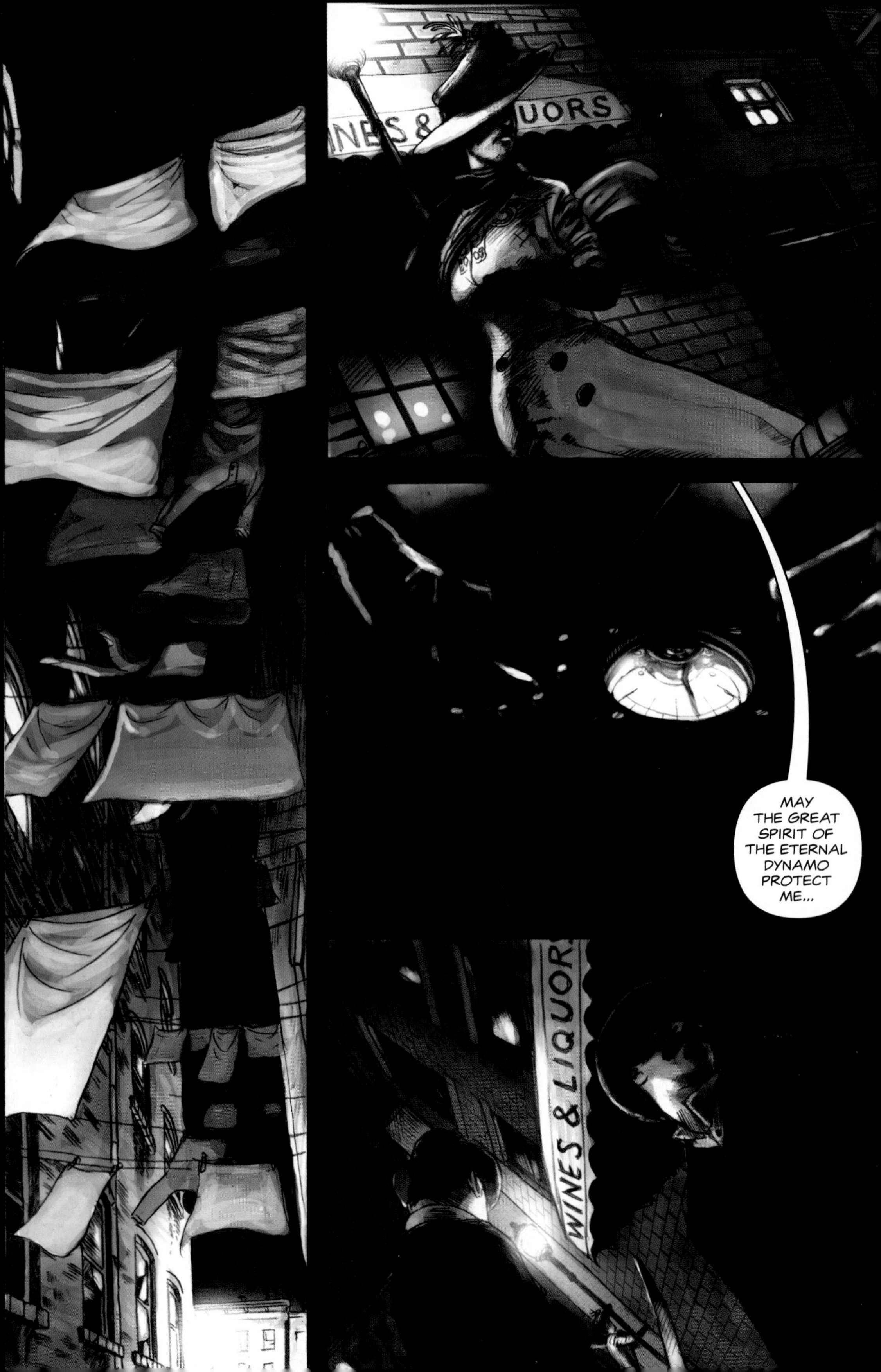

INES & UORS
MAY THE GREAT SPIRIT OF THE ETERNAL DYNAMO PROTECT ME...
WINES & LIQUORS

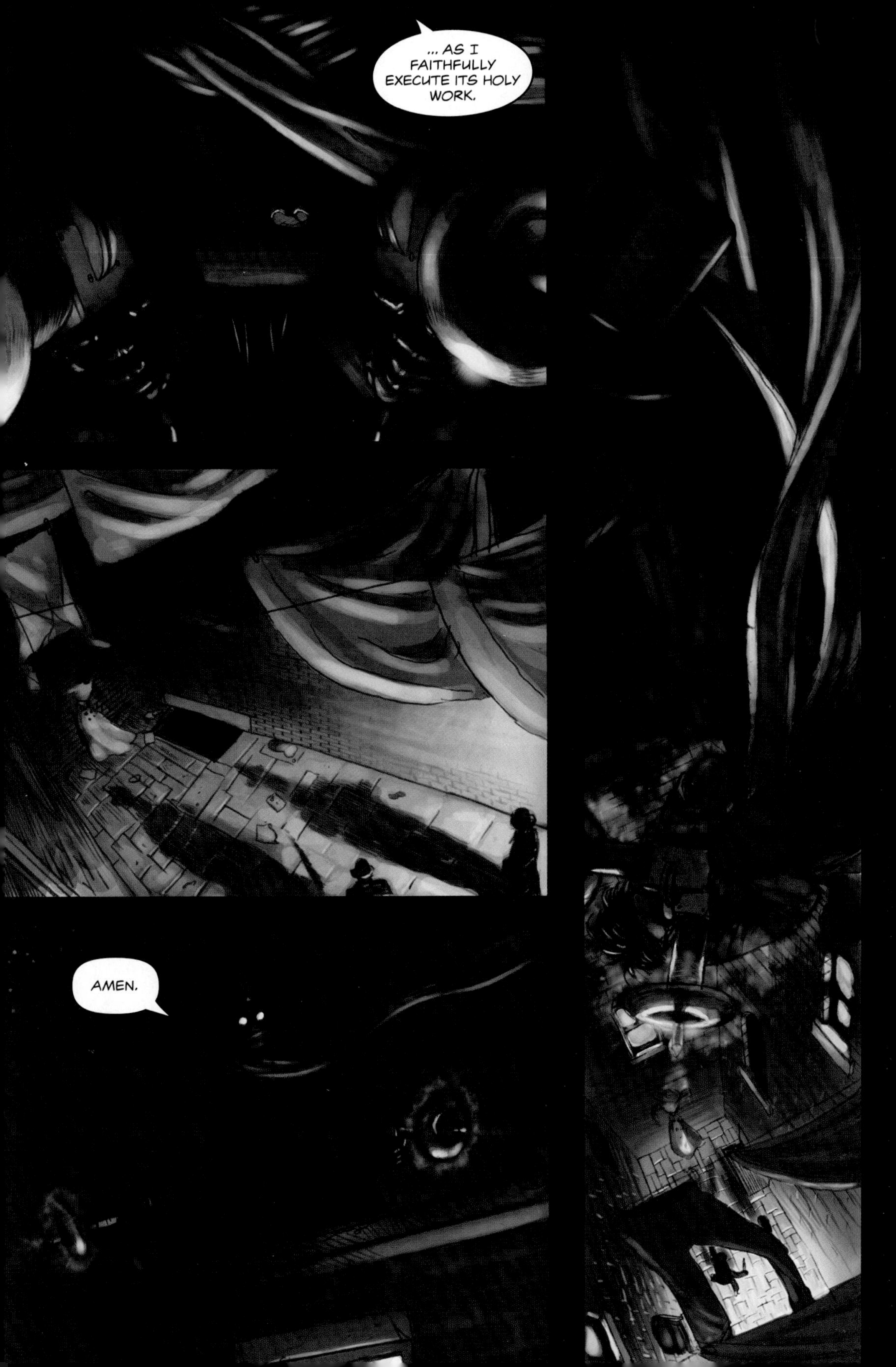
... AS I FAITHFULLY EXECUTE ITS HOLY WORK.
AMEN.

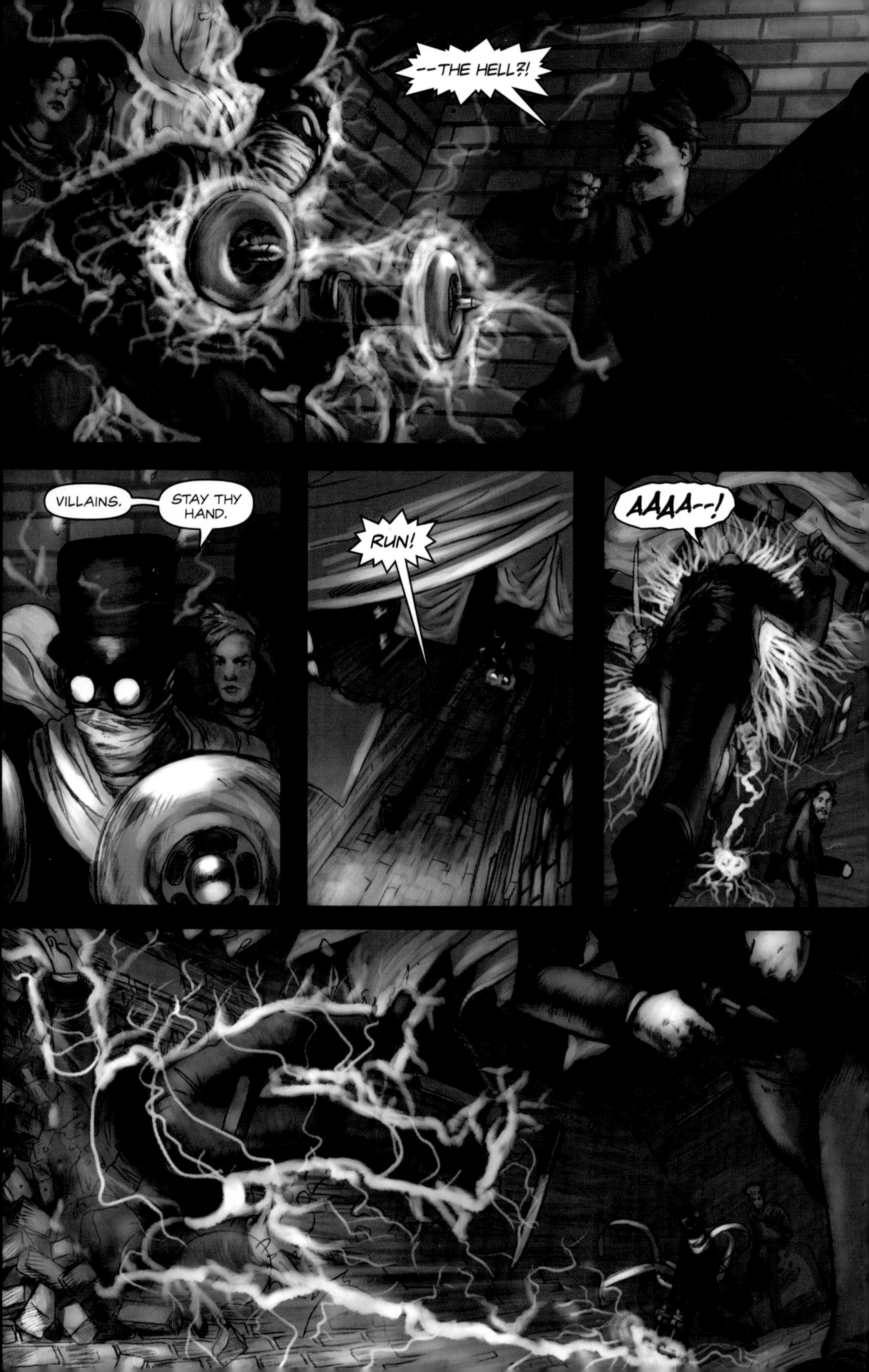
--THE HELL?!
VILLAINS.
STAY THY HAND.
RUN!
AAAA--!

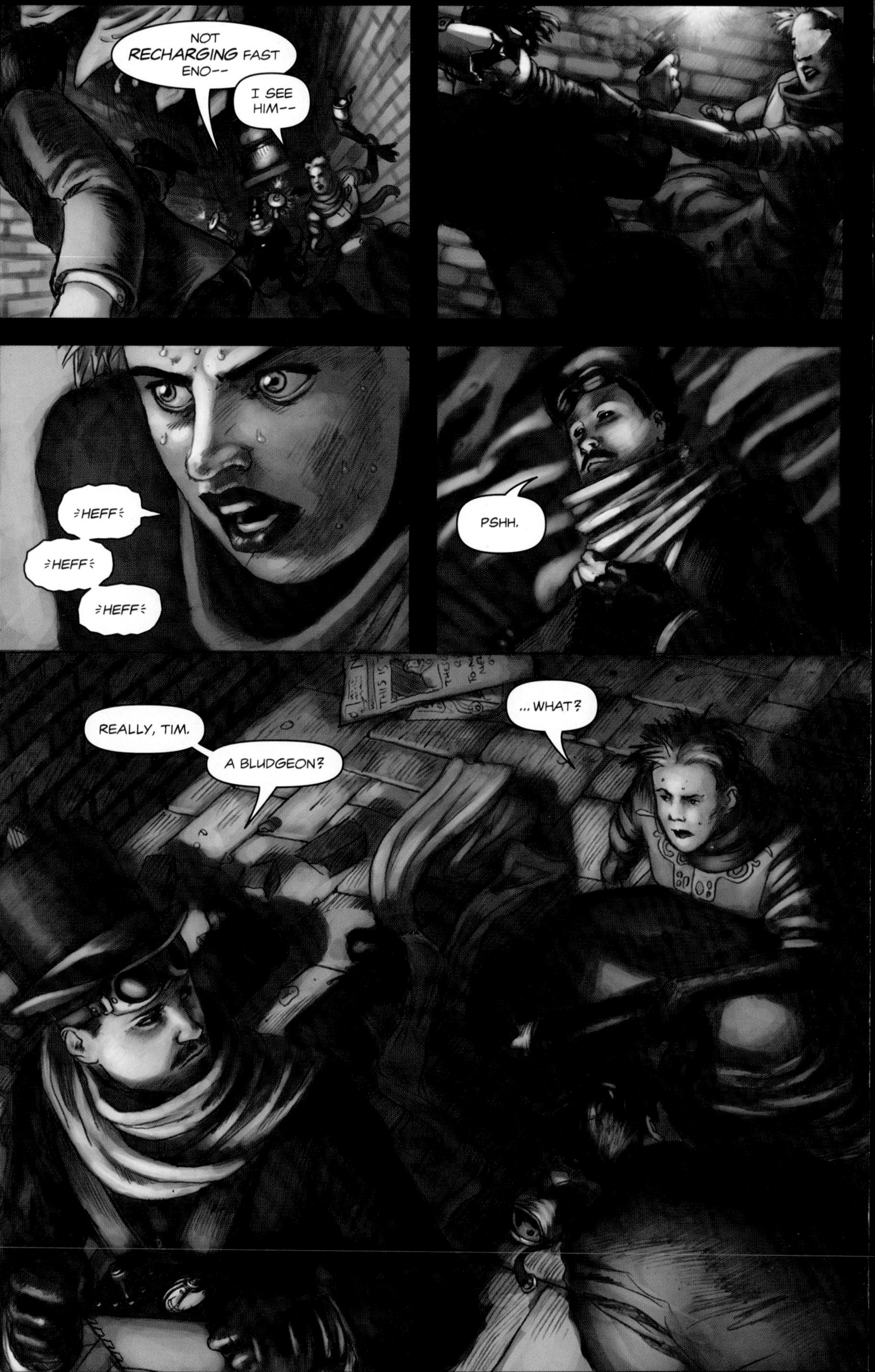
NOT RECHARGING FAST ENO--
I SEE HIM--
HEFF
HEFF
HEFF
PSHH.
REALLY, TIM.
A BLUDGEON?
...WHAT?

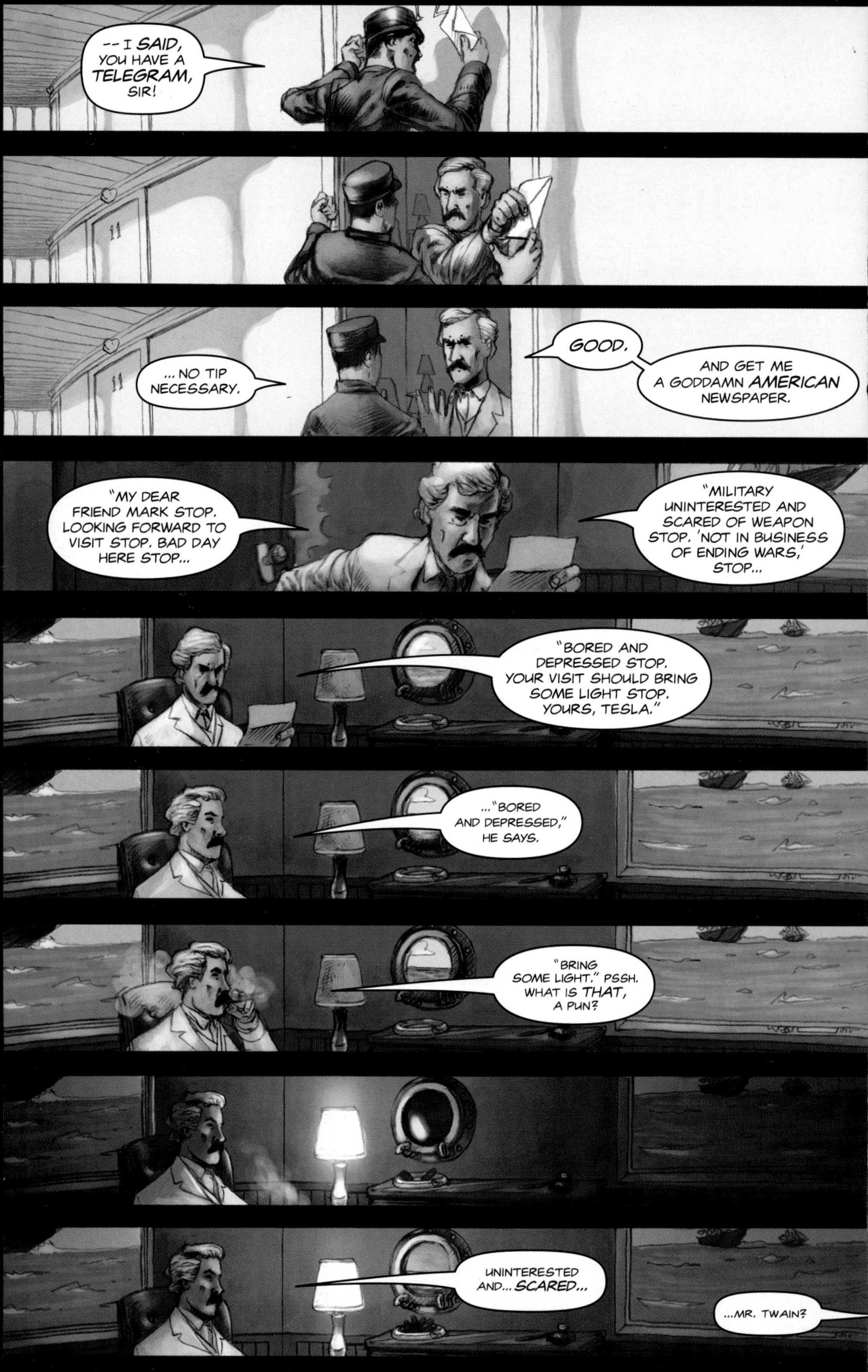

-- I SAID, YOU HAVE A TELEGRAM, SIR!
...NO TIP NECESSARY.
GOOD.
AND GET ME A GODDAMN AMERICAN NEWSPAPER.
"MY DEAR FRIEND MARK STOP. LOOKING FORWARD TO VISIT STOP. BAD DAY HERE STOP...
"MILITARY UNINTERESTED AND SCARED OF WEAPON STOP. 'NOT IN BUSINESS OF ENDING WARS,' STOP...
"BORED AND DEPRESSED STOP. YOUR VISIT SHOULD BRING SOME LIGHT STOP. YOURS, TESLA."
..."BORED AND DEPRESSED," HE SAYS.
"BRING SOME LIGHT." PSSH. WHAT IS THAT, A PUN?
UNINTERESTED AND... SCARED...
...MR. TWAIN?

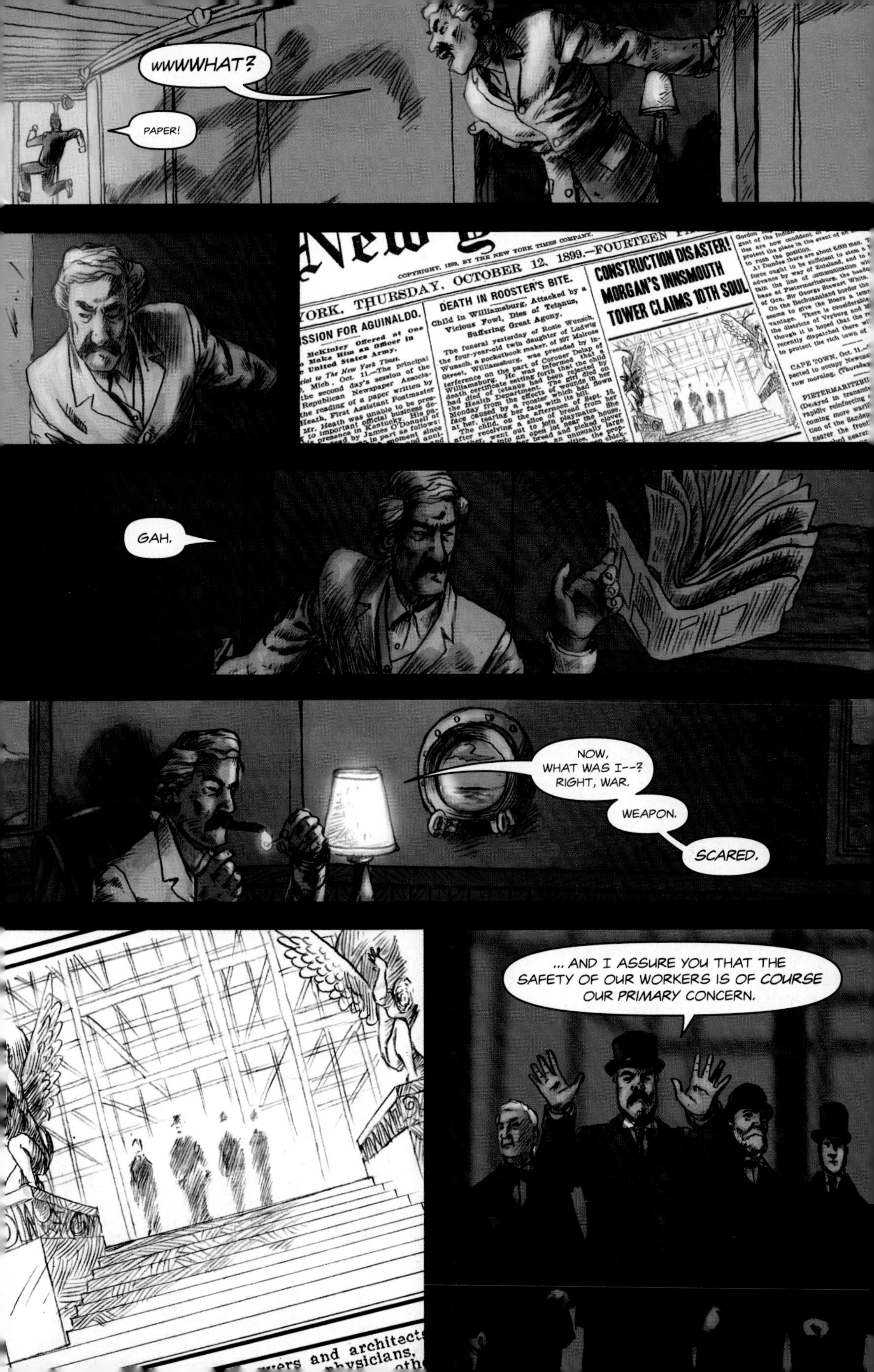
WWWWHAT?
PAPER!
COPYRIGHT, 1899, BY THE NEW YORK TIMES COMPANY.
YORK, THURSDAY, OCTOBER 12, 1899.—FOURTEEN
DEATH IN ROOSTER'S BITE.
CONSTRUCTION DISASTER!
MORGAN'S INNSMOUTH
TOWER CLAIMS 10TH SOUL
GAH.
NOW, WHAT WAS I--? RIGHT, WAR.
WEAPON.
SCARED.
... AND I ASSURE YOU THAT THE SAFETY OF OUR WORKERS IS OF COURSE OUR PRIMARY CONCERN.

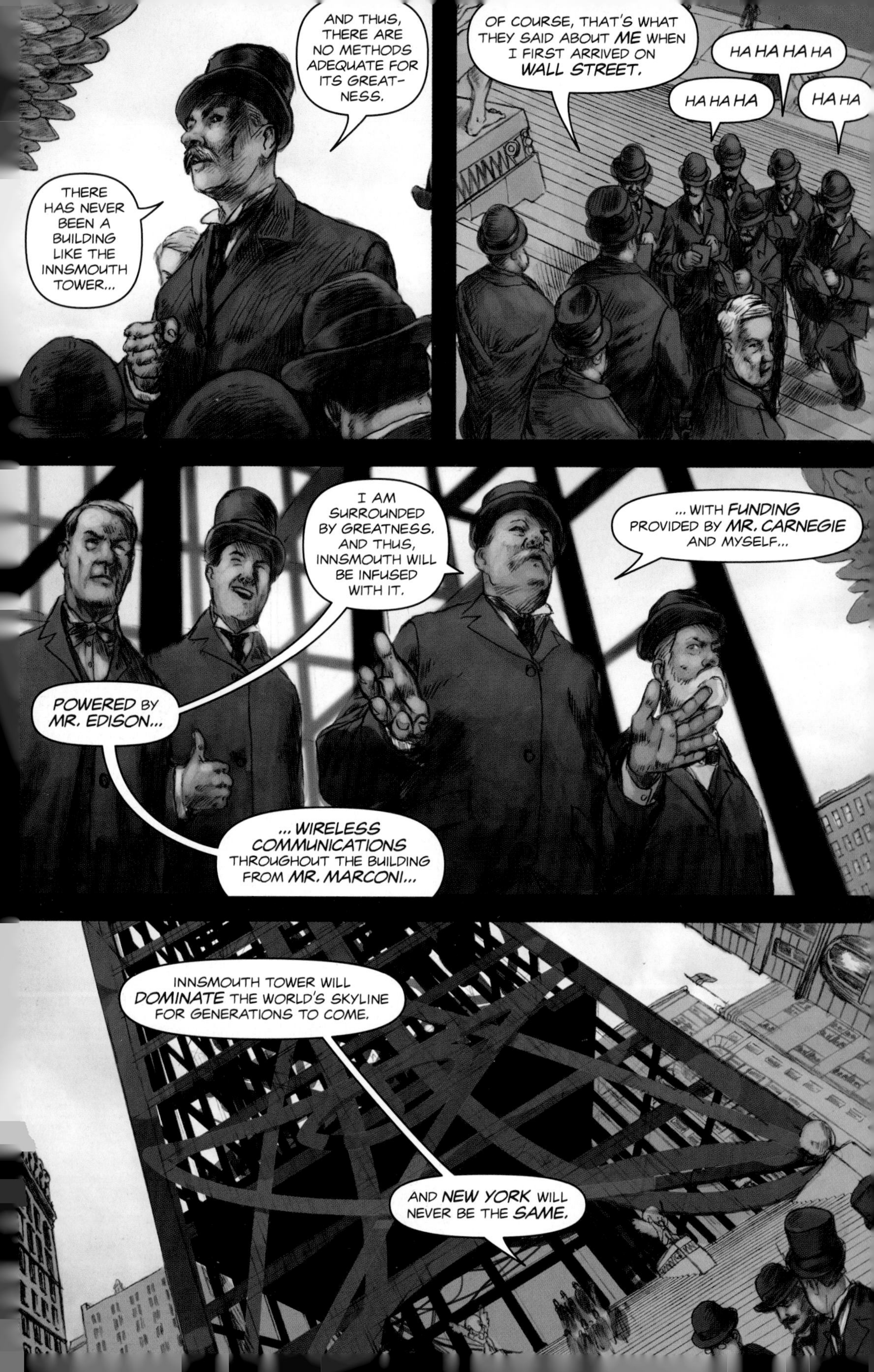
THERE HAS NEVER BEEN A BUILDING LIKE THE INNSMOUTH TOWER...
AND THUS, THERE ARE NO METHODS ADEQUATE FOR ITS GREATNESS.
OF COURSE, THAT'S WHAT THEY SAID ABOUT ME WHEN I FIRST ARRIVED ON WALL STREET.
HA HA HA HA
HA HA HA HA
HA HA
I AM SURROUNDED BY GREATNESS. AND THUS, INNSMOUTH WILL BE INFUSED WITH IT.
POWERED BY MR. EDISON...
...WIRELESS COMMUNICATIONS THROUGHOUT THE BUILDING FROM MR. MARCONI...
...WITH FUNDING PROVIDED BY MR. CARNEGIE AND MYSELF...
INNSMOUTH TOWER WILL DOMINATE THE WORLD'S SKYLINE FOR GENERATIONS TO COME.
AND NEW YORK WILL NEVER BE THE SAME.

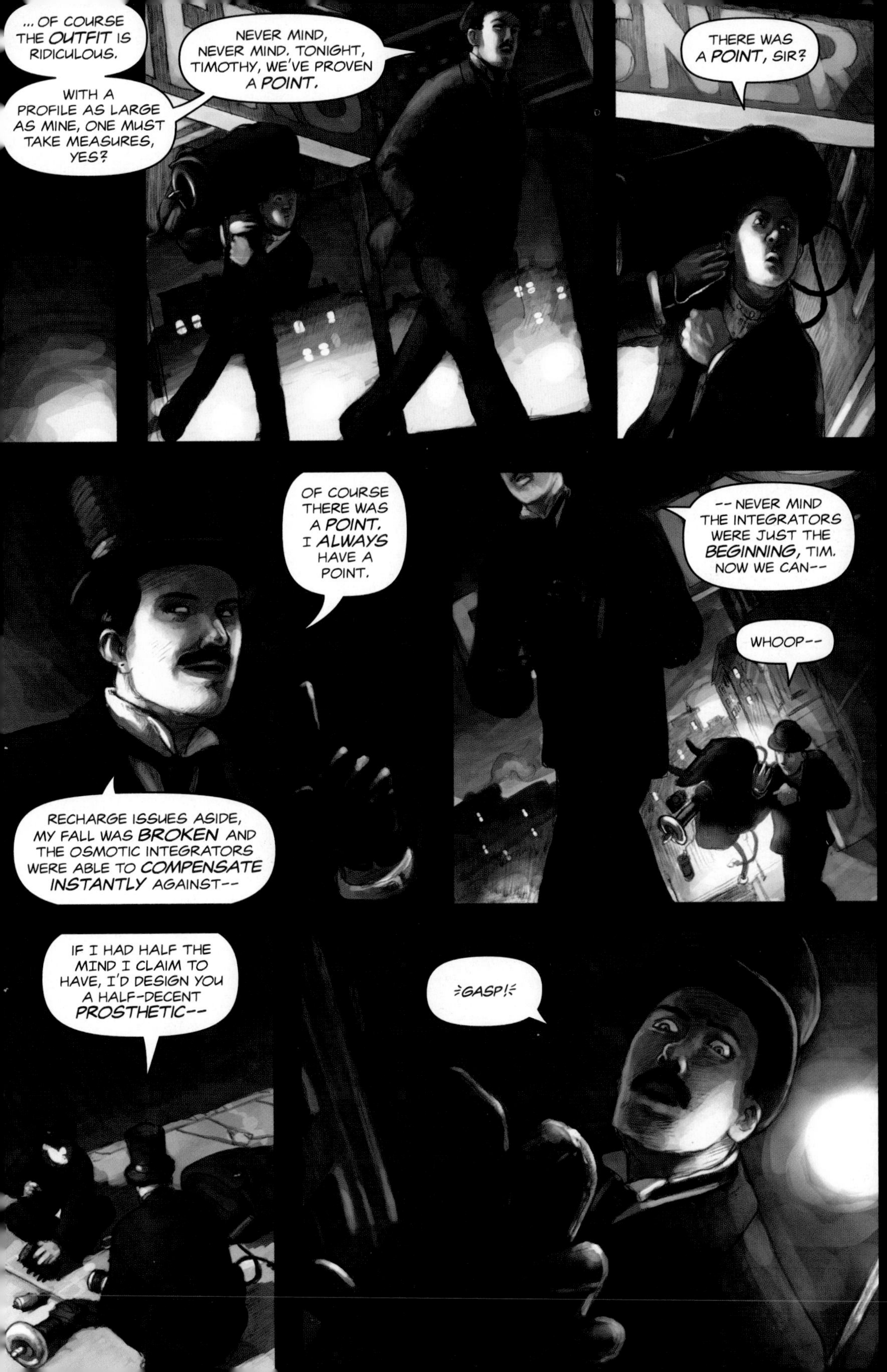
...OF COURSE THE OUTFIT IS RIDICULOUS.
WITH A PROFILE AS LARGE AS MINE, ONE MUST TAKE MEASURES, YES?
NEVER MIND, NEVER MIND. TONIGHT, TIMOTHY, WE'VE PROVEN A POINT.
THERE WAS A POINT, SIR?
OF COURSE THERE WAS A POINT. I ALWAYS HAVE A POINT.
RECHARGE ISSUES ASIDE, MY FALL WAS BROKEN AND THE OSMOTIC INTEGRATORS WERE ABLE TO COMPENSATE INSTANTLY AGAINST--
--NEVER MIND THE INTEGRATORS WERE JUST THE BEGINNING, TIM. NOW WE CAN--
WHOOP--
IF I HAD HALF THE MIND I CLAIM TO HAVE, I'D DESIGN YOU A HALF-DECENT PROSTHETIC--
GASP!

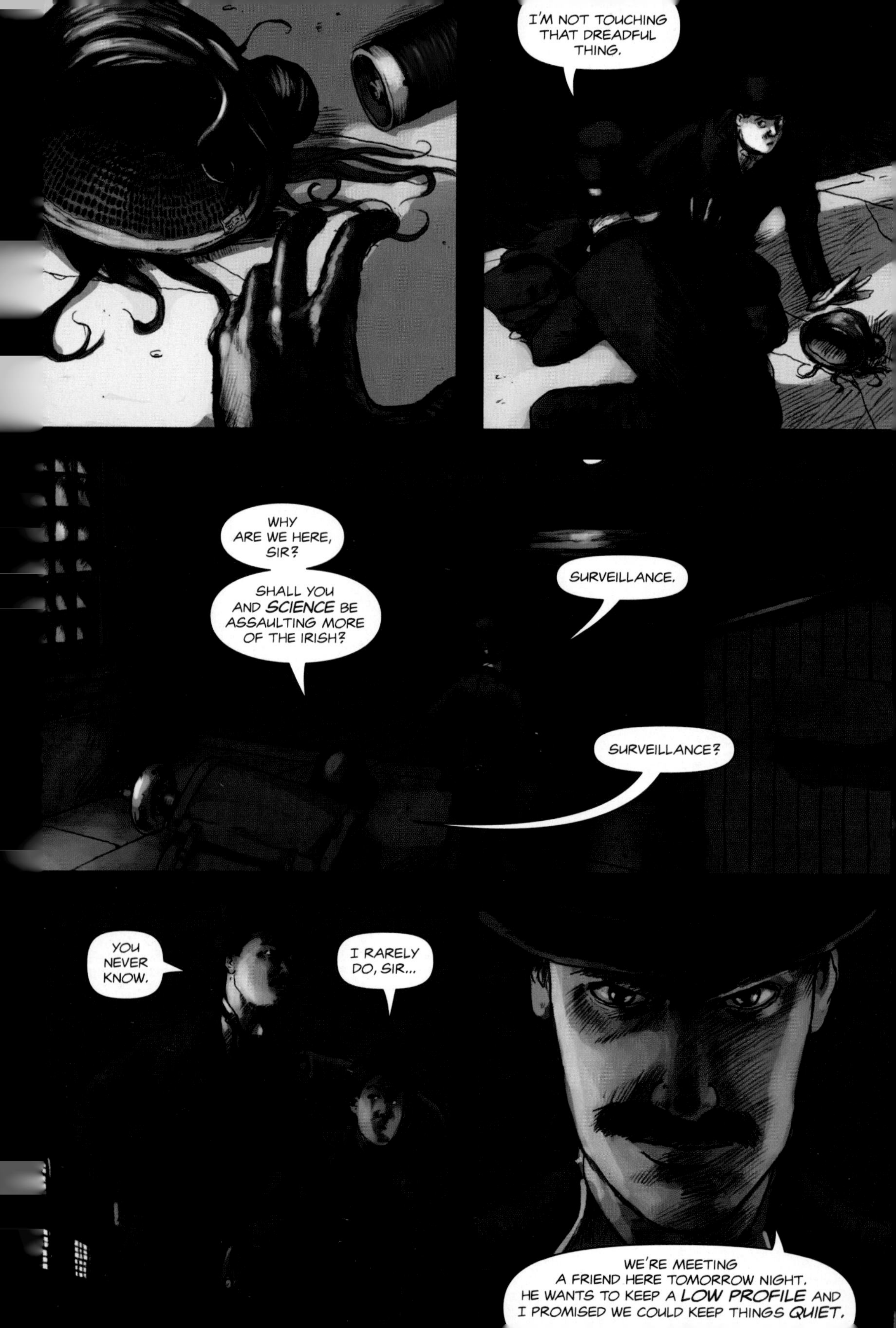
I'M NOT TOUCHING THAT DREADFUL THING.
WHY ARE WE HERE, SIR?
SHALL YOU AND SCIENCE BE ASSAULTING MORE OF THE IRISH?
SURVEILLANCE.
SURVEILLANCE?
YOU NEVER KNOW.
I RARELY DO, SIR...
WE'RE MEETING A FRIEND HERE TOMORROW NIGHT. HE WANTS TO KEEP A LOW PROFILE AND I PROMISED WE COULD KEEP THINGS QUIET.

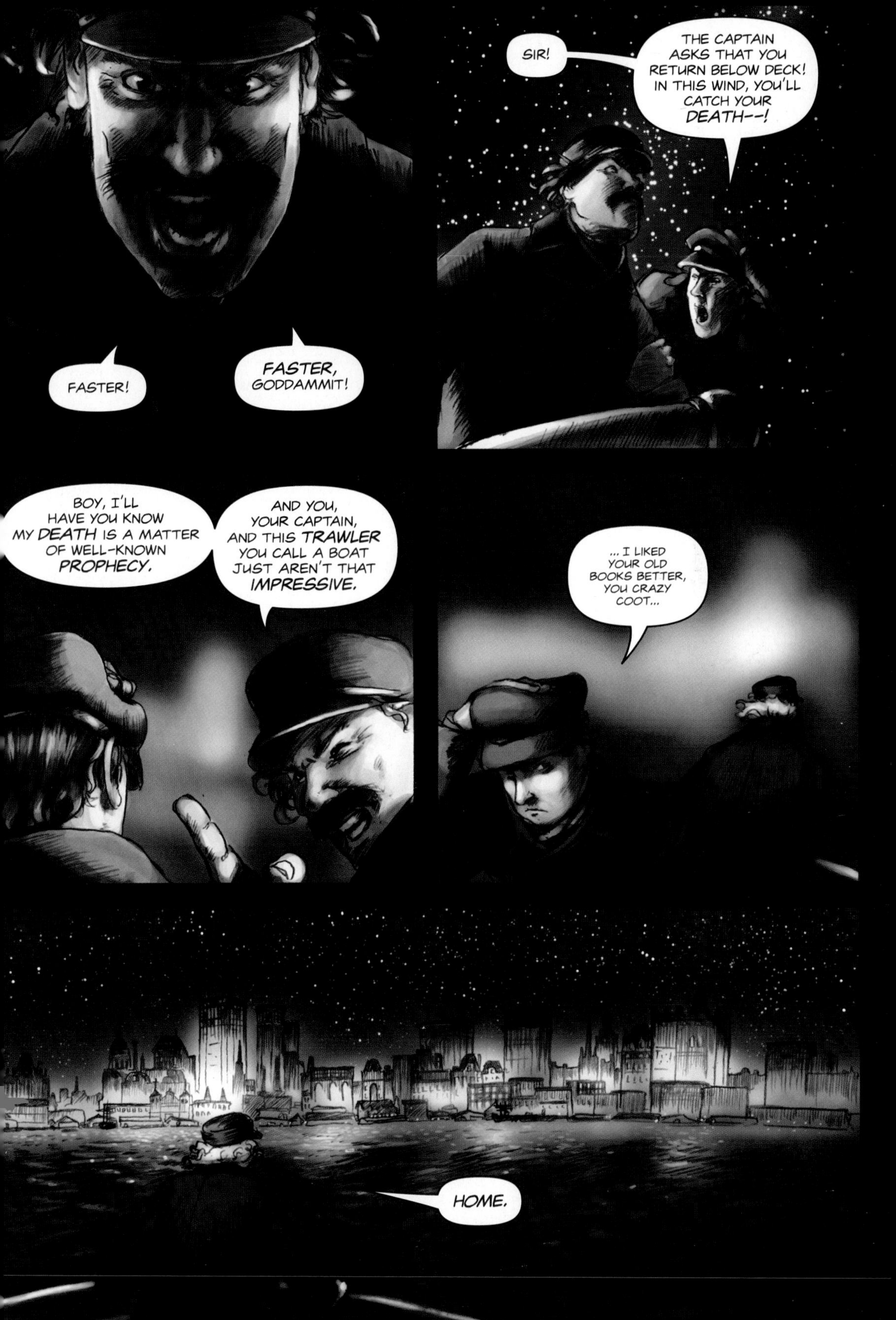
FASTER!
FASTER, GODDAMMIT!
SIR!
THE CAPTAIN ASKS THAT YOU RETURN BELOW DECK! IN THIS WIND, YOU'LL CATCH YOUR DEATH--!
BOY, I'LL HAVE YOU KNOW MY DEATH IS A MATTER OF WELL-KNOWN PROPHECY.
AND YOU, YOUR CAPTAIN, AND THIS TRAWLER YOU CALL A BOAT JUST AREN'T THAT IMPRESSIVE.
... I LIKED YOUR OLD BOOKS BETTER, YOU CRAZY COOT...
HOME.

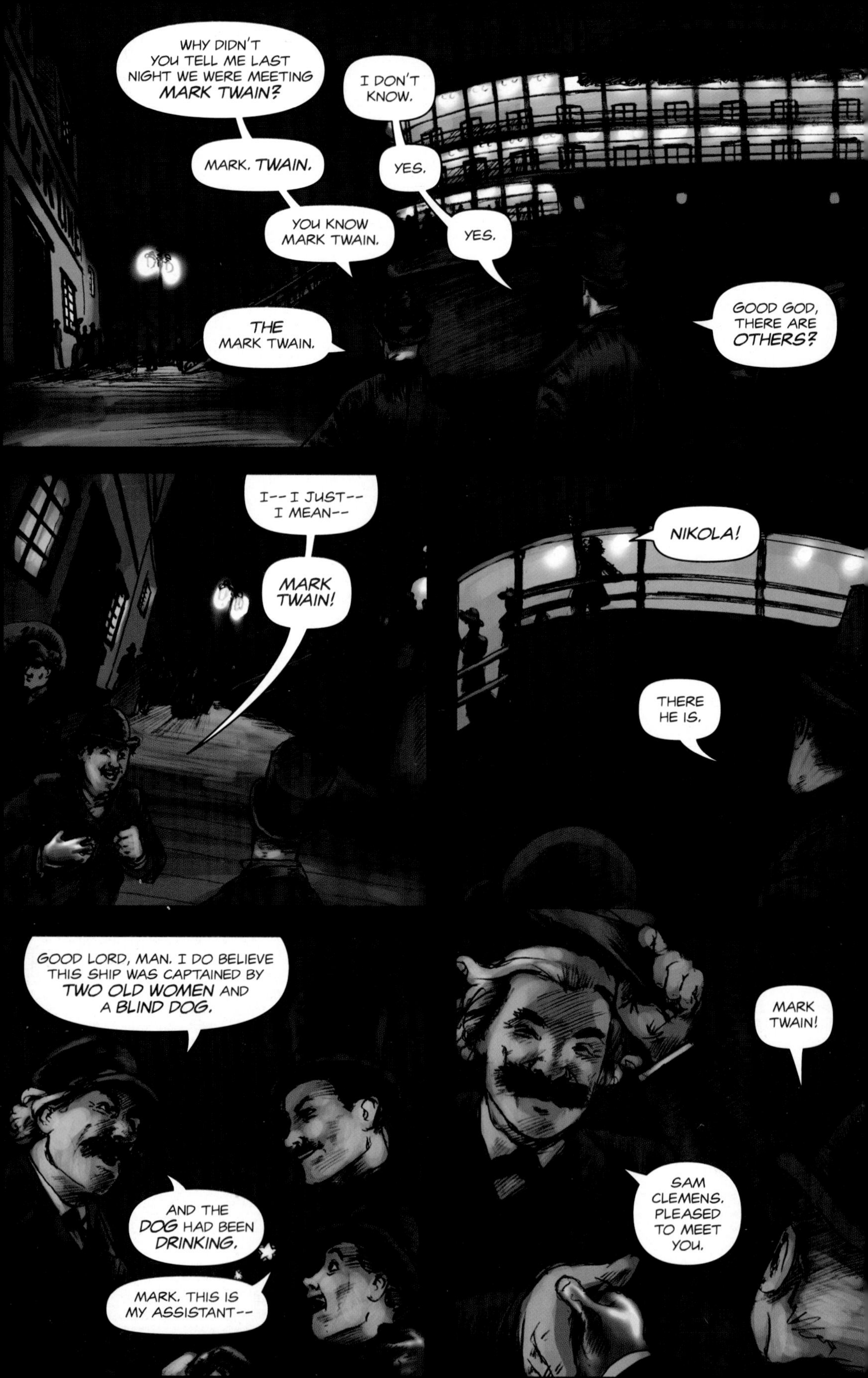
WHY DIDN'T YOU TELL ME LAST NIGHT WE WERE MEETING MARK TWAIN?
I DON'T KNOW.
MARK. TWAIN.
YES.
YOU KNOW MARK TWAIN.
YES.
THE MARK TWAIN.
GOOD GOD, THERE ARE OTHERS?
I-- I JUST-- I MEAN--
MARK TWAIN!
NIKOLA!
THERE HE IS.
GOOD LORD, MAN. I DO BELIEVE THIS SHIP WAS CAPTAINED BY TWO OLD WOMEN AND A BLIND DOG.
AND THE DOG HAD BEEN DRINKING.
MARK. THIS IS MY ASSISTANT--
MARK TWAIN!
SAM CLEMENS. PLEASED TO MEET YOU.

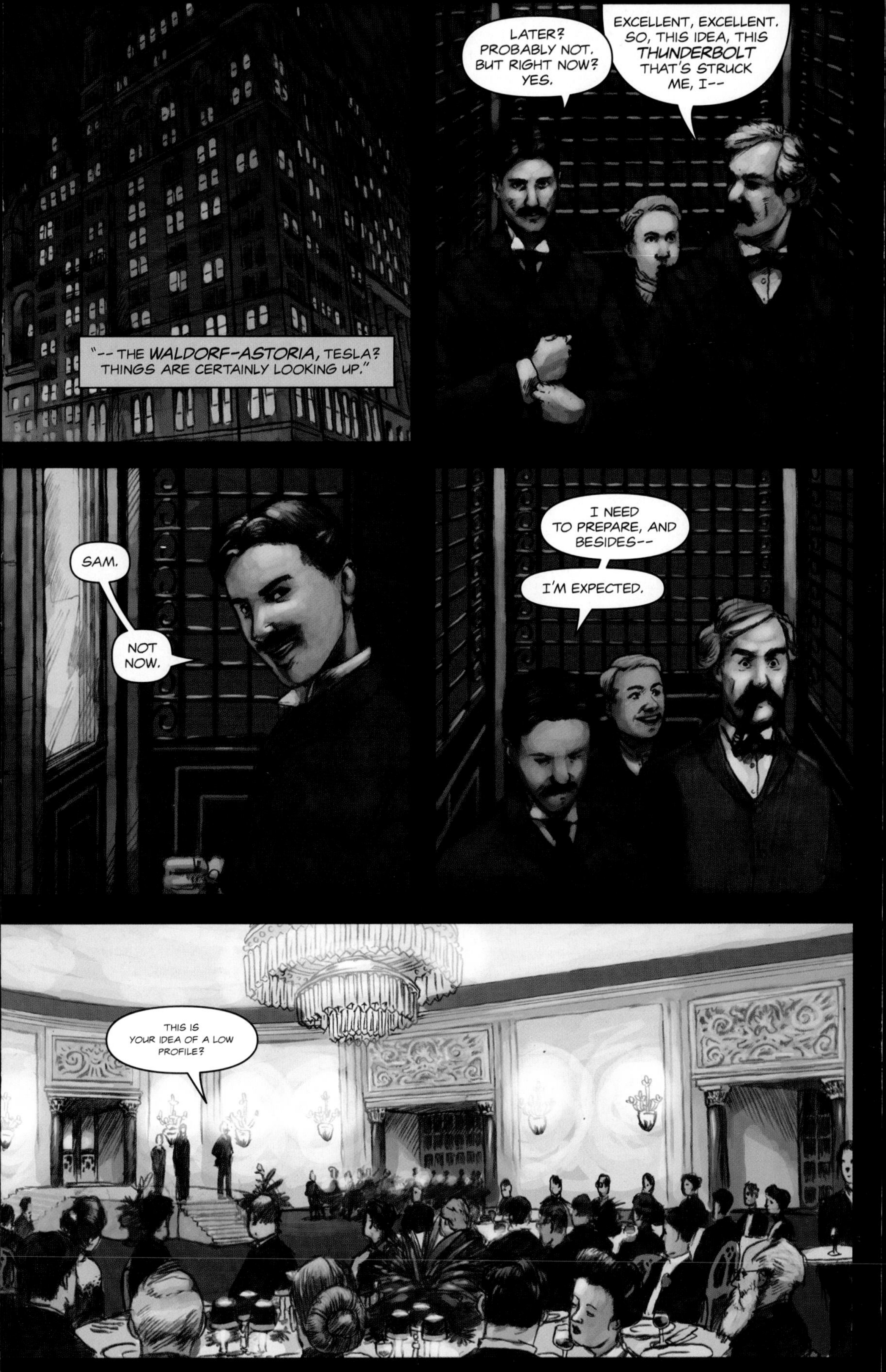
"-- THE WALDORF-ASTORIA, TESLA? THINGS ARE CERTAINLY LOOKING UP."
LATER? PROBABLY NOT. BUT RIGHT NOW? YES.
EXCELLENT, EXCELLENT. SO, THIS IDEA, THIS THUNDERBOLT THAT'S STRUCK ME, I--
SAM.
NOT NOW.
I NEED TO PREPARE, AND BESIDES--
I'M EXPECTED.
THIS IS YOUR IDEA OF A LOW PROFILE?

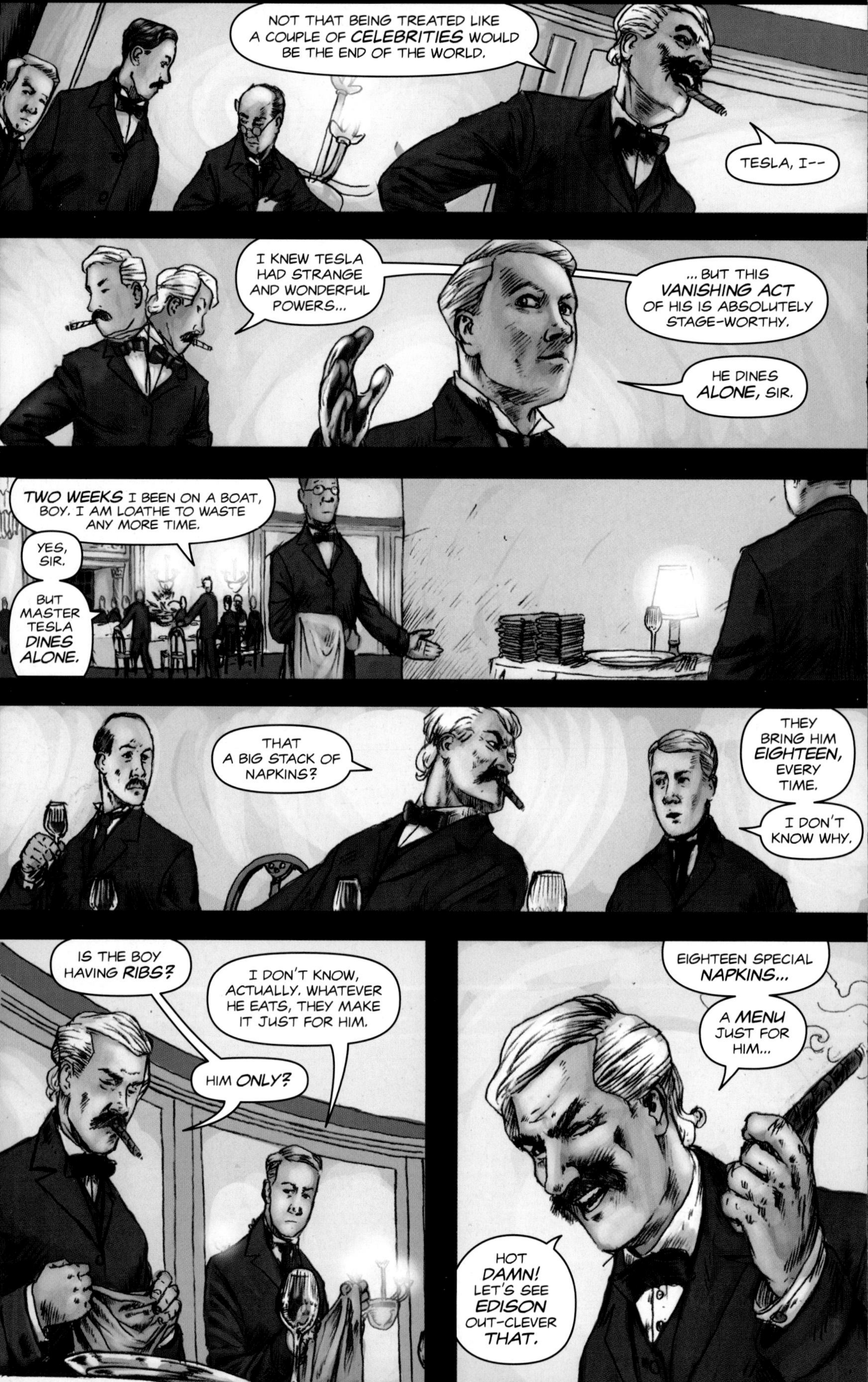
NOT THAT BEING TREATED LIKE A COUPLE OF **CELEBRITIES** WOULD BE THE END OF THE WORLD.
TESLA, I--
I KNEW TESLA HAD STRANGE AND WONDERFUL POWERS...
... BUT THIS **VANISHING ACT** OF HIS IS ABSOLUTELY STAGE-WORTHY.
HE DINES **ALONE,** SIR.
**TWO WEEKS** I BEEN ON A BOAT, BOY. I AM LOATHE TO WASTE ANY MORE TIME.
YES, SIR.
BUT MASTER TESLA **DINES ALONE.**
THAT A BIG STACK OF NAPKINS?
THEY BRING HIM **EIGHTEEN,** EVERY TIME.
I DON'T KNOW WHY.
IS THE BOY HAVING **RIBS?**
I DON'T KNOW, ACTUALLY. WHATEVER HE EATS, THEY MAKE IT JUST FOR HIM.
HIM **ONLY?**
EIGHTEEN SPECIAL **NAPKINS...**
A **MENU** JUST FOR HIM...
HOT **DAMN!** LET'S SEE **EDISON** OUT-CLEVER **THAT.**

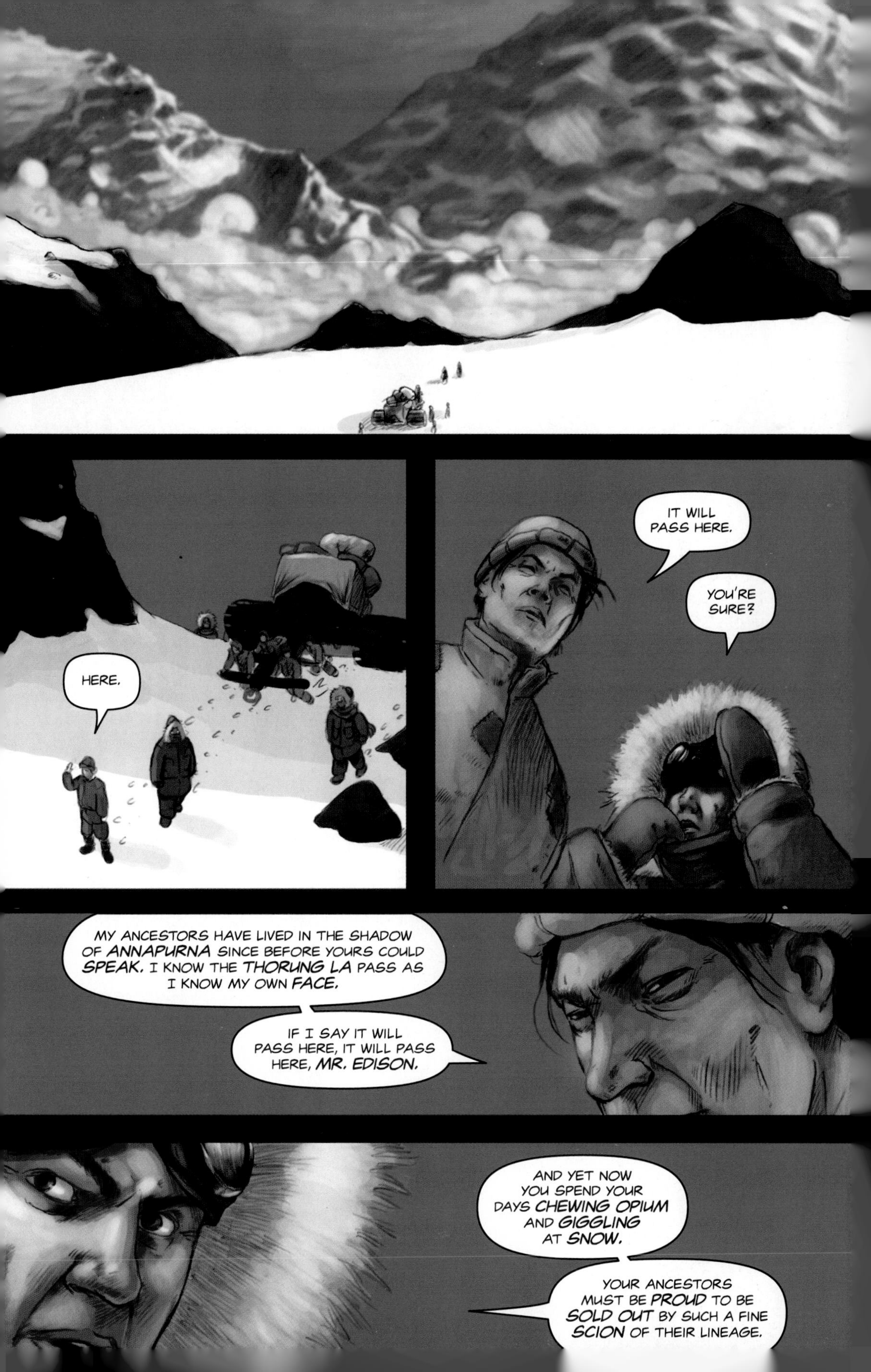
HERE.
IT WILL PASS HERE.
YOU'RE SURE?
MY ANCESTORS HAVE LIVED IN THE SHADOW OF ANNAPURNA SINCE BEFORE YOURS COULD SPEAK. I KNOW THE THORUNG LA PASS AS I KNOW MY OWN FACE.
IF I SAY IT WILL PASS HERE, IT WILL PASS HERE, MR. EDISON.
AND YET NOW YOU SPEND YOUR DAYS CHEWING OPIUM AND GIGGLING AT SNOW.
YOUR ANCESTORS MUST BE PROUD TO BE SOLD OUT BY SUCH A FINE SCION OF THEIR LINEAGE.

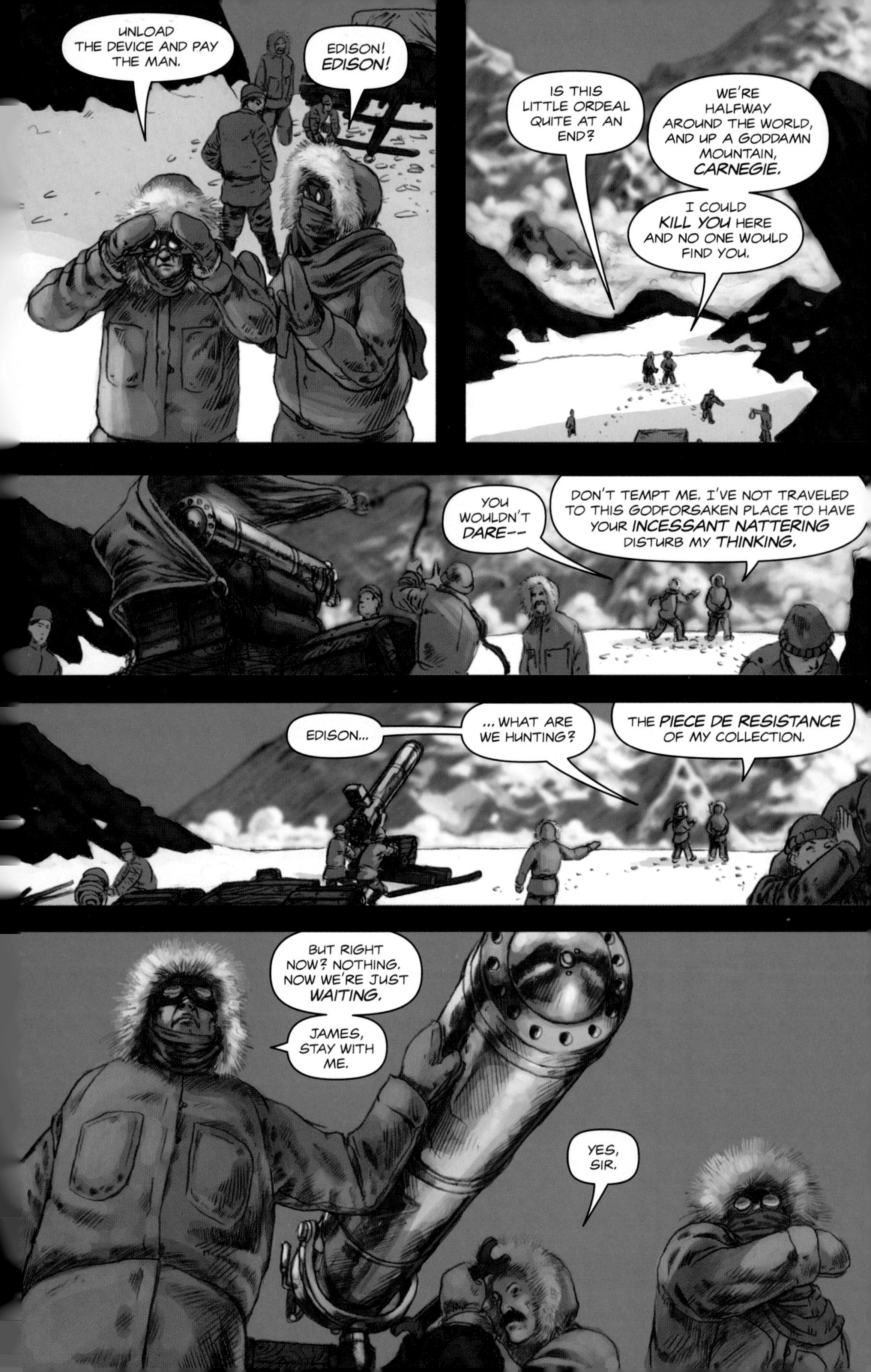
UNLOAD THE DEVICE AND PAY THE MAN.
EDISON! EDISON!
IS THIS LITTLE ORDEAL QUITE AT AN END?
WE'RE HALFWAY AROUND THE WORLD, AND UP A GODDAMN MOUNTAIN, CARNEGIE.
I COULD KILL YOU HERE AND NO ONE WOULD FIND YOU.
YOU WOULDN'T DARE--
DON'T TEMPT ME. I'VE NOT TRAVELED TO THIS GODFORSAKEN PLACE TO HAVE YOUR INCESSANT NATTERING DISTURB MY THINKING.
EDISON...
...WHAT ARE WE HUNTING?
THE PIECE DE RESISTANCE OF MY COLLECTION.
BUT RIGHT NOW? NOTHING. NOW WE'RE JUST WAITING.
JAMES, STAY WITH ME.
YES, SIR.

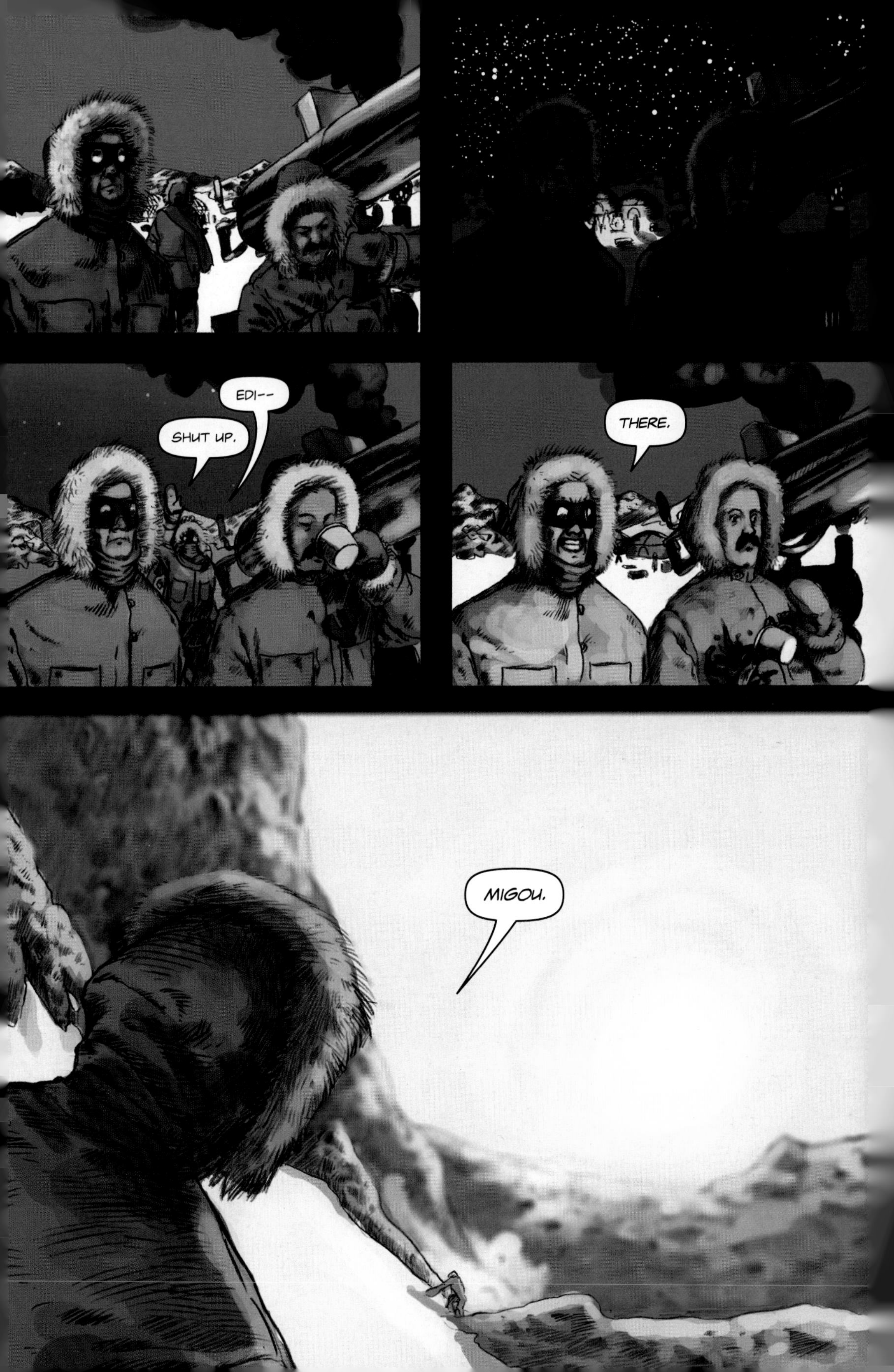
EDI--
SHUT UP.
THERE.
MIGOU.

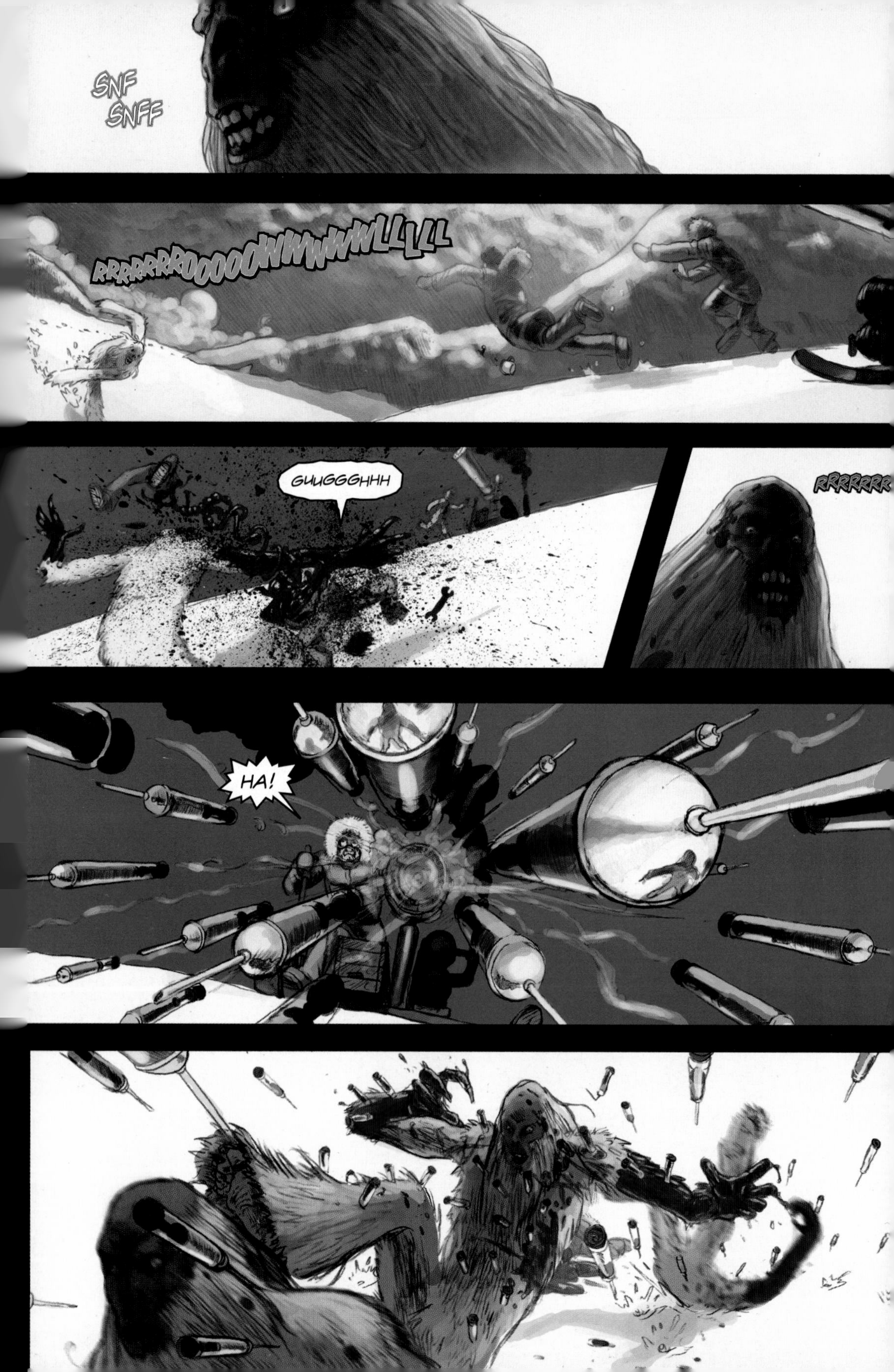
SNF
SNFF
RRRRRRROOOOOOWWWWWLLLLL
GUUGGGHHH
RRRRRRR
HA!

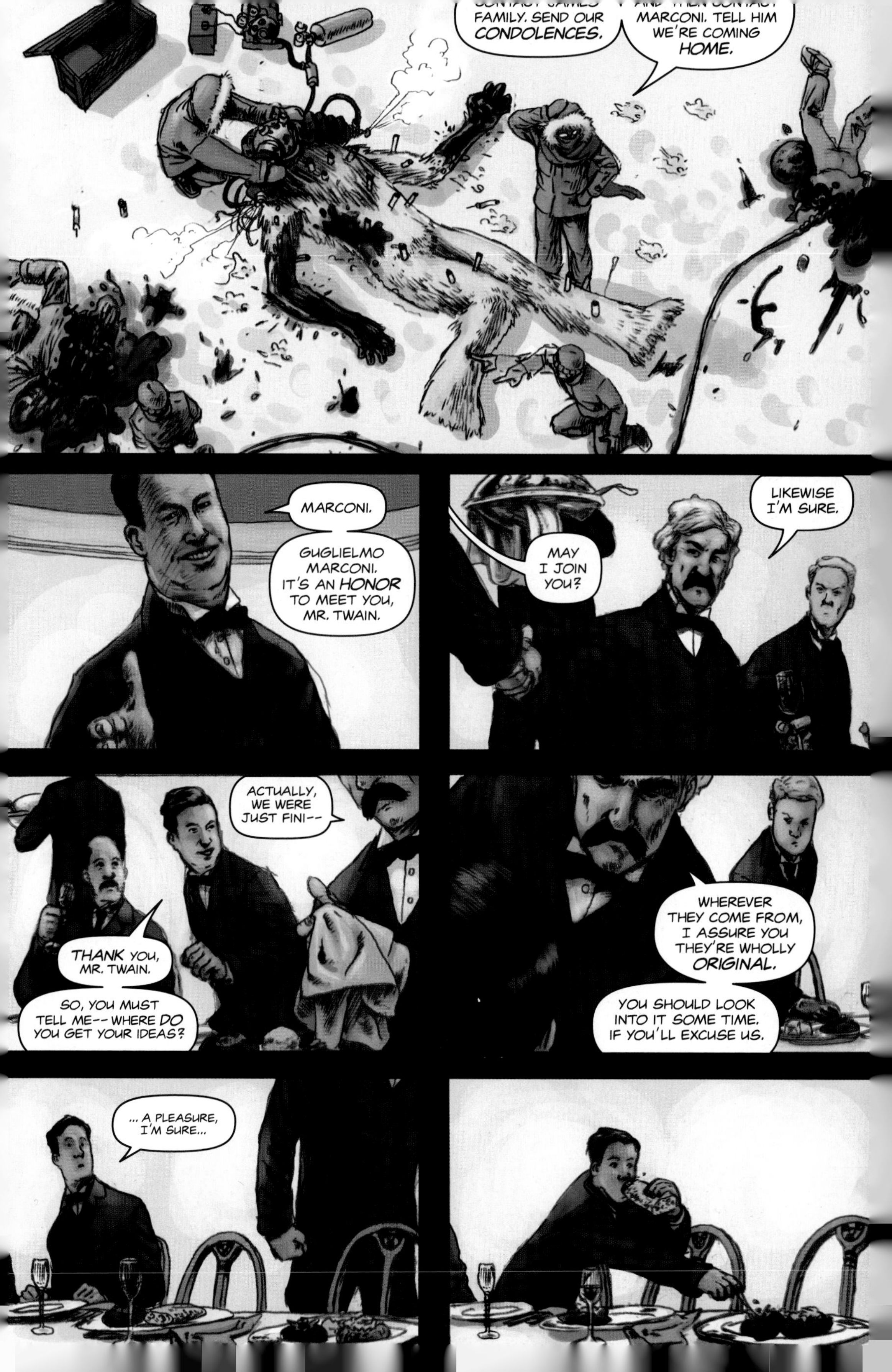
FAMILY. SEND OUR CONDOLENCES.
MARCONI. TELL HIM WE'RE COMING HOME.
MARCONI.
GUGLIELMO MARCONI. IT'S AN HONOR TO MEET YOU, MR. TWAIN.
MAY I JOIN YOU?
LIKEWISE I'M SURE.
ACTUALLY, WE WERE JUST FINI--
THANK YOU, MR. TWAIN.
SO, YOU MUST TELL ME-- WHERE DO YOU GET YOUR IDEAS?
WHEREVER THEY COME FROM, I ASSURE YOU THEY'RE WHOLLY ORIGINAL.
YOU SHOULD LOOK INTO IT SOME TIME. IF YOU'LL EXCUSE US.
... A PLEASURE, I'M SURE...

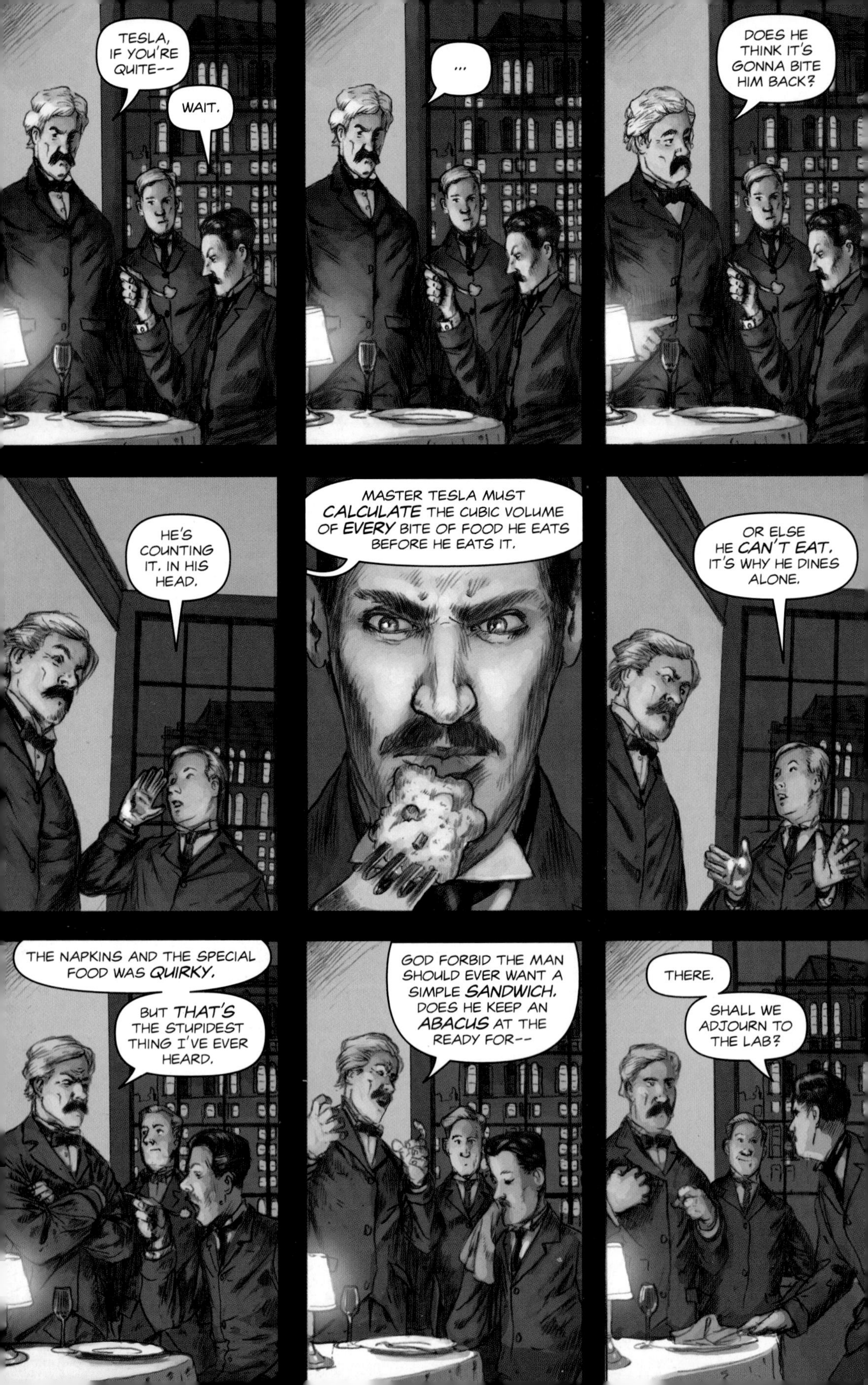
TESLA, IF YOU'RE QUITE--
WAIT.
...
DOES HE THINK IT'S GONNA BITE HIM BACK?
HE'S COUNTING IT. IN HIS HEAD.
MASTER TESLA MUST CALCULATE THE CUBIC VOLUME OF EVERY BITE OF FOOD HE EATS BEFORE HE EATS IT.
OR ELSE HE CAN'T EAT. IT'S WHY HE DINES ALONE.
THE NAPKINS AND THE SPECIAL FOOD WAS QUIRKY.
BUT THAT'S THE STUPIDEST THING I'VE EVER HEARD.
GOD FORBID THE MAN SHOULD EVER WANT A SIMPLE SANDWICH. DOES HE KEEP AN ABACUS AT THE READY FOR--
THERE.
SHALL WE ADJOURN TO THE LAB?

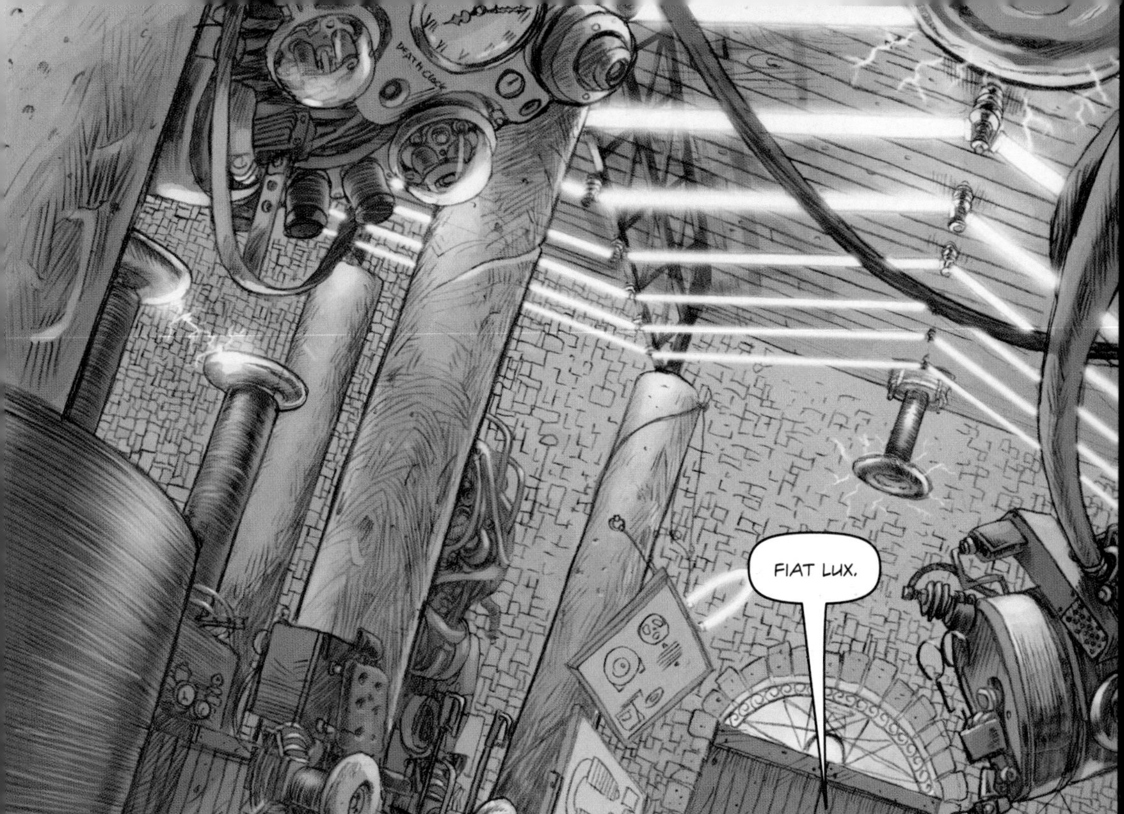
FIAT LUX.

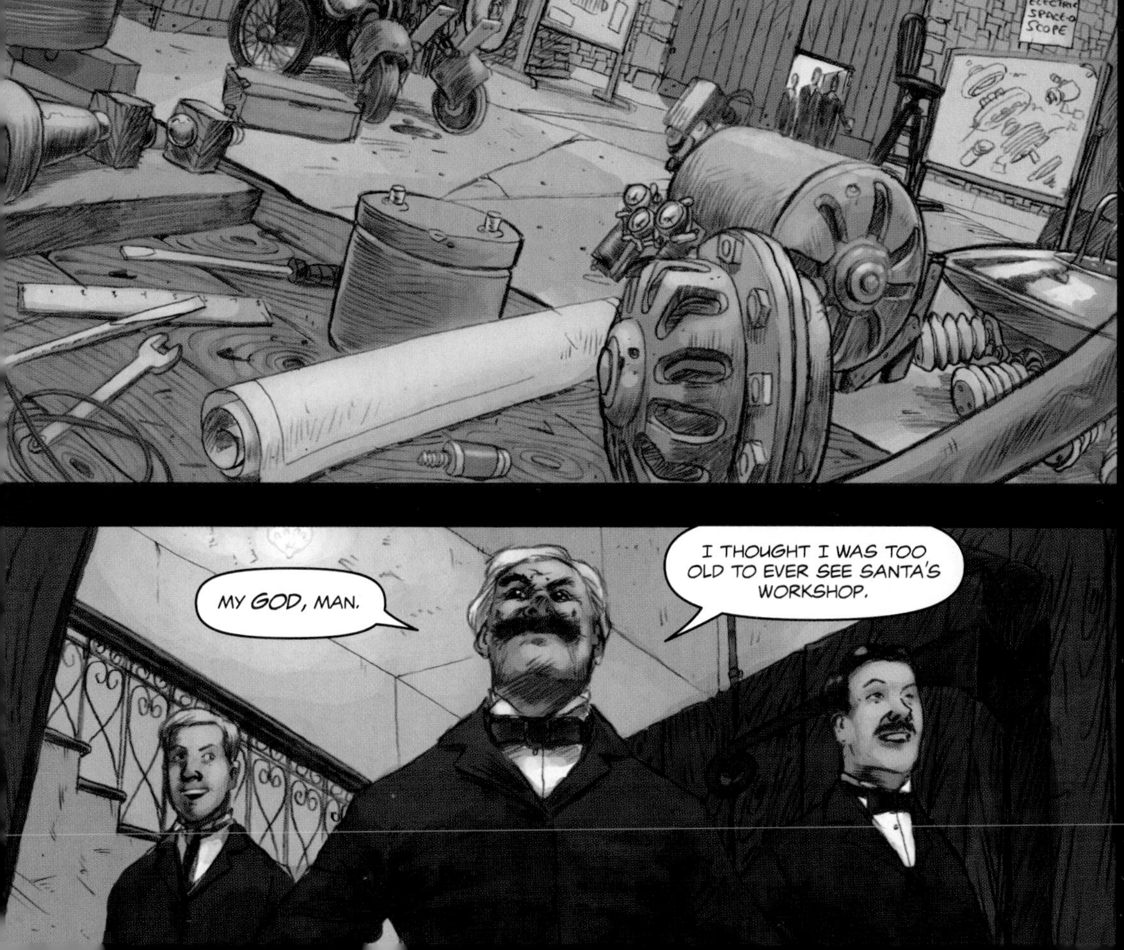
MY *GOD*, MAN.
I THOUGHT I WAS TOO OLD TO EVER SEE SANTA'S WORKSHOP.

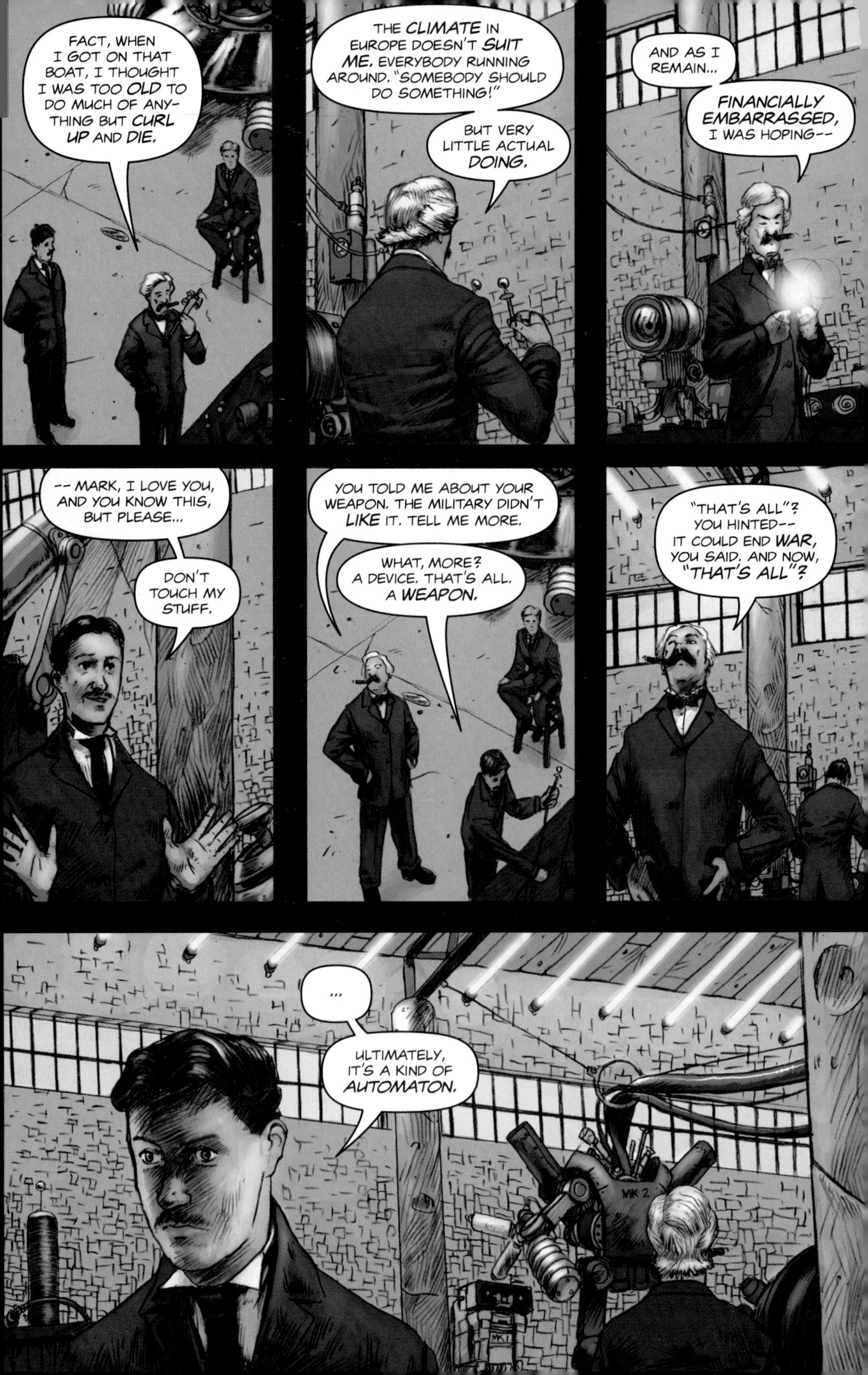
FACT, WHEN I GOT ON THAT BOAT, I THOUGHT I WAS TOO OLD TO DO MUCH OF ANY-THING BUT CURL UP AND DIE.
THE CLIMATE IN EUROPE DOESN'T SUIT ME. EVERYBODY RUNNING AROUND. "SOMEBODY SHOULD DO SOMETHING!"
BUT VERY LITTLE ACTUAL DOING.
AND AS I REMAIN...
FINANCIALLY EMBARRASSED, I WAS HOPING--
-- MARK, I LOVE YOU, AND YOU KNOW THIS, BUT PLEASE...
DON'T TOUCH MY STUFF.
YOU TOLD ME ABOUT YOUR WEAPON. THE MILITARY DIDN'T LIKE IT. TELL ME MORE.
WHAT, MORE? A DEVICE. THAT'S ALL. A WEAPON.
"THAT'S ALL"? YOU HINTED-- IT COULD END WAR, YOU SAID, AND NOW, "THAT'S ALL"?
...
ULTIMATELY, IT'S A KIND OF AUTOMATON.
MK 2
MK 1

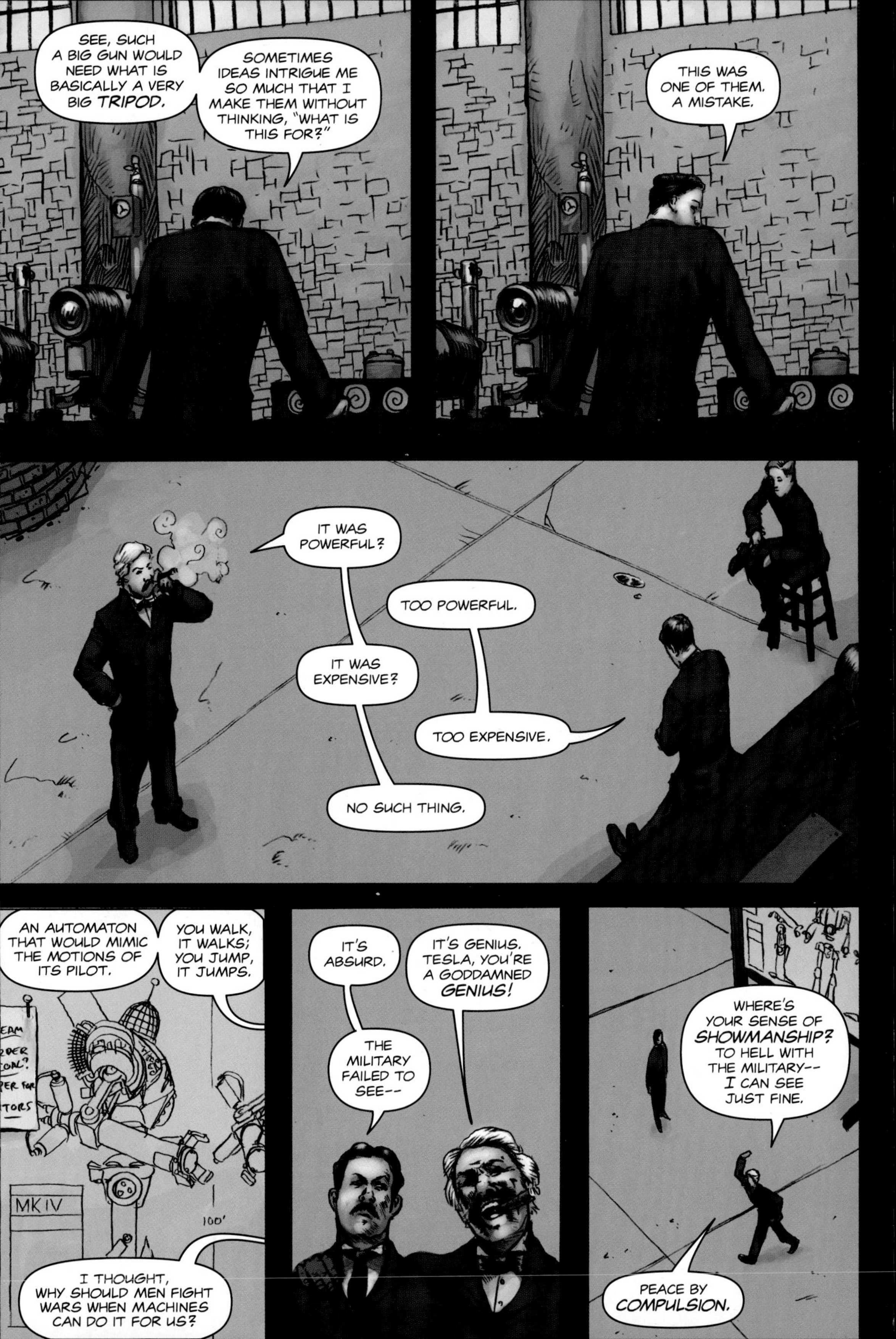
SEE, SUCH A BIG GUN WOULD NEED WHAT IS BASICALLY A VERY BIG TRIPOD.
SOMETIMES IDEAS INTRIGUE ME SO MUCH THAT I MAKE THEM WITHOUT THINKING, "WHAT IS THIS FOR?"
THIS WAS ONE OF THEM. A MISTAKE.
IT WAS POWERFUL?
TOO POWERFUL.
IT WAS EXPENSIVE?
TOO EXPENSIVE.
NO SUCH THING.
AN AUTOMATON THAT WOULD MIMIC THE MOTIONS OF ITS PILOT.
YOU WALK, IT WALKS; YOU JUMP, IT JUMPS.
MK IV
100'
I THOUGHT, WHY SHOULD MEN FIGHT WARS WHEN MACHINES CAN DO IT FOR US?
IT'S ABSURD.
IT'S GENIUS. TESLA, YOU'RE A GODDAMNED GENIUS!
THE MILITARY FAILED TO SEE--
WHERE'S YOUR SENSE OF SHOWMANSHIP? TO HELL WITH THE MILITARY-- I CAN SEE JUST FINE.
PEACE BY COMPULSION.

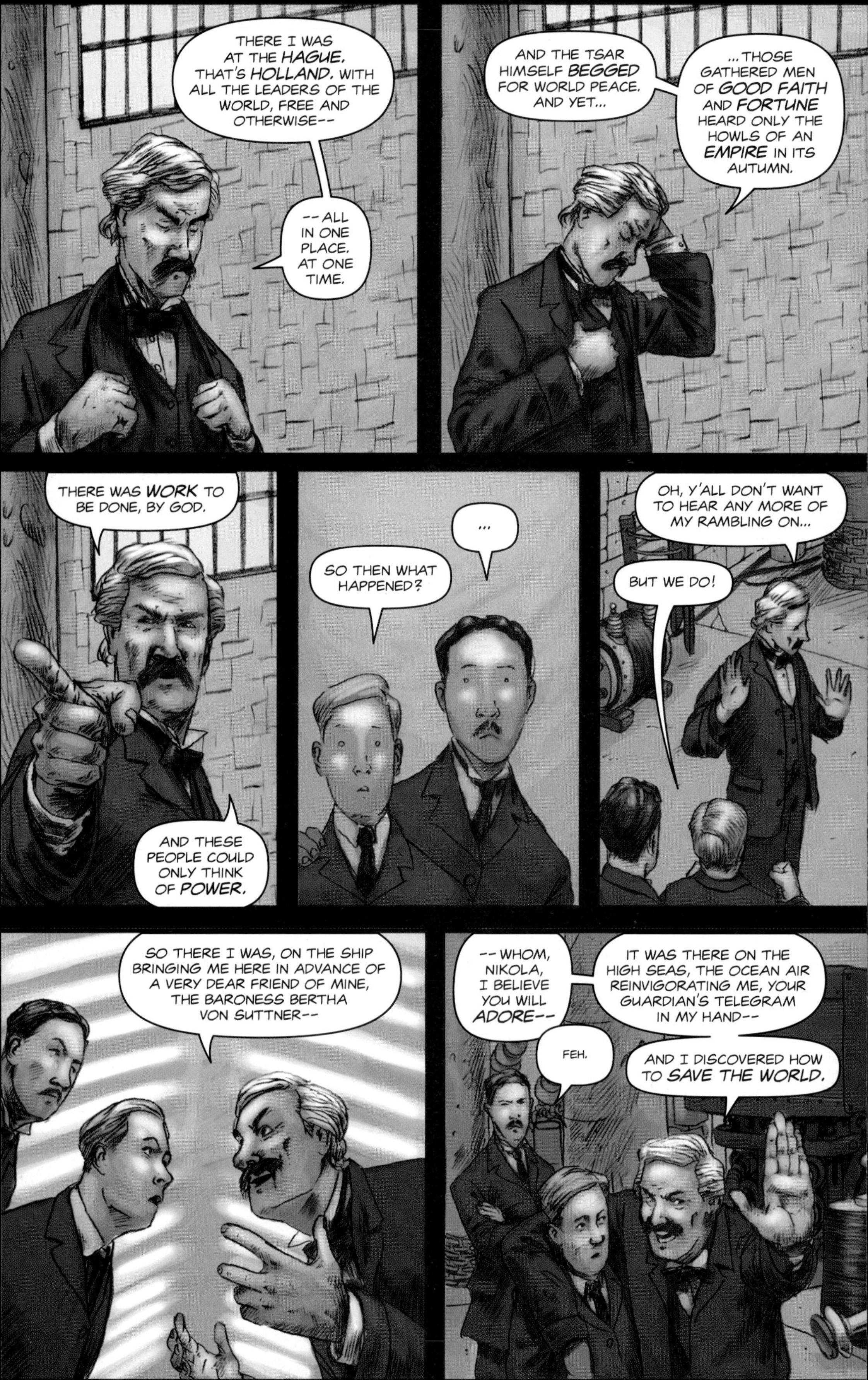
THERE I WAS AT THE HAGUE. THAT'S HOLLAND. WITH ALL THE LEADERS OF THE WORLD, FREE AND OTHERWISE--
--ALL IN ONE PLACE. AT ONE TIME.
AND THE TSAR HIMSELF BEGGED FOR WORLD PEACE. AND YET...
...THOSE GATHERED MEN OF GOOD FAITH AND FORTUNE HEARD ONLY THE HOWLS OF AN EMPIRE IN ITS AUTUMN.
THERE WAS WORK TO BE DONE, BY GOD.
AND THESE PEOPLE COULD ONLY THINK OF POWER.
...
SO THEN WHAT HAPPENED?
OH, Y'ALL DON'T WANT TO HEAR ANY MORE OF MY RAMBLING ON...
BUT WE DO!
SO THERE I WAS, ON THE SHIP BRINGING ME HERE IN ADVANCE OF A VERY DEAR FRIEND OF MINE, THE BARONESS BERTHA VON SUTTNER--
--WHOM, NIKOLA, I BELIEVE YOU WILL ADORE--
FEH.
IT WAS THERE ON THE HIGH SEAS, THE OCEAN AIR REINVIGORATING ME, YOUR GUARDIAN'S TELEGRAM IN MY HAND--
AND I DISCOVERED HOW TO SAVE THE WORLD.

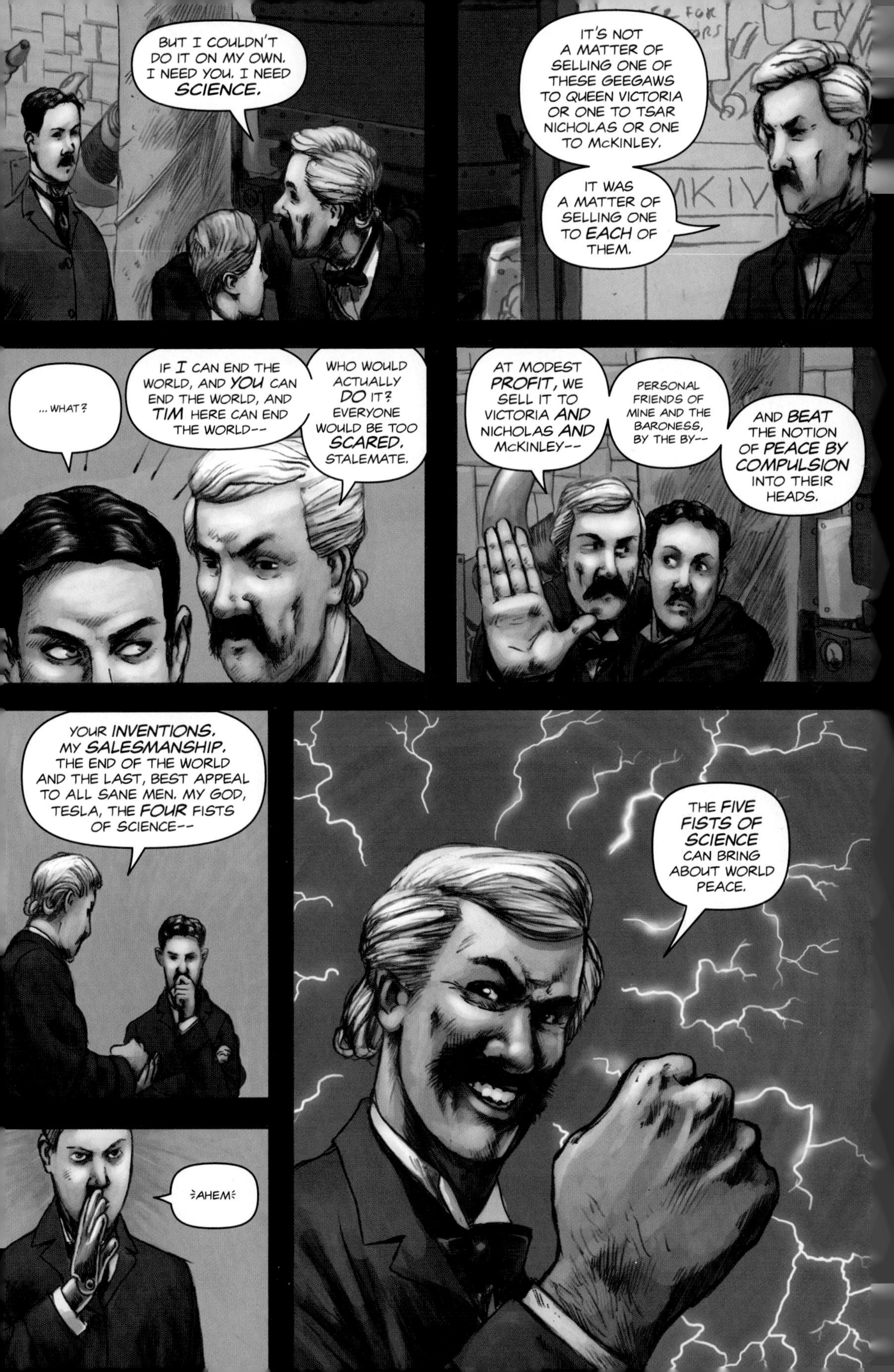
BUT I COULDN'T DO IT ON MY OWN. I NEED YOU. I NEED SCIENCE.
IT'S NOT A MATTER OF SELLING ONE OF THESE GEEGAWS TO QUEEN VICTORIA OR ONE TO TSAR NICHOLAS OR ONE TO McKINLEY.
IT WAS A MATTER OF SELLING ONE TO EACH OF THEM.
...WHAT?
IF I CAN END THE WORLD, AND YOU CAN END THE WORLD, AND TIM HERE CAN END THE WORLD--
WHO WOULD ACTUALLY DO IT? EVERYONE WOULD BE TOO SCARED. STALEMATE.
AT MODEST PROFIT, WE SELL IT TO VICTORIA AND NICHOLAS AND McKINLEY--
PERSONAL FRIENDS OF MINE AND THE BARONESS, BY THE BY--
AND BEAT THE NOTION OF PEACE BY COMPULSION INTO THEIR HEADS.
YOUR INVENTIONS. MY SALESMANSHIP. THE END OF THE WORLD AND THE LAST, BEST APPEAL TO ALL SANE MEN. MY GOD, TESLA, THE FOUR FISTS OF SCIENCE--
AHEM
THE FIVE FISTS OF SCIENCE CAN BRING ABOUT WORLD PEACE.

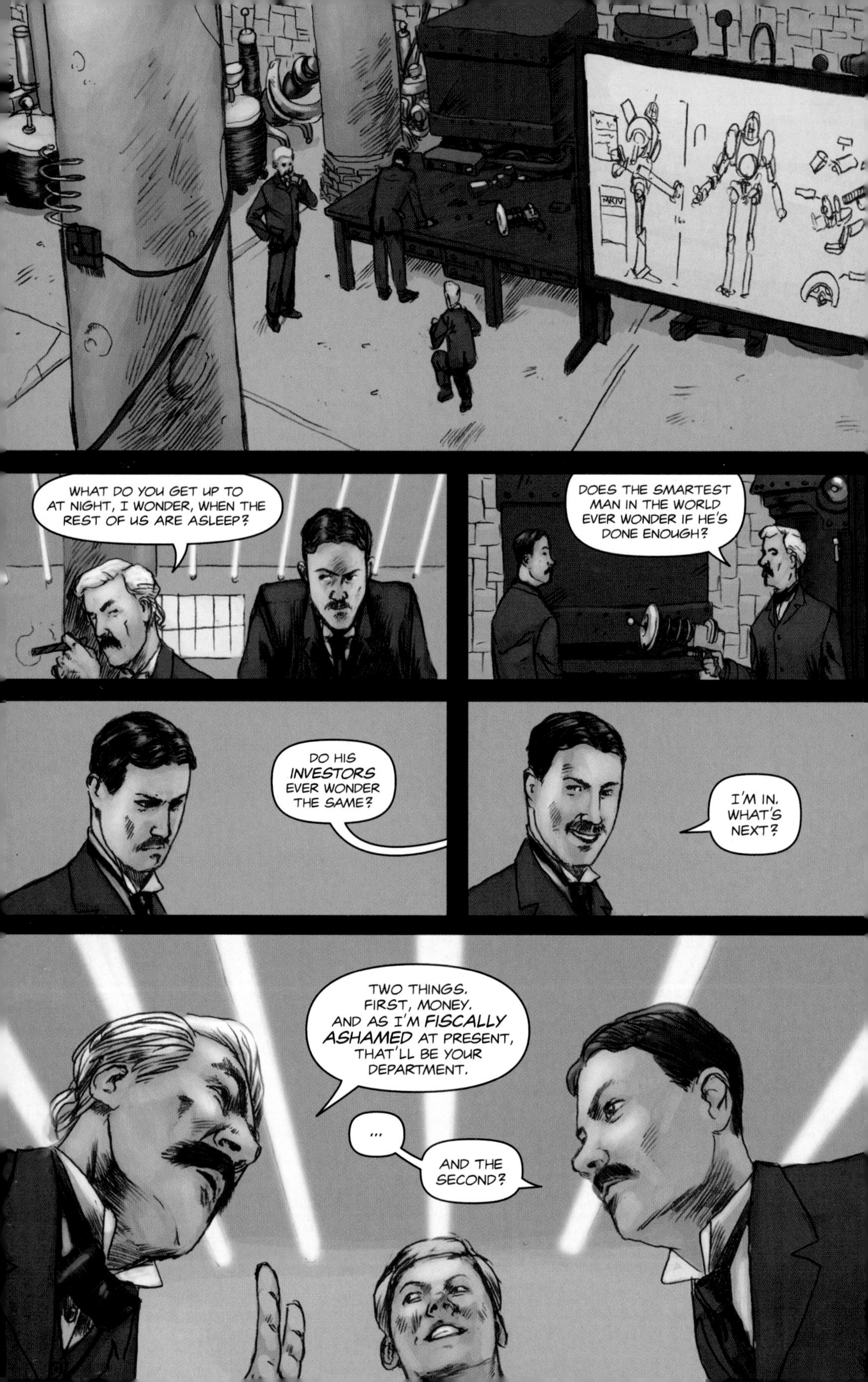
WHAT DO YOU GET UP TO AT NIGHT, I WONDER, WHEN THE REST OF US ARE ASLEEP?
DOES THE SMARTEST MAN IN THE WORLD EVER WONDER IF HE'S DONE ENOUGH?
DO HIS INVESTORS EVER WONDER THE SAME?
I'M IN. WHAT'S NEXT?
TWO THINGS. FIRST, MONEY. AND AS I'M FISCALLY ASHAMED AT PRESENT, THAT'LL BE YOUR DEPARTMENT.
...
AND THE SECOND?

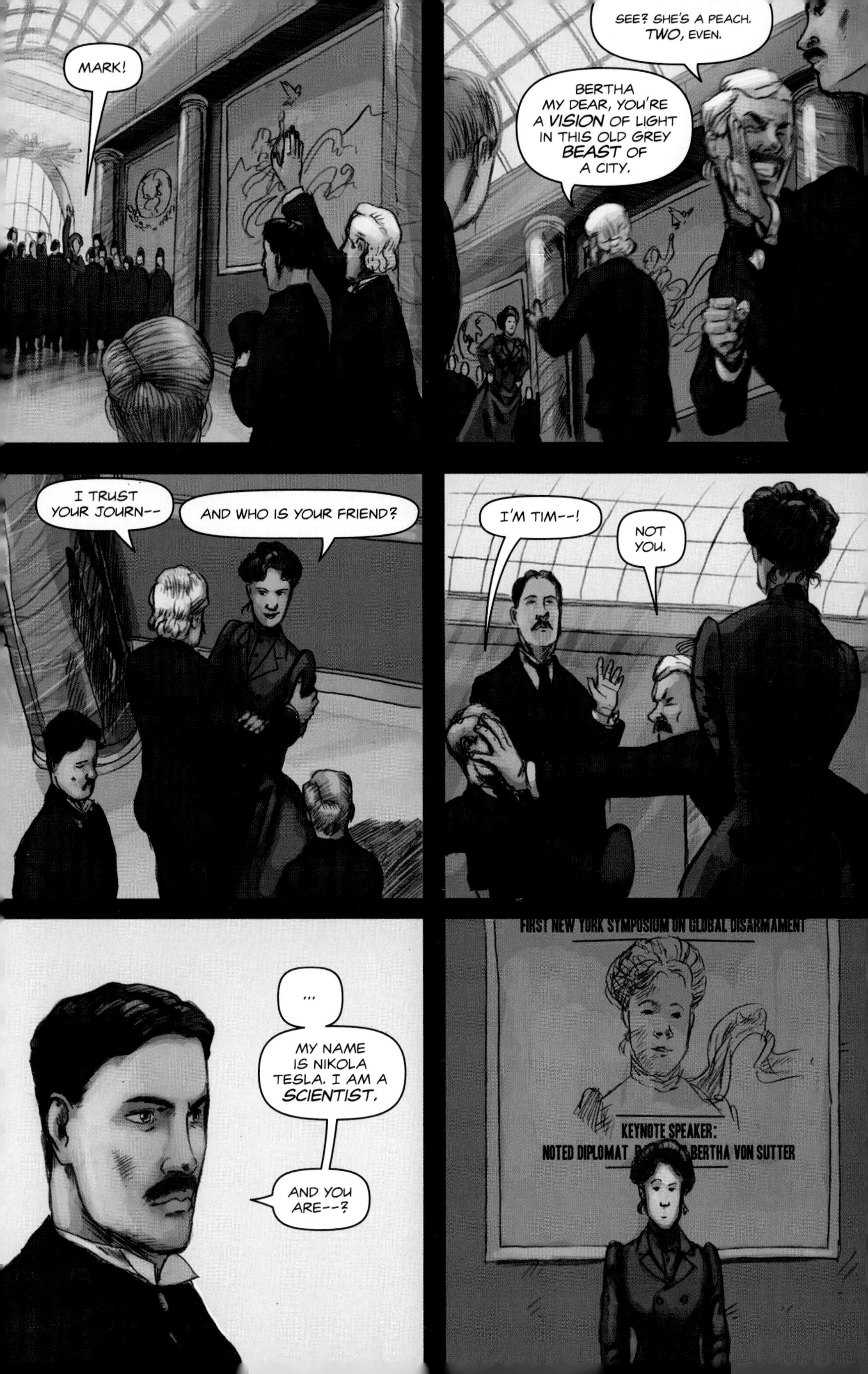
MARK!
SEE? SHE'S A PEACH. TWO, EVEN.
BERTHA MY DEAR, YOU'RE A VISION OF LIGHT IN THIS OLD GREY BEAST OF A CITY.
I TRUST YOUR JOURN--
AND WHO IS YOUR FRIEND?
I'M TIM--!
NOT YOU.
...
MY NAME IS NIKOLA TESLA. I AM A SCIENTIST.
AND YOU ARE--?
FIRST NEW YORK SYMPOSIUM ON GLOBAL DISARMAMENT
KEYNOTE SPEAKER:
NOTED DIPLOMAT
BERTHA VON SUTTER

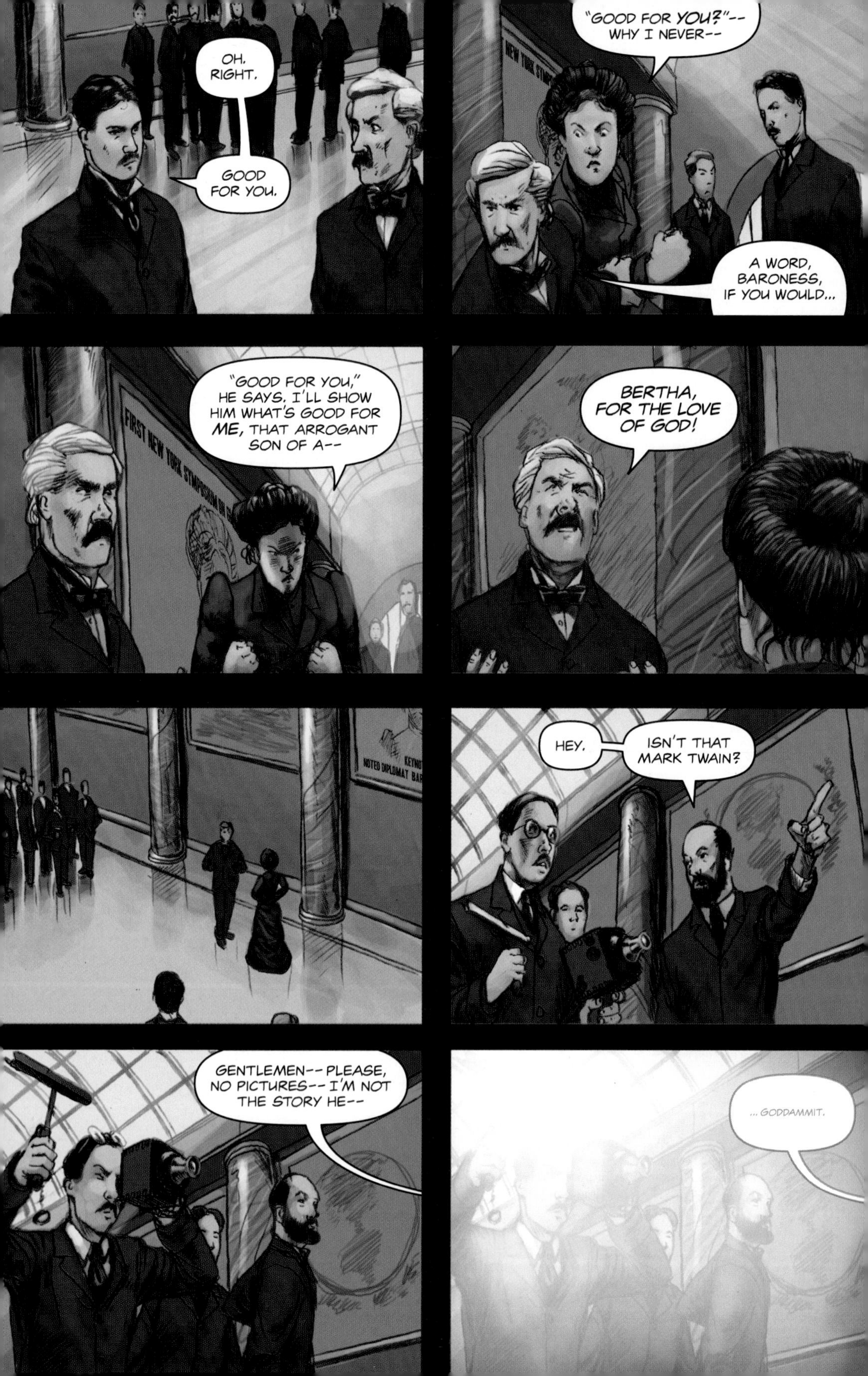
OH. RIGHT.
GOOD FOR YOU.
"GOOD FOR YOU?"-- WHY I NEVER--
A WORD, BARONESS, IF YOU WOULD...
"GOOD FOR YOU," HE SAYS. I'LL SHOW HIM WHAT'S GOOD FOR ME, THAT ARROGANT SON OF A--
BERTHA, FOR THE LOVE OF GOD!
HEY.
ISN'T THAT MARK TWAIN?
GENTLEMEN-- PLEASE, NO PICTURES-- I'M NOT THE STORY HE--
...GODDAMMIT.

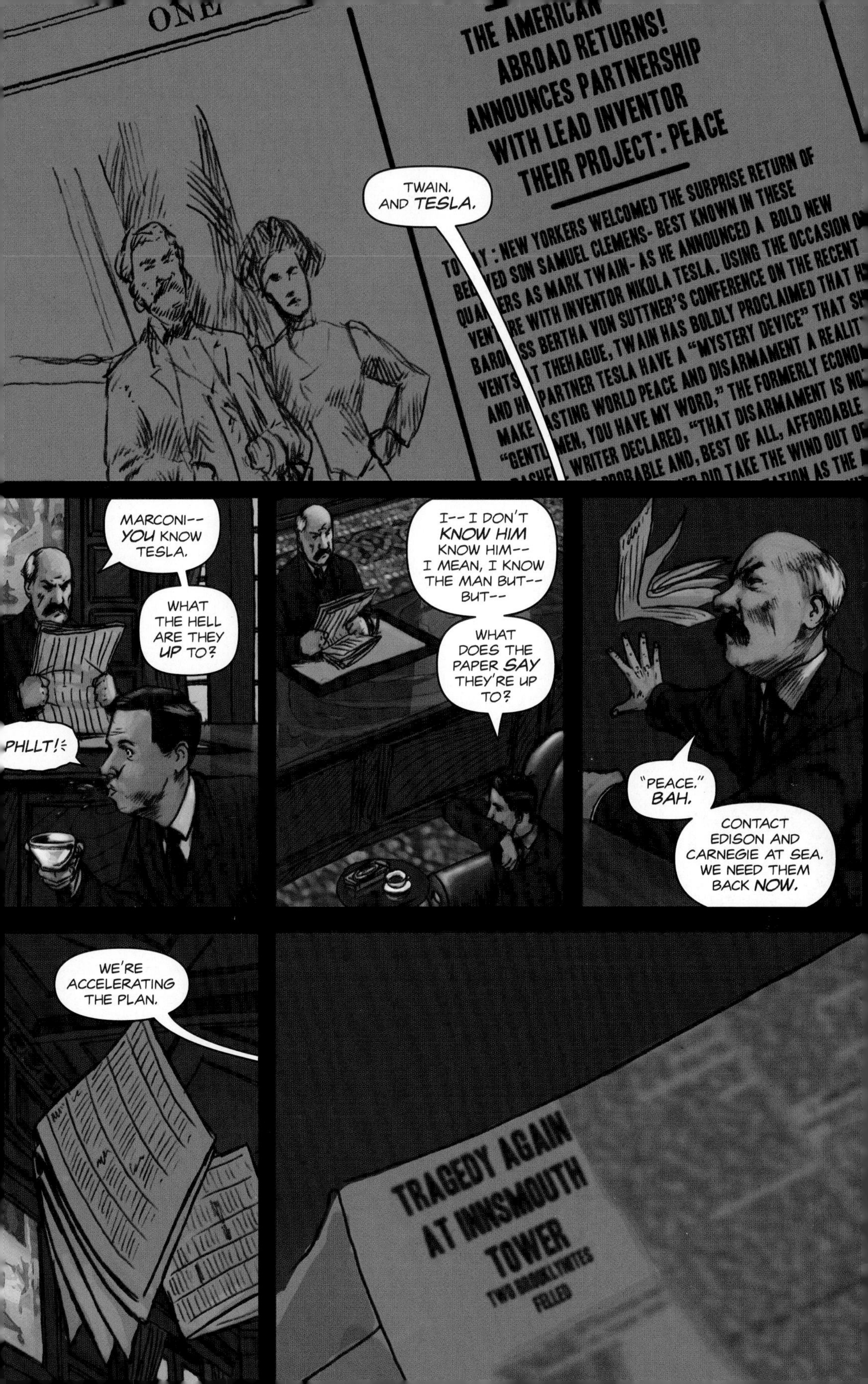
ONE
THE AMERICAN ABROAD RETURNS! ANNOUNCES PARTNERSHIP WITH LEAD INVENTOR THEIR PROJECT: PEACE
TWAIN. AND TESLA.
MARCONI-- YOU KNOW TESLA.
WHAT THE HELL ARE THEY UP TO?
PHLLT!
I-- I DON'T KNOW HIM KNOW HIM-- I MEAN, I KNOW THE MAN BUT-- BUT--
WHAT DOES THE PAPER SAY THEY'RE UP TO?
"PEACE." BAH.
CONTACT EDISON AND CARNEGIE AT SEA. WE NEED THEM BACK NOW.
WE'RE ACCELERATING THE PLAN.
TRAGEDY AGAIN AT INNSMOUTH TOWER

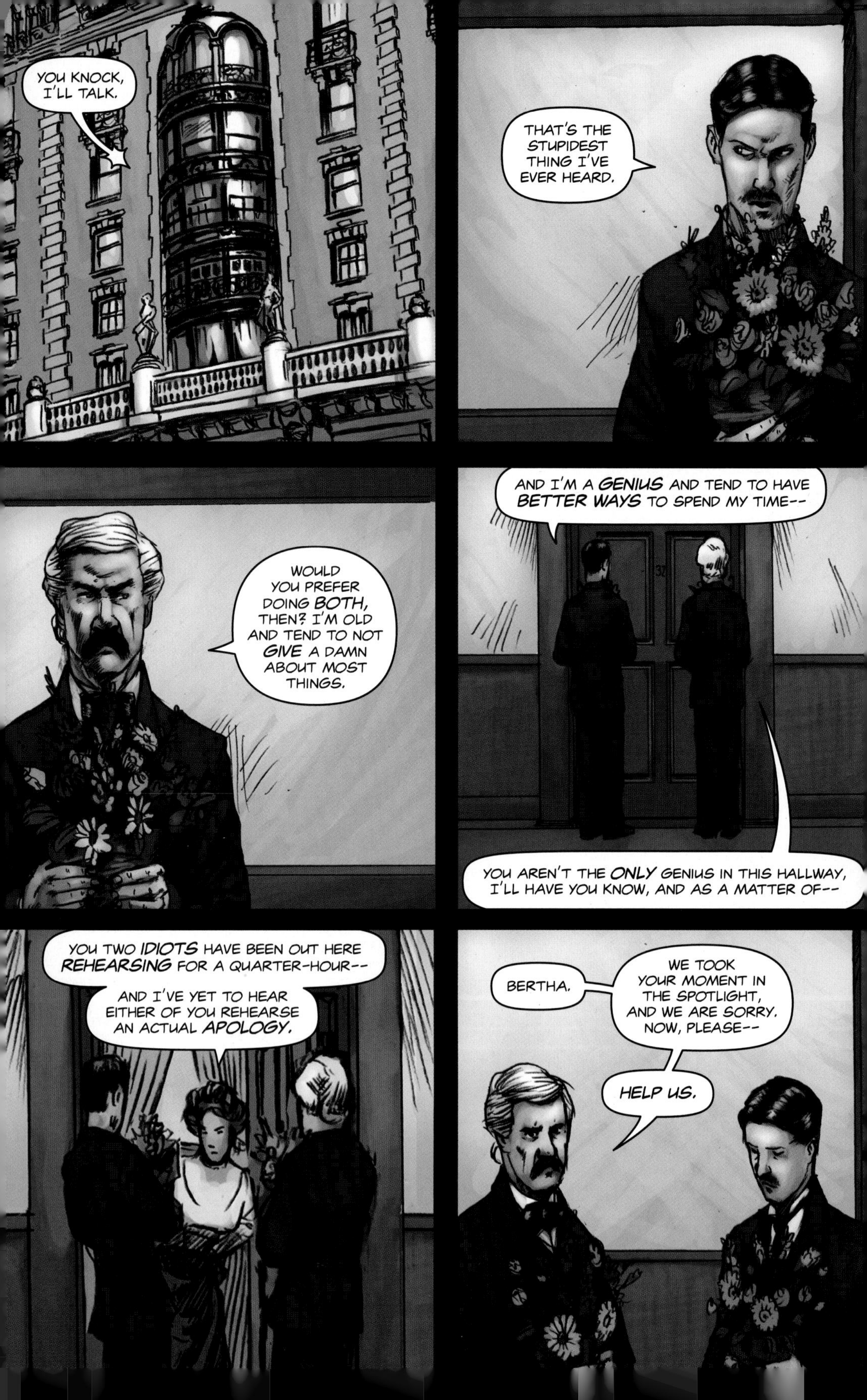
YOU KNOCK, I'LL TALK.
THAT'S THE STUPIDEST THING I'VE EVER HEARD.
WOULD YOU PREFER DOING BOTH, THEN? I'M OLD AND TEND TO NOT GIVE A DAMN ABOUT MOST THINGS.
AND I'M A GENIUS AND TEND TO HAVE BETTER WAYS TO SPEND MY TIME--
YOU AREN'T THE ONLY GENIUS IN THIS HALLWAY, I'LL HAVE YOU KNOW, AND AS A MATTER OF--
YOU TWO IDIOTS HAVE BEEN OUT HERE REHEARSING FOR A QUARTER-HOUR--
AND I'VE YET TO HEAR EITHER OF YOU REHEARSE AN ACTUAL APOLOGY.
BERTHA.
WE TOOK YOUR MOMENT IN THE SPOTLIGHT, AND WE ARE SORRY. NOW, PLEASE--
HELP US.

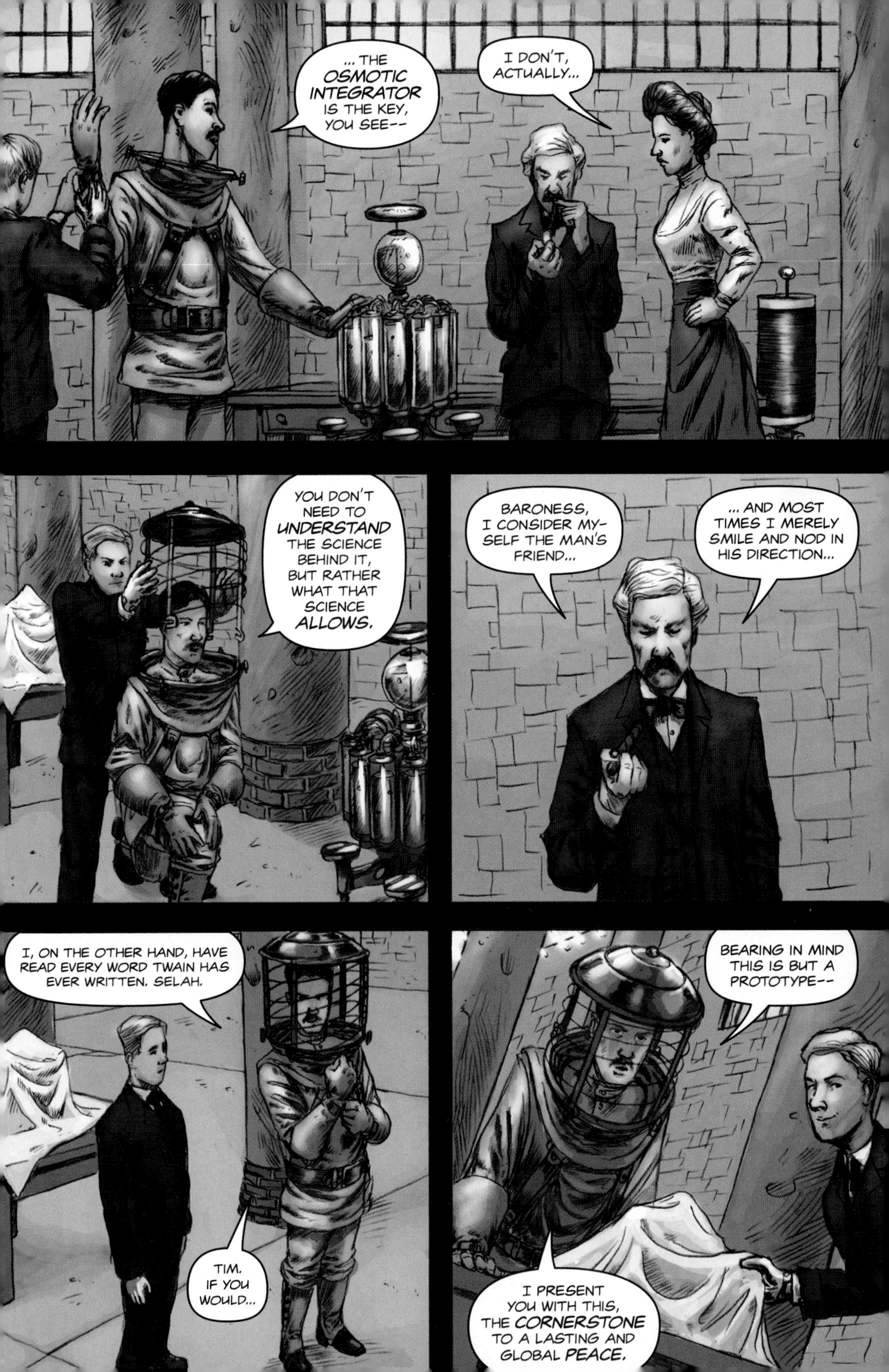
... THE OSMOTIC INTEGRATOR IS THE KEY, YOU SEE--
I DON'T, ACTUALLY...
YOU DON'T NEED TO UNDERSTAND THE SCIENCE BEHIND IT, BUT RATHER WHAT THAT SCIENCE ALLOWS.
BARONESS, I CONSIDER MY-SELF THE MAN'S FRIEND...
... AND MOST TIMES I MERELY SMILE AND NOD IN HIS DIRECTION...
I, ON THE OTHER HAND, HAVE READ EVERY WORD TWAIN HAS EVER WRITTEN. SELAH.
TIM, IF YOU WOULD...
BEARING IN MIND THIS IS BUT A PROTOTYPE--
I PRESENT YOU WITH THIS, THE CORNERSTONE TO A LASTING AND GLOBAL PEACE.

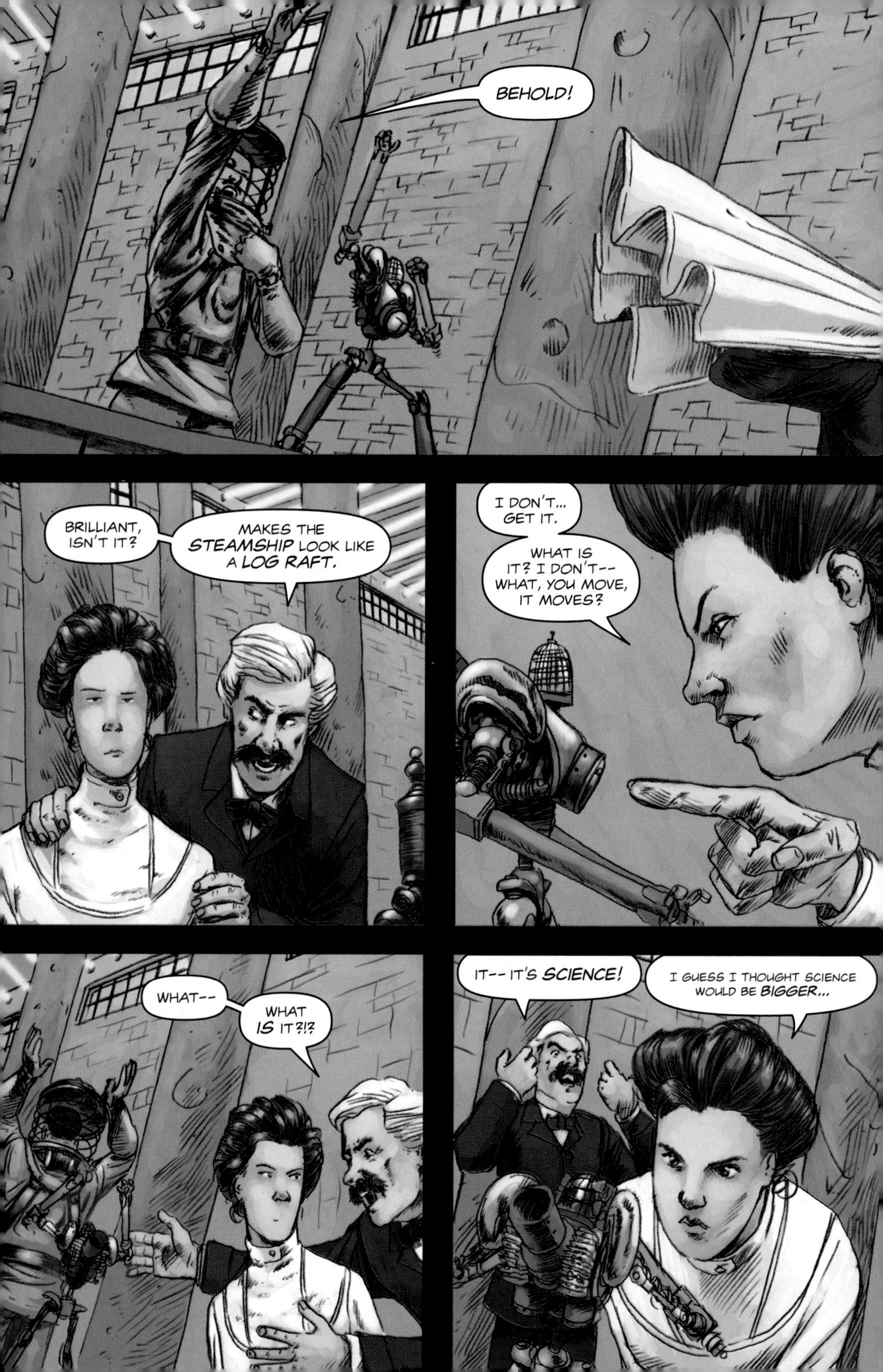

BEHOLD!
BRILLIANT, ISN'T IT?
MAKES THE STEAMSHIP LOOK LIKE A LOG RAFT.
I DON'T... GET IT.
WHAT IS IT? I DON'T-- WHAT, YOU MOVE, IT MOVES?
WHAT--
WHAT IS IT?!?
IT-- IT'S SCIENCE!
I GUESS I THOUGHT SCIENCE WOULD BE BIGGER...

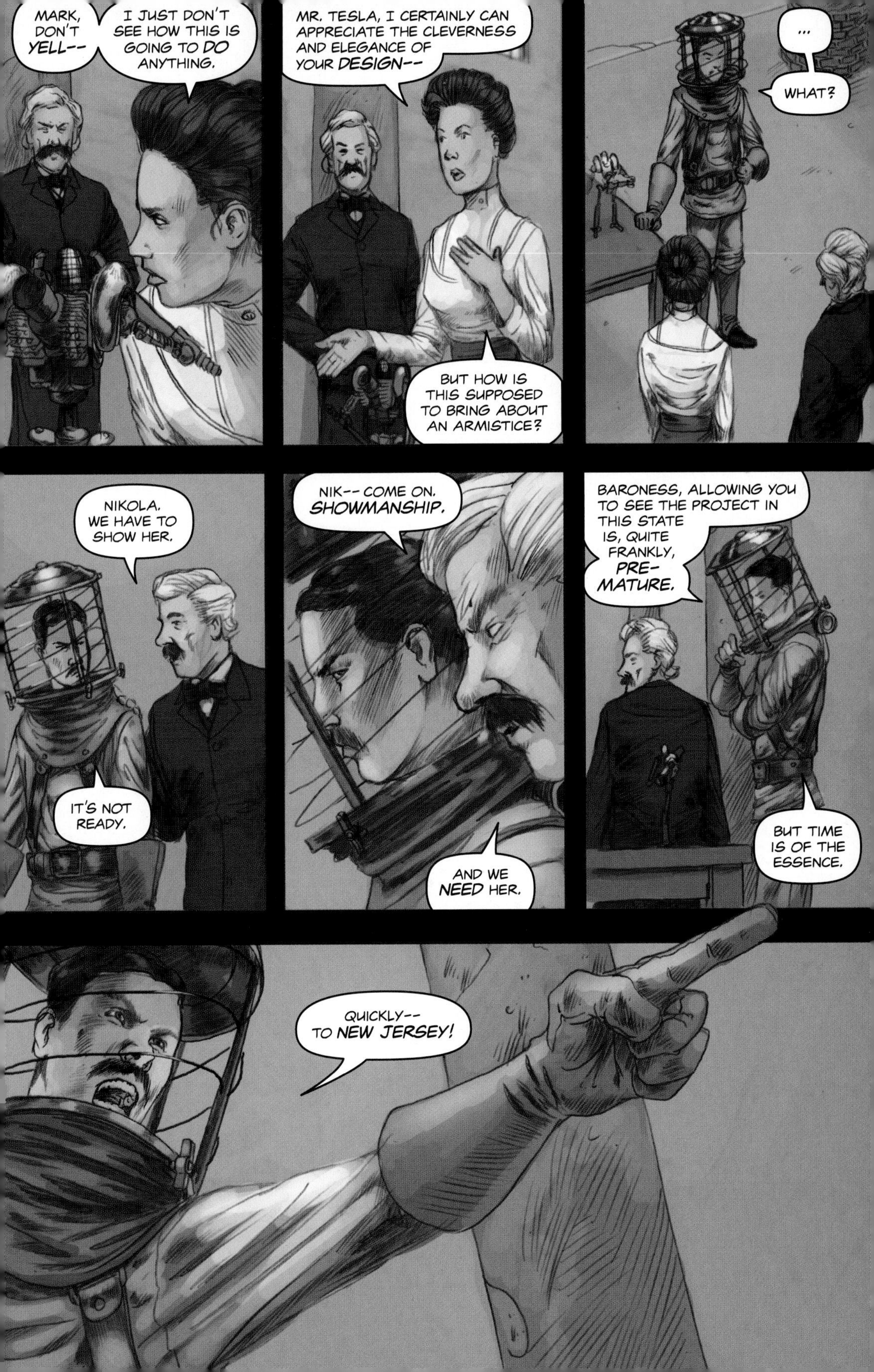
MARK, DON'T YELL--
I JUST DON'T SEE HOW THIS IS GOING TO DO ANYTHING.
MR. TESLA, I CERTAINLY CAN APPRECIATE THE CLEVERNESS AND ELEGANCE OF YOUR DESIGN--
BUT HOW IS THIS SUPPOSED TO BRING ABOUT AN ARMISTICE?
...
WHAT?
NIKOLA. WE HAVE TO SHOW HER.
IT'S NOT READY.
NIK-- COME ON. SHOWMANSHIP.
AND WE NEED HER.
BARONESS, ALLOWING YOU TO SEE THE PROJECT IN THIS STATE IS, QUITE FRANKLY, PRE-MATURE.
BUT TIME IS OF THE ESSENCE.
QUICKLY-- TO NEW JERSEY!

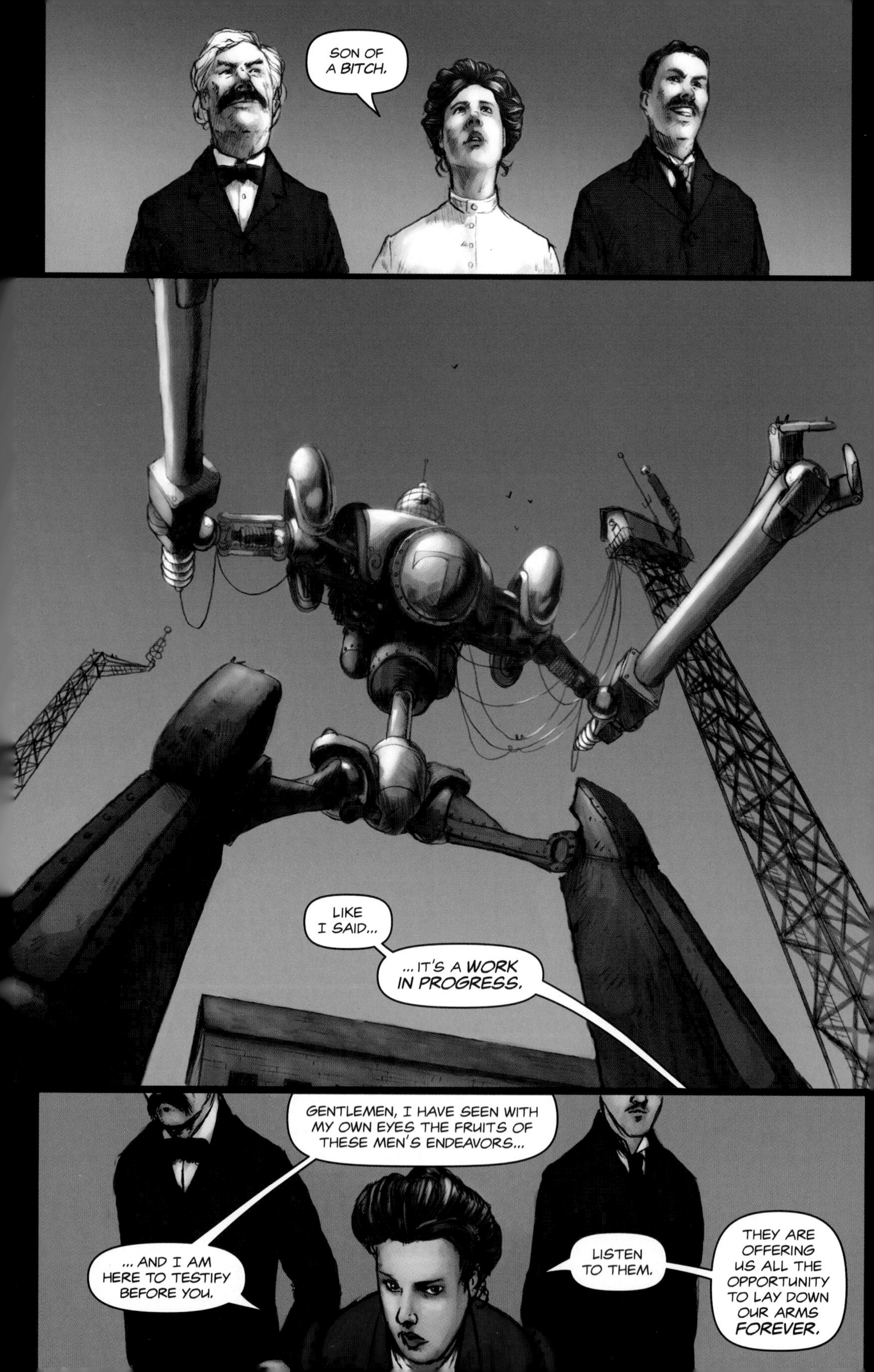
SON OF A BITCH.
LIKE I SAID...
... IT'S A WORK IN PROGRESS.
GENTLEMEN, I HAVE SEEN WITH MY OWN EYES THE FRUITS OF THESE MEN'S ENDEAVORS...
... AND I AM HERE TO TESTIFY BEFORE YOU.
LISTEN TO THEM.
THEY ARE OFFERING US ALL THE OPPORTUNITY TO LAY DOWN OUR ARMS FOREVER.

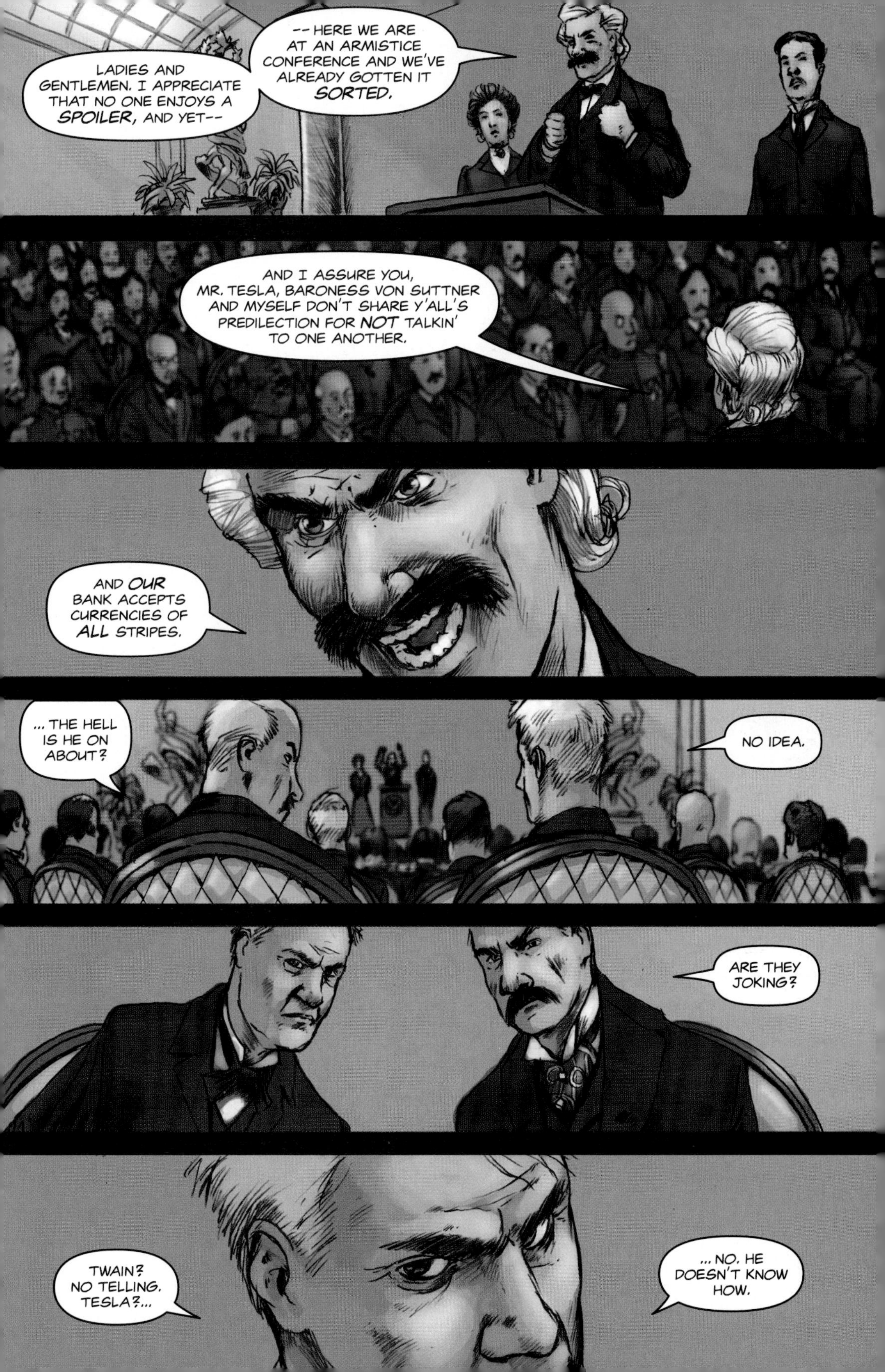
LADIES AND GENTLEMEN. I APPRECIATE THAT NO ONE ENJOYS A SPOILER, AND YET--
--HERE WE ARE AT AN ARMISTICE CONFERENCE AND WE'VE ALREADY GOTTEN IT SORTED.
AND I ASSURE YOU, MR. TESLA, BARONESS VON SUTTNER AND MYSELF DON'T SHARE Y'ALL'S PREDILECTION FOR NOT TALKIN' TO ONE ANOTHER.
AND OUR BANK ACCEPTS CURRENCIES OF ALL STRIPES.
...THE HELL IS HE ON ABOUT?
NO IDEA.
ARE THEY JOKING?
TWAIN? NO TELLING. TESLA?...
...NO. HE DOESN'T KNOW HOW.

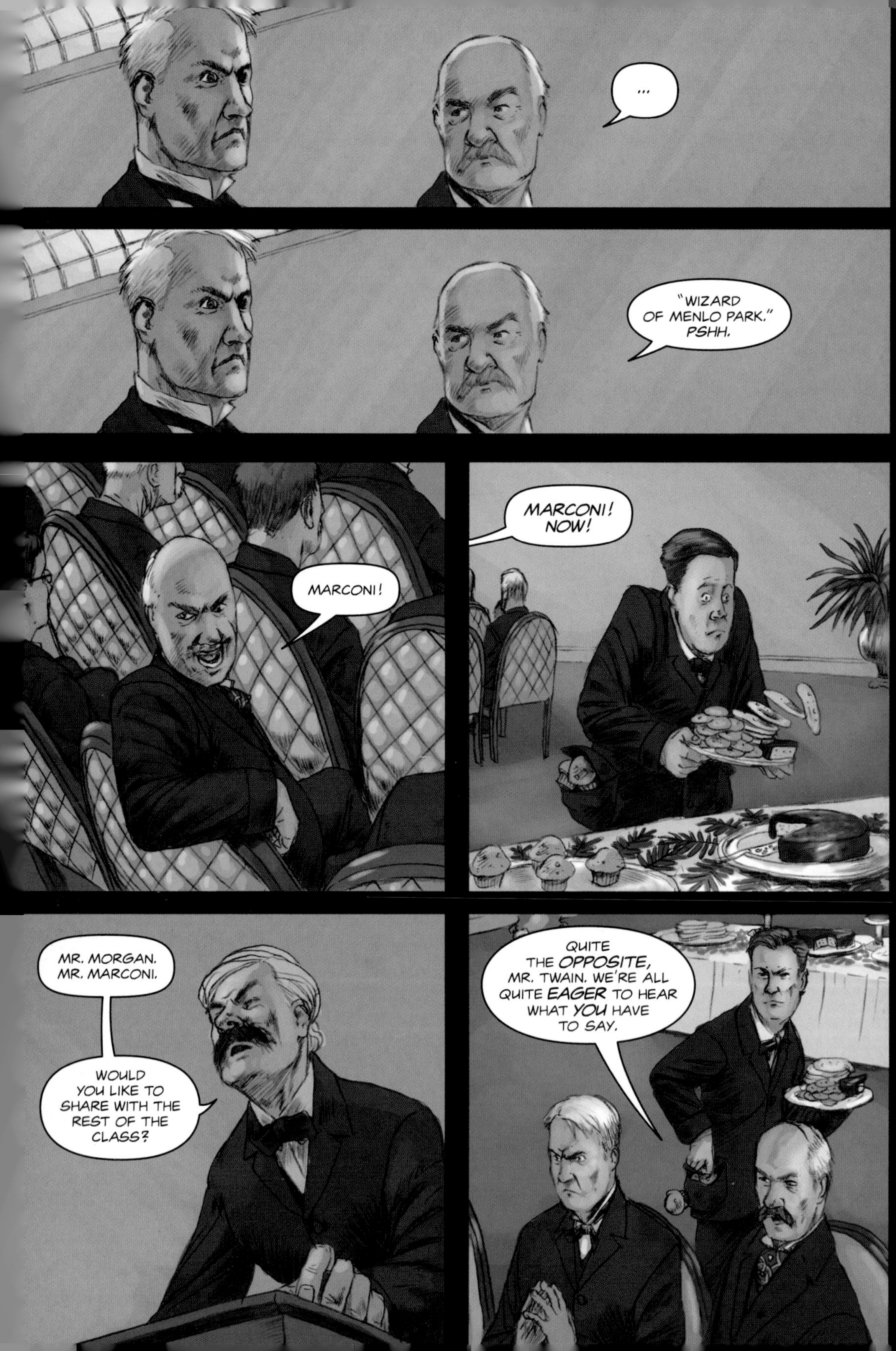
...
"WIZARD OF MENLO PARK." PSHH.
MARCONI!
MARCONI! NOW!
MR. MORGAN. MR. MARCONI.
WOULD YOU LIKE TO SHARE WITH THE REST OF THE CLASS?
QUITE THE OPPOSITE, MR. TWAIN. WE'RE ALL QUITE EAGER TO HEAR WHAT YOU HAVE TO SAY.

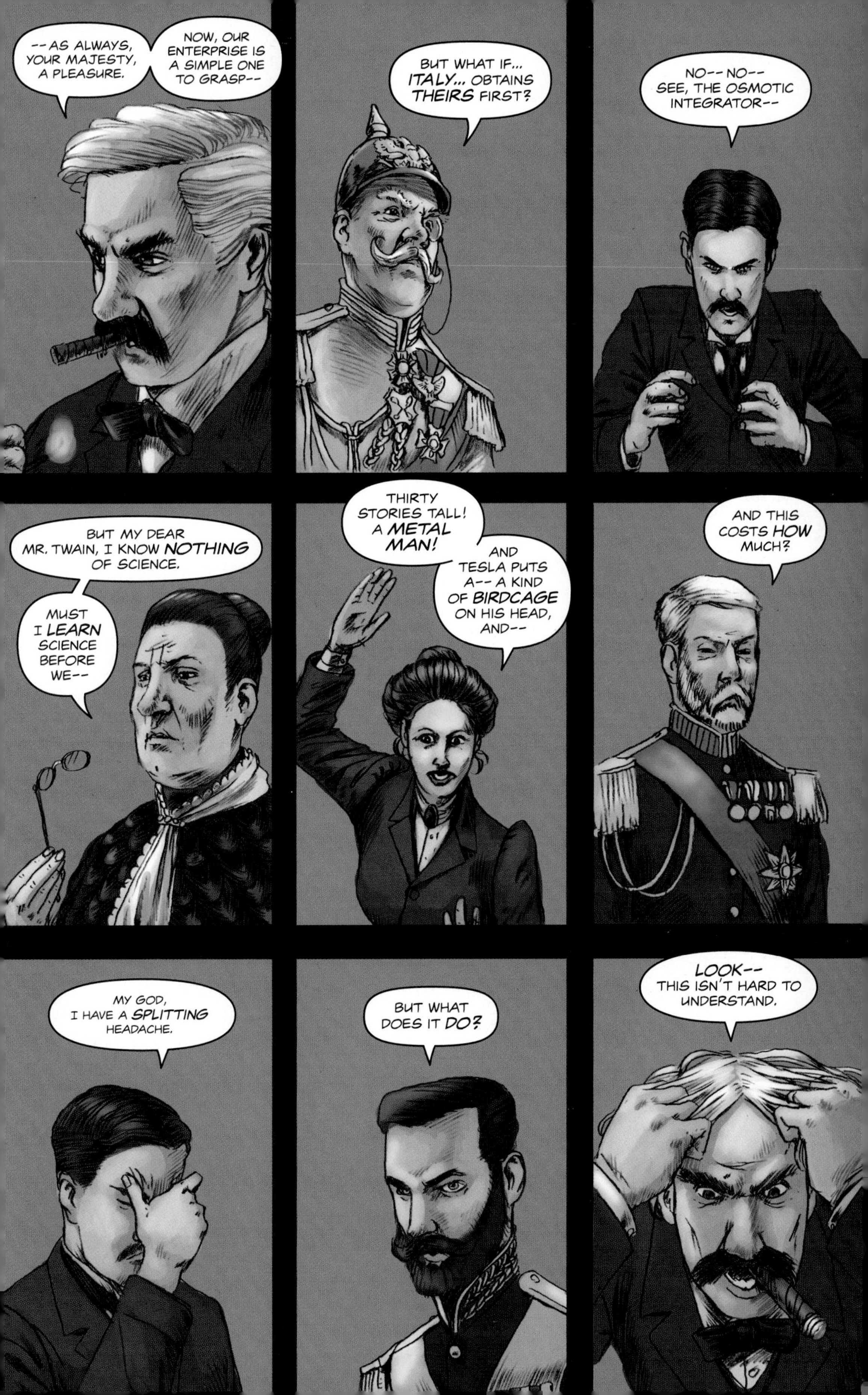
--AS ALWAYS, YOUR MAJESTY, A PLEASURE.
NOW, OUR ENTERPRISE IS A SIMPLE ONE TO GRASP--
BUT WHAT IF... ITALY... OBTAINS THEIRS FIRST?
NO--NO-- SEE, THE OSMOTIC INTEGRATOR--
BUT MY DEAR MR. TWAIN, I KNOW NOTHING OF SCIENCE.
MUST I LEARN SCIENCE BEFORE WE--
THIRTY STORIES TALL! A METAL MAN!
AND TESLA PUTS A-- A KIND OF BIRDCAGE ON HIS HEAD, AND--
AND THIS COSTS HOW MUCH?
MY GOD, I HAVE A SPLITTING HEADACHE.
BUT WHAT DOES IT DO?
LOOK-- THIS ISN'T HARD TO UNDERSTAND.

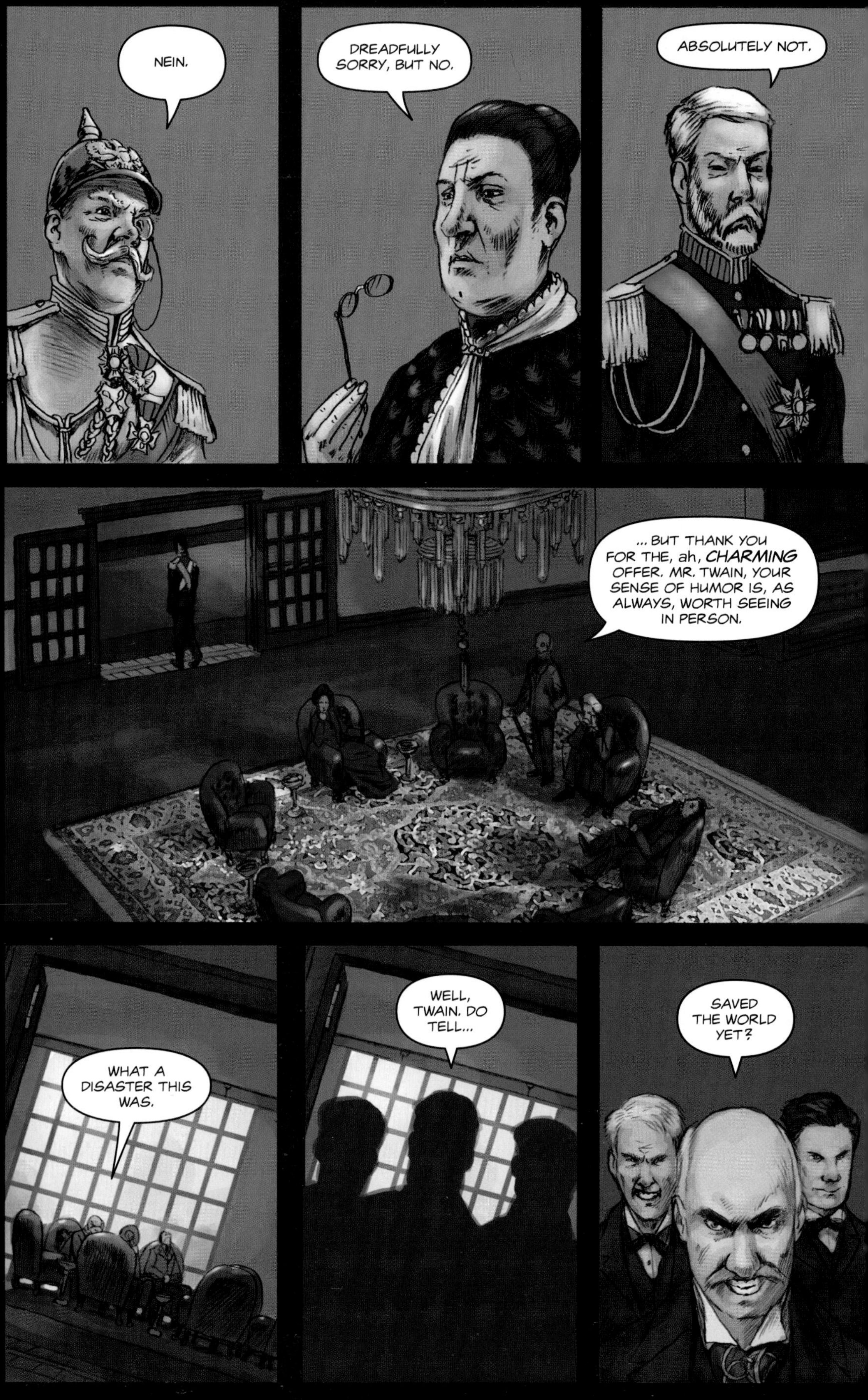
NEIN.
DREADFULLY SORRY, BUT NO.
ABSOLUTELY NOT.
... BUT THANK YOU FOR THE, ah, CHARMING OFFER. MR. TWAIN, YOUR SENSE OF HUMOR IS, AS ALWAYS, WORTH SEEING IN PERSON.
WHAT A DISASTER THIS WAS.
WELL, TWAIN. DO TELL...
SAVED THE WORLD YET?

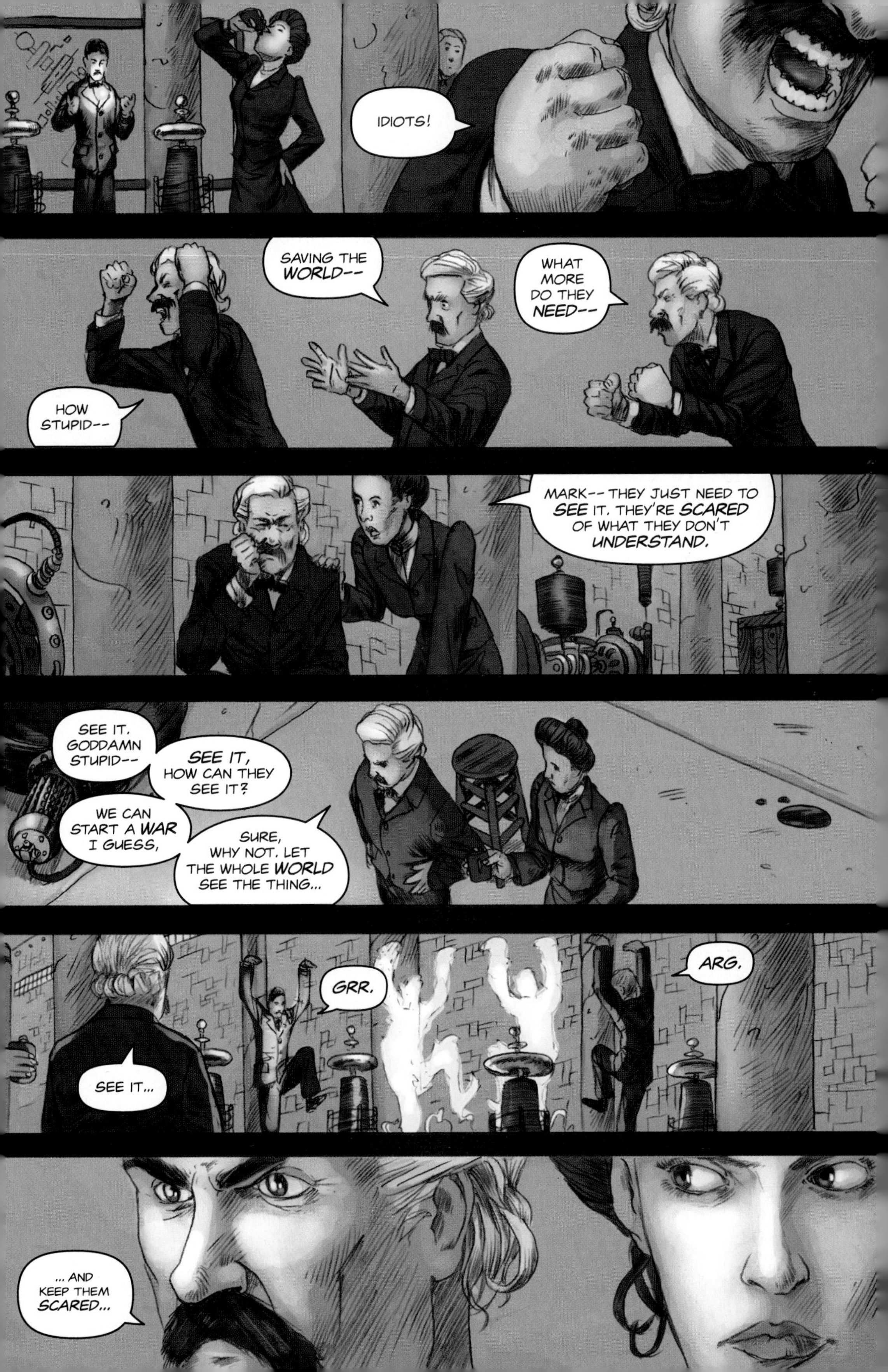
IDIOTS!
HOW STUPID--
SAVING THE WORLD--
WHAT MORE DO THEY NEED--
MARK-- THEY JUST NEED TO SEE IT. THEY'RE SCARED OF WHAT THEY DON'T UNDERSTAND.
SEE IT. GODDAMN STUPID--
SEE IT, HOW CAN THEY SEE IT?
WE CAN START A WAR I GUESS,
SURE, WHY NOT. LET THE WHOLE WORLD SEE THE THING...
GRR.
ARG.
SEE IT...
... AND KEEP THEM SCARED...

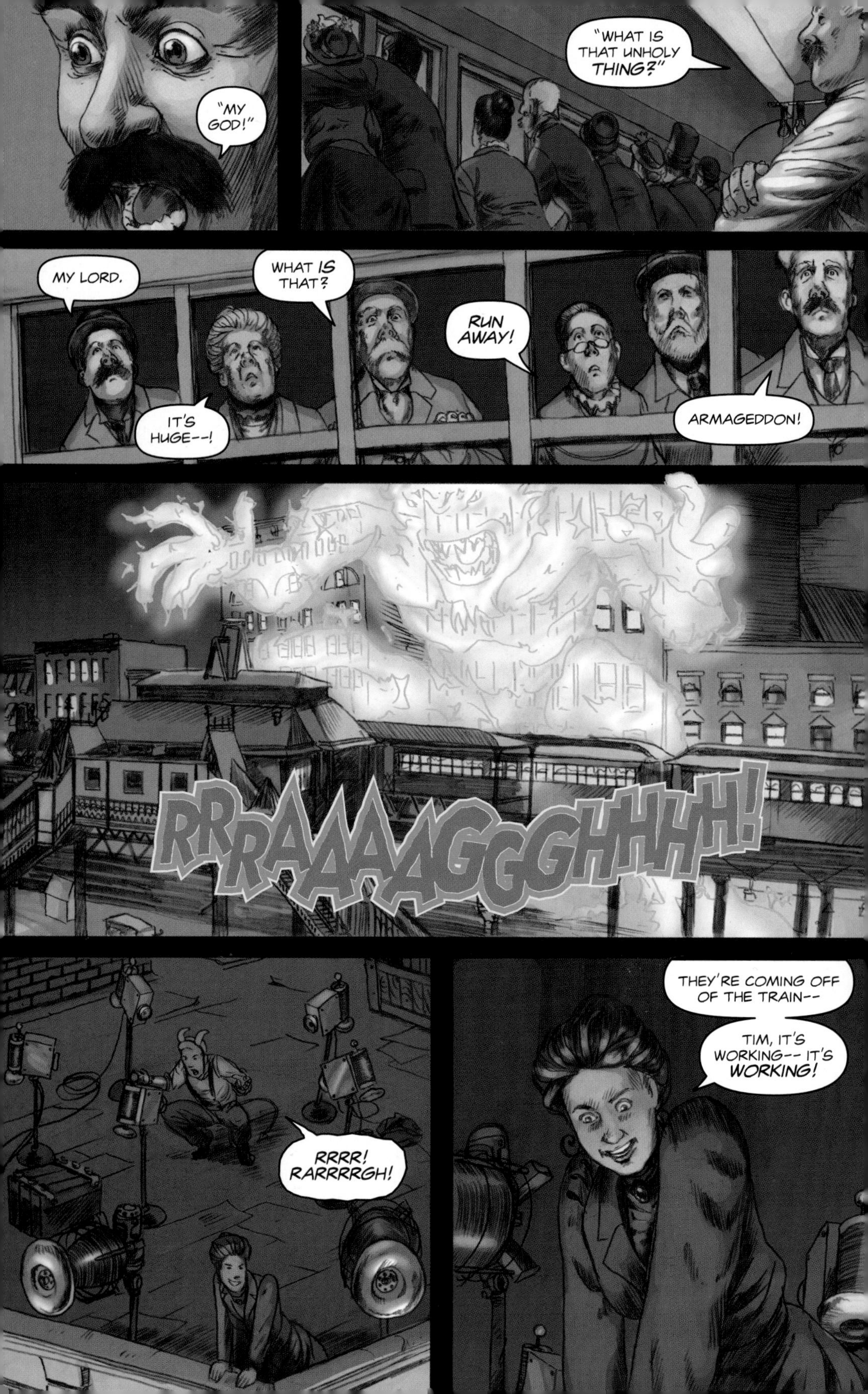
"MY GOD!"
"WHAT IS THAT UNHOLY THING?"
MY LORD.
WHAT IS THAT?
IT'S HUGE--!
RUN AWAY!
ARMAGEDDON!
RRRAAAAGGGHHHH!
RRRR! RARRRRGH!
THEY'RE COMING OFF OF THE TRAIN--
TIM, IT'S WORKING-- IT'S WORKING!

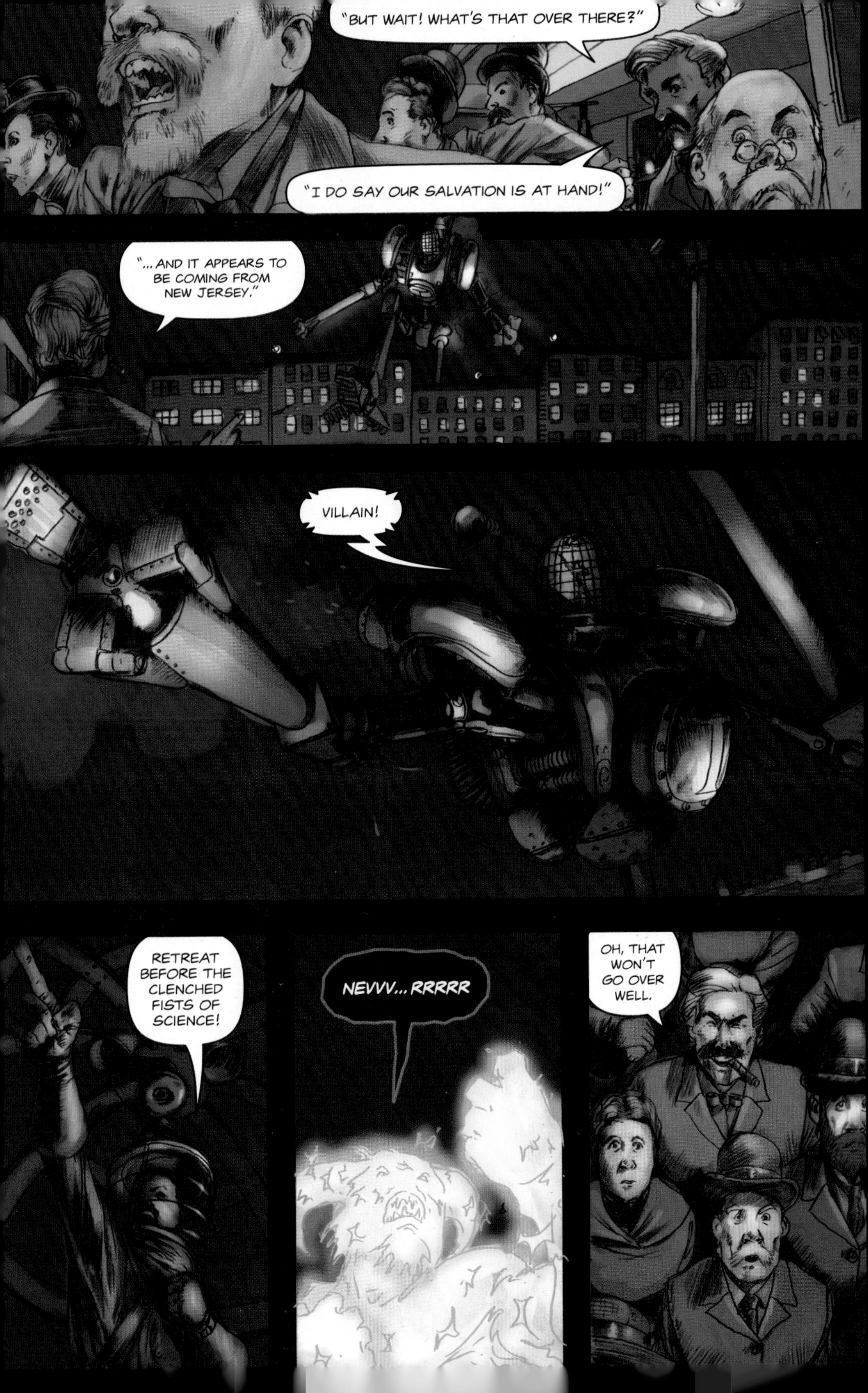
"BUT WAIT! WHAT'S THAT OVER THERE?"
"I DO SAY OUR SALVATION IS AT HAND!"
"...AND IT APPEARS TO BE COMING FROM NEW JERSEY."
VILLAIN!
RETREAT BEFORE THE CLENCHED FISTS OF SCIENCE!
NEVVV... RRRRR
OH, THAT WON'T GO OVER WELL.

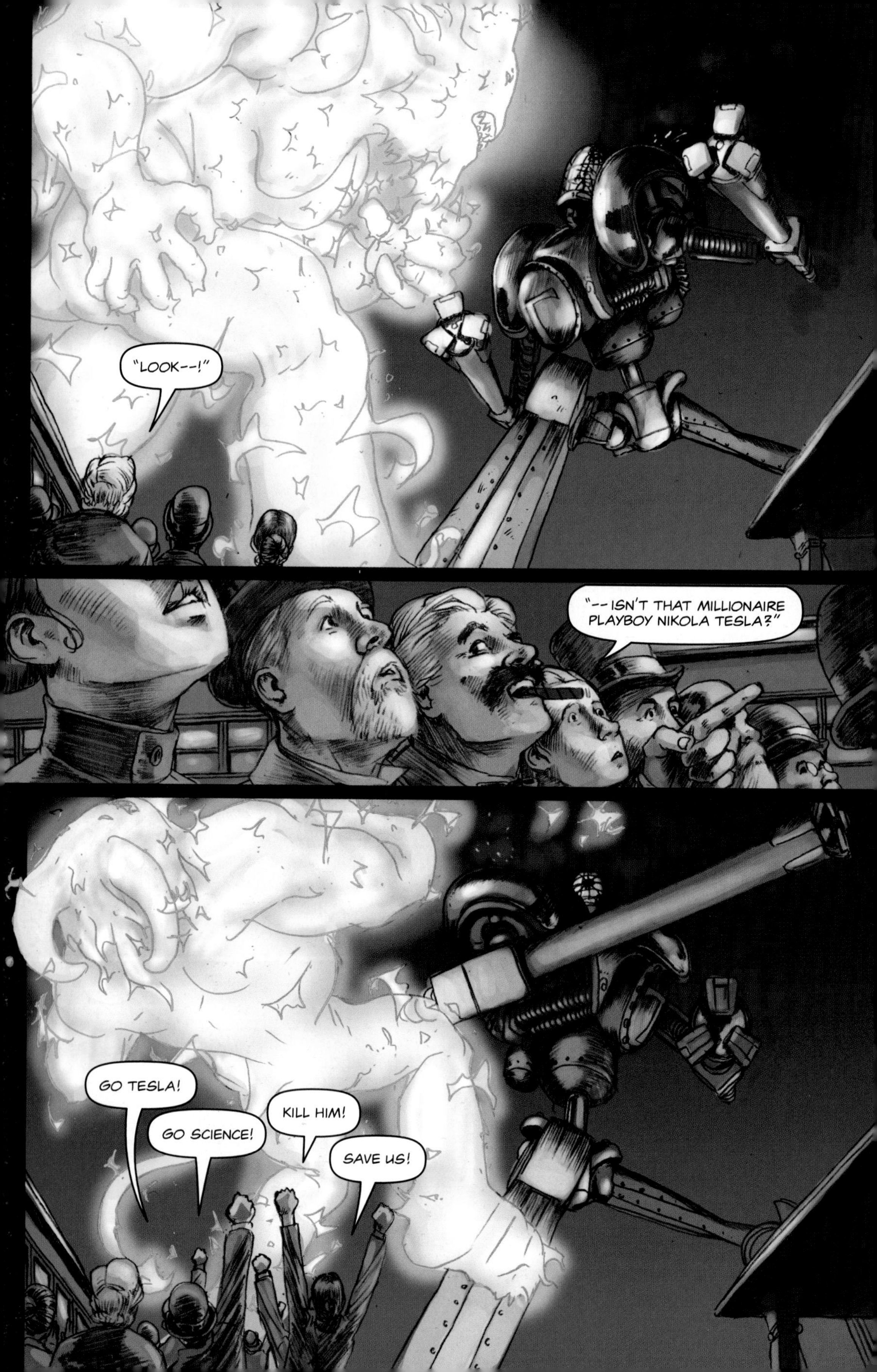
"LOOK--!"
"--ISN'T THAT MILLIONAIRE PLAYBOY NIKOLA TESLA?"
GO TESLA!
GO SCIENCE!
KILL HIM!
SAVE US!

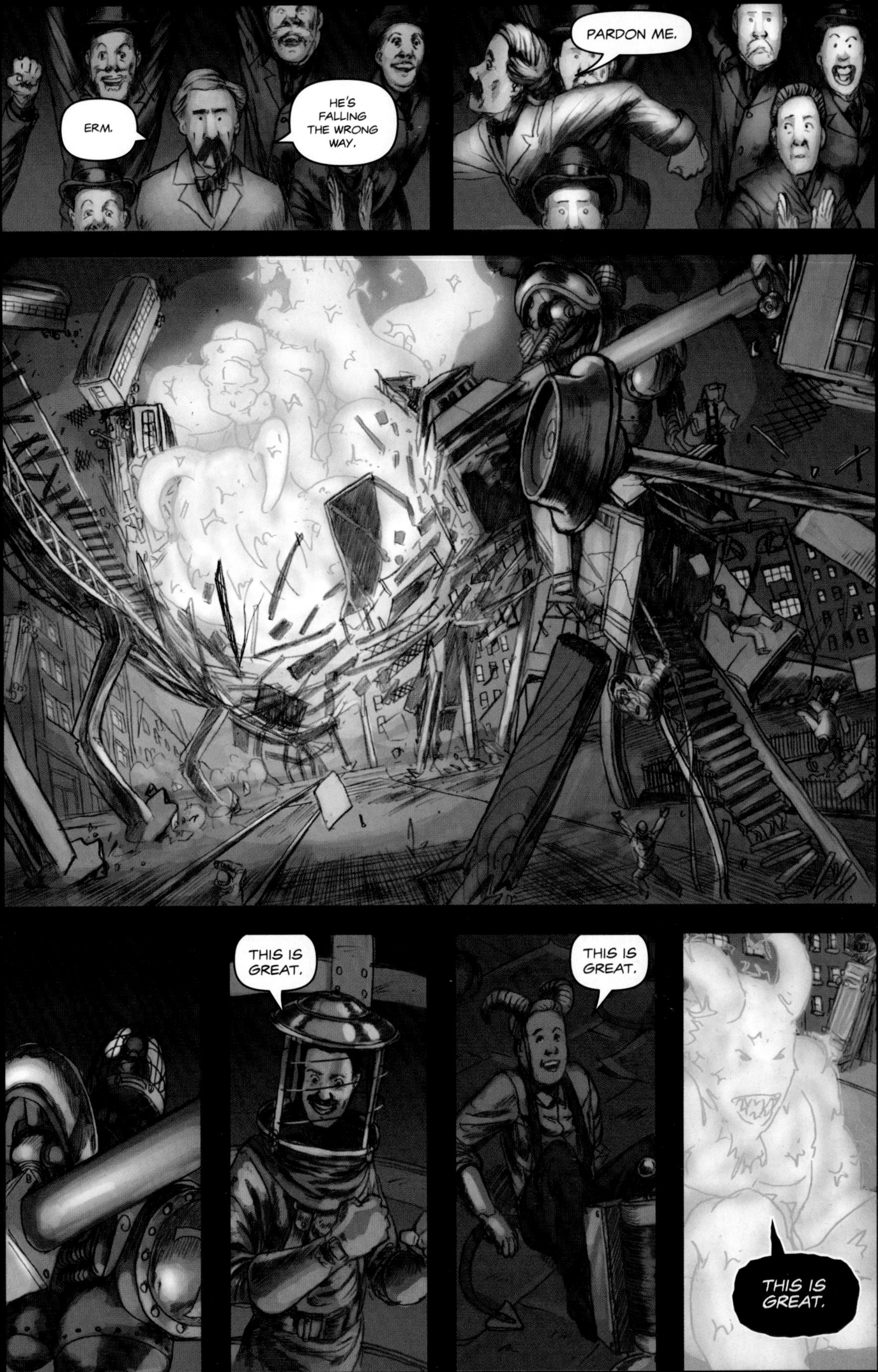
ERM.
HE'S FALLING THE WRONG WAY.
PARDON ME.
THIS IS GREAT.
THIS IS GREAT.
THIS IS GREAT.

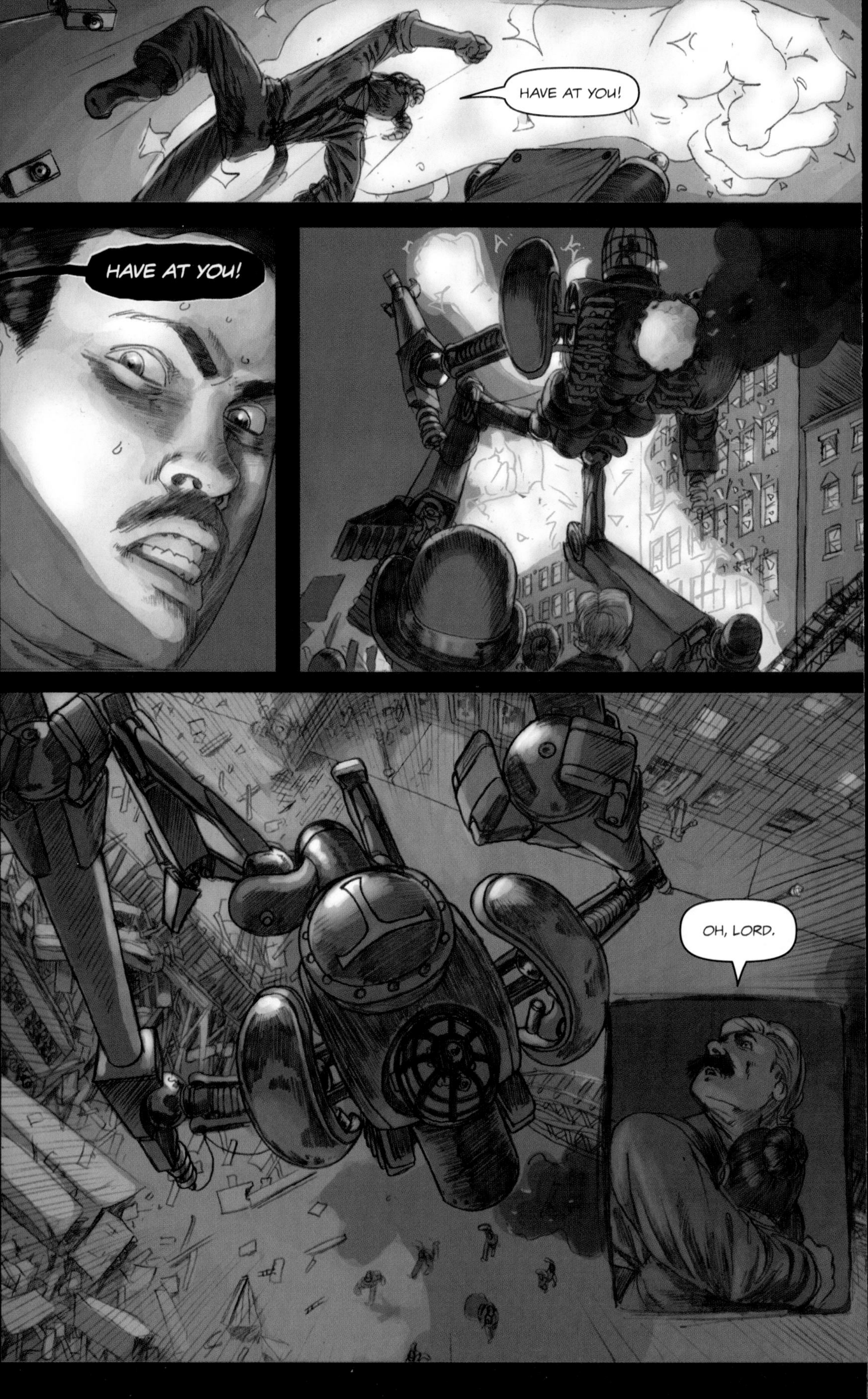
HAVE AT YOU!
HAVE AT YOU!
OH, LORD.

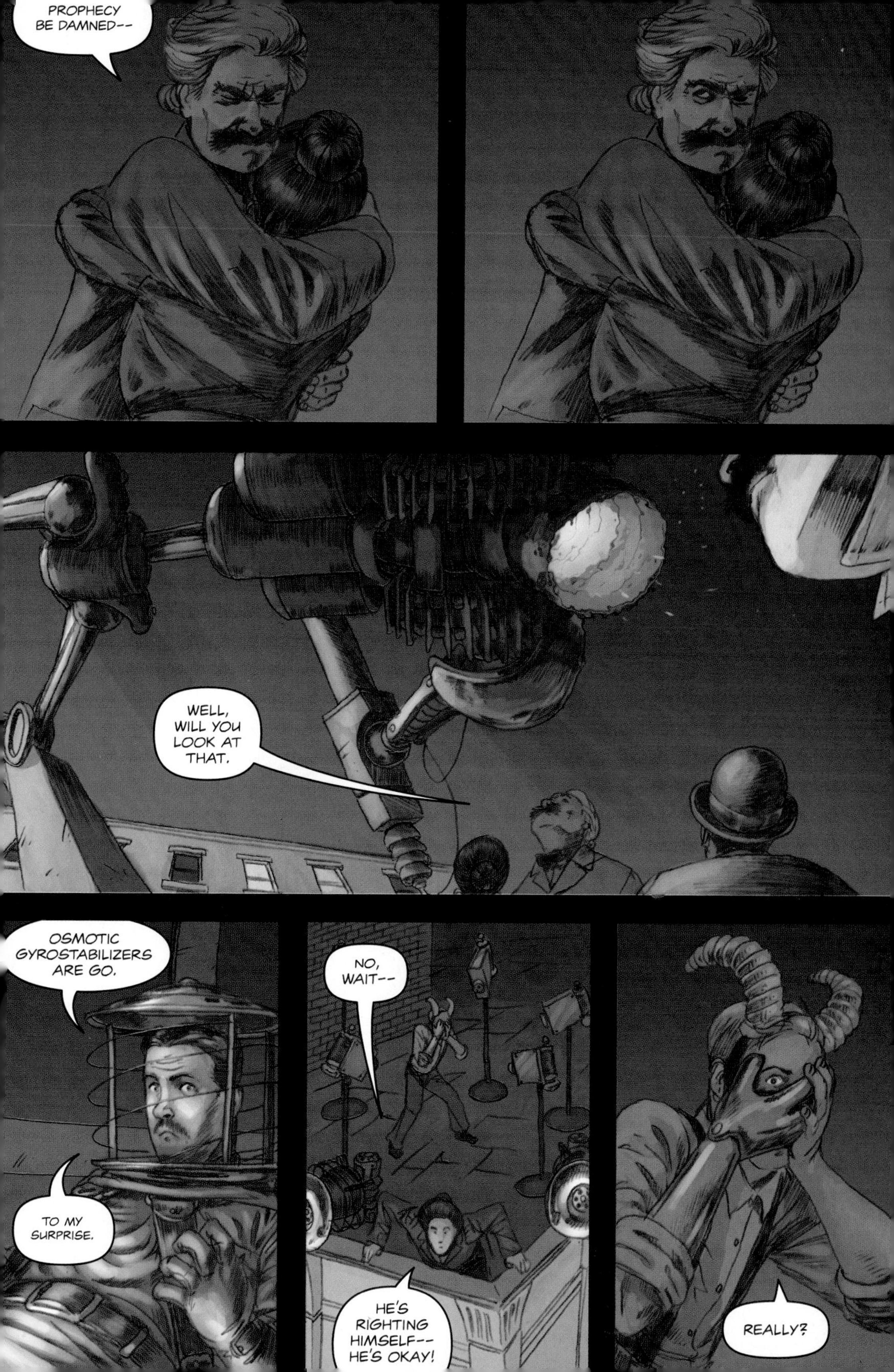
PROPHECY BE DAMNED--
WELL, WILL YOU LOOK AT THAT.
OSMOTIC GYROSTABILIZERS ARE GO.
TO MY SURPRISE.
NO, WAIT--
HE'S RIGHTING HIMSELF-- HE'S OKAY!
REALLY?

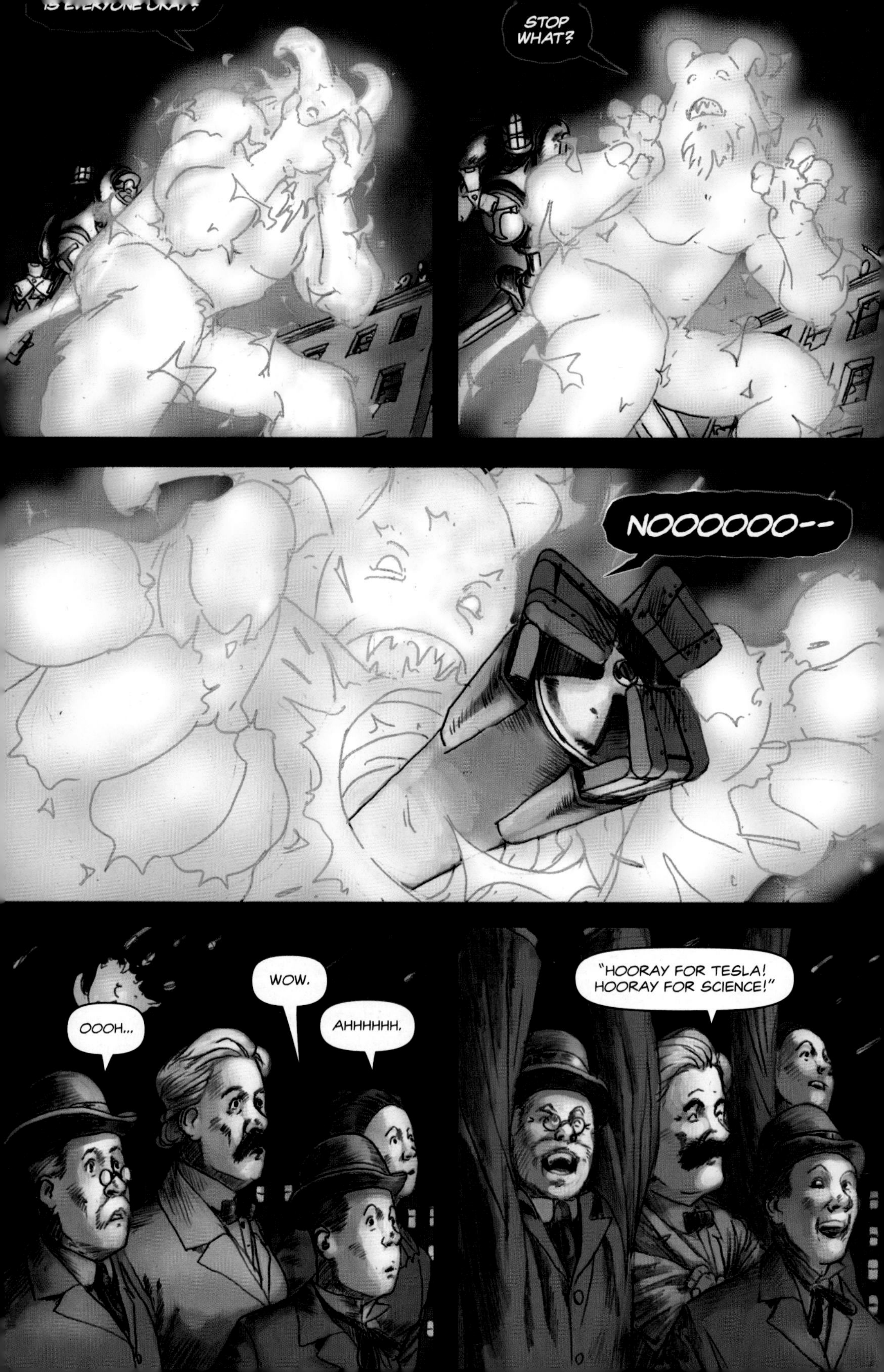
STOP WHAT?
NOOOOOO--
OOOH...
WOW.
AHHHHHH.
"HOORAY FOR TESLA! HOORAY FOR SCIENCE!"

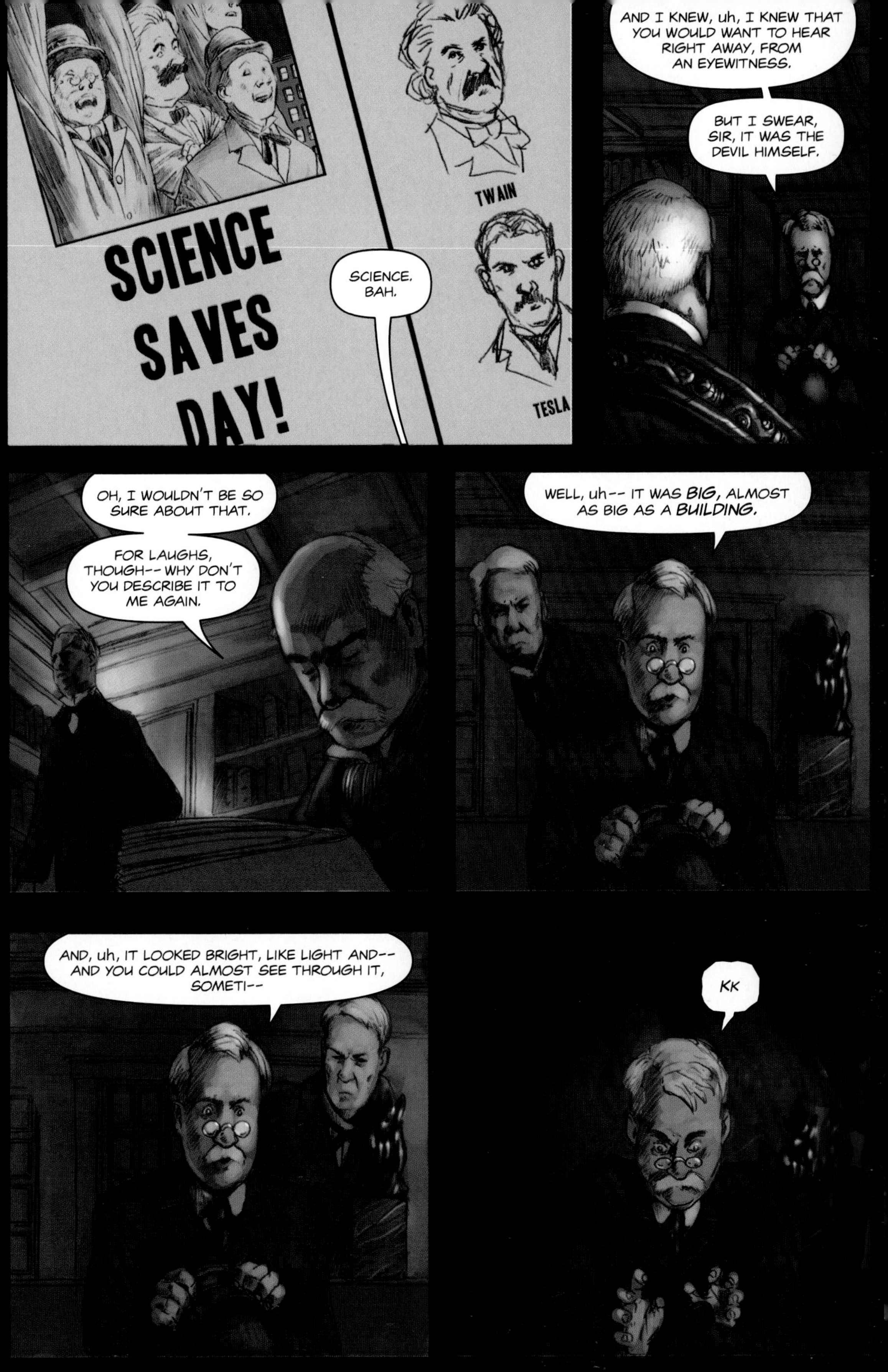
SCIENCE SAVES DAY!
TWAIN
TESLA
SCIENCE. BAH.
AND I KNEW, uh, I KNEW THAT YOU WOULD WANT TO HEAR RIGHT AWAY, FROM AN EYEWITNESS.
BUT I SWEAR, SIR, IT WAS THE DEVIL HIMSELF.
OH, I WOULDN'T BE SO SURE ABOUT THAT.
FOR LAUGHS, THOUGH-- WHY DON'T YOU DESCRIBE IT TO ME AGAIN.
WELL, uh-- IT WAS BIG, ALMOST AS BIG AS A BUILDING.
AND, uh, IT LOOKED BRIGHT, LIKE LIGHT AND-- AND YOU COULD ALMOST SEE THROUGH IT, SOMETI--
KK

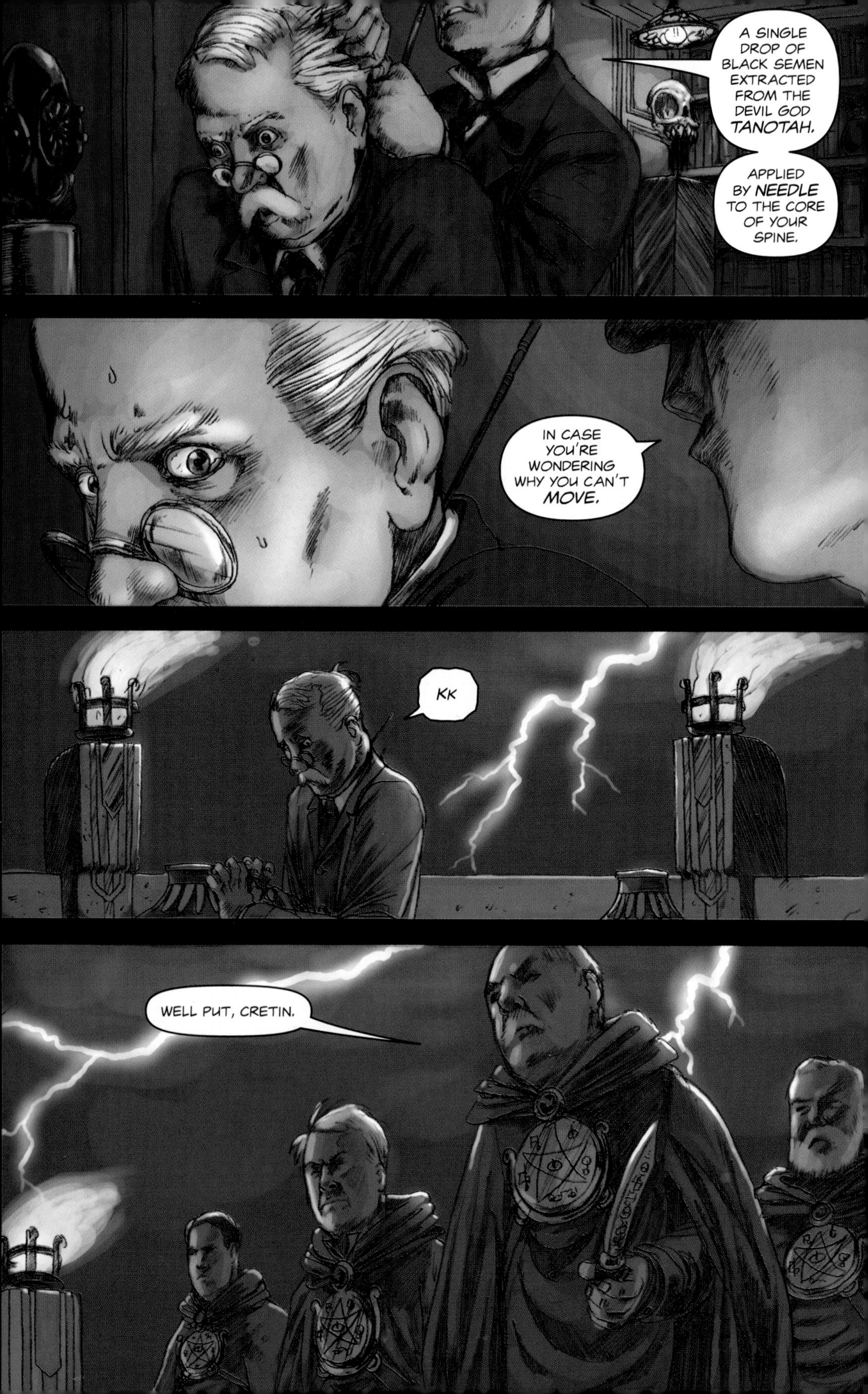
A SINGLE DROP OF BLACK SEMEN EXTRACTED FROM THE DEVIL GOD TANOTAH.
APPLIED BY NEEDLE TO THE CORE OF YOUR SPINE.
IN CASE YOU'RE WONDERING WHY YOU CAN'T MOVE.
KK
WELL PUT, CRETIN.

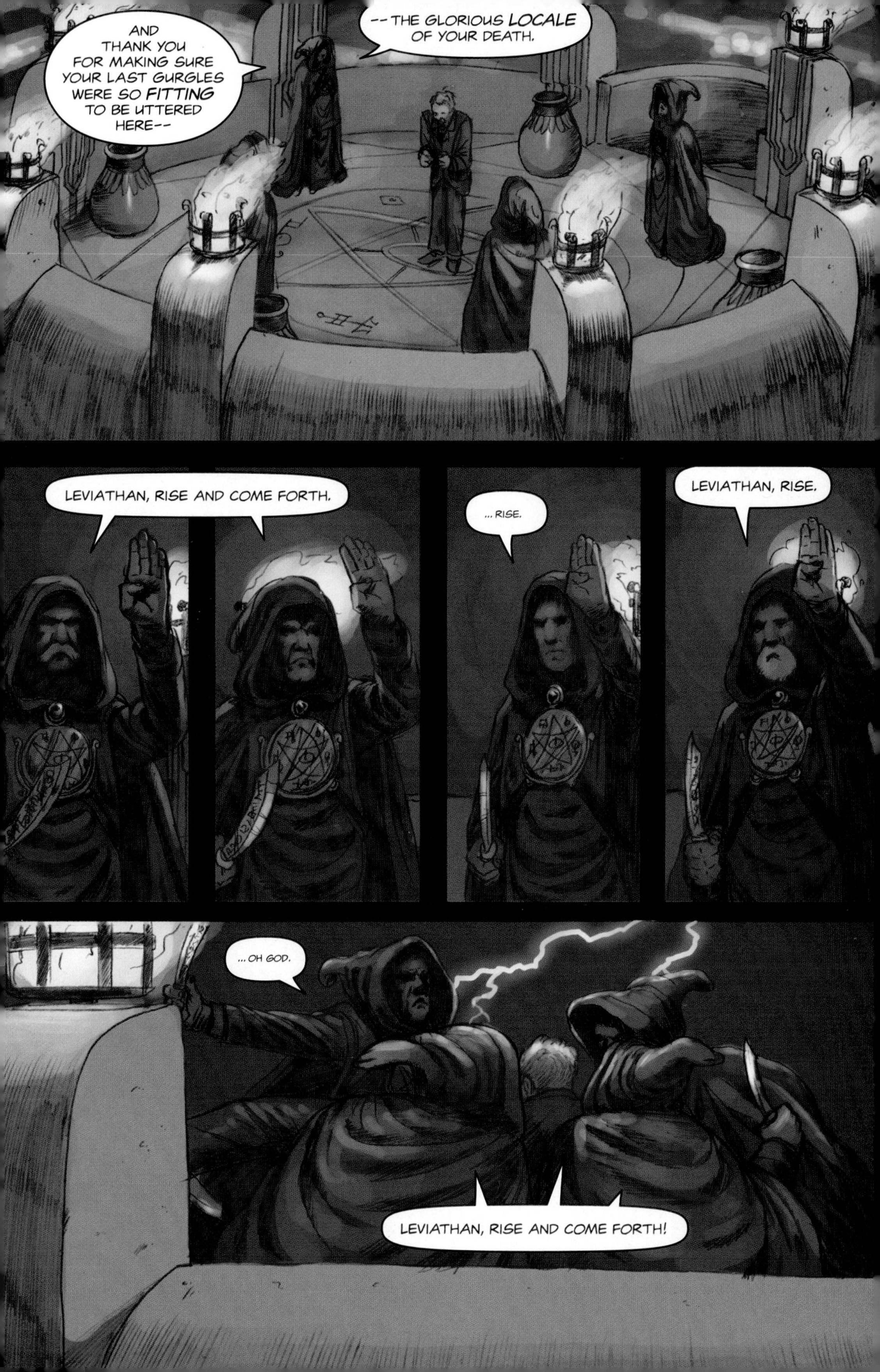
AND THANK YOU FOR MAKING SURE YOUR LAST GURGLES WERE SO FITTING TO BE UTTERED HERE--
--THE GLORIOUS LOCALE OF YOUR DEATH.
LEVIATHAN, RISE AND COME FORTH.
... RISE.
LEVIATHAN, RISE.
... OH GOD.
LEVIATHAN, RISE AND COME FORTH!

WAIT FOR IT.

HERE IT COMES--

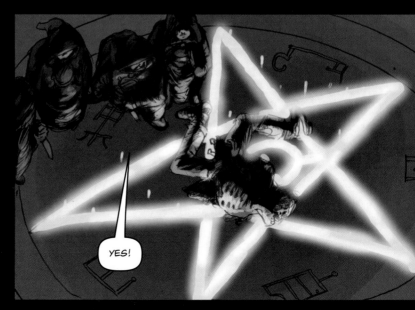
YES!

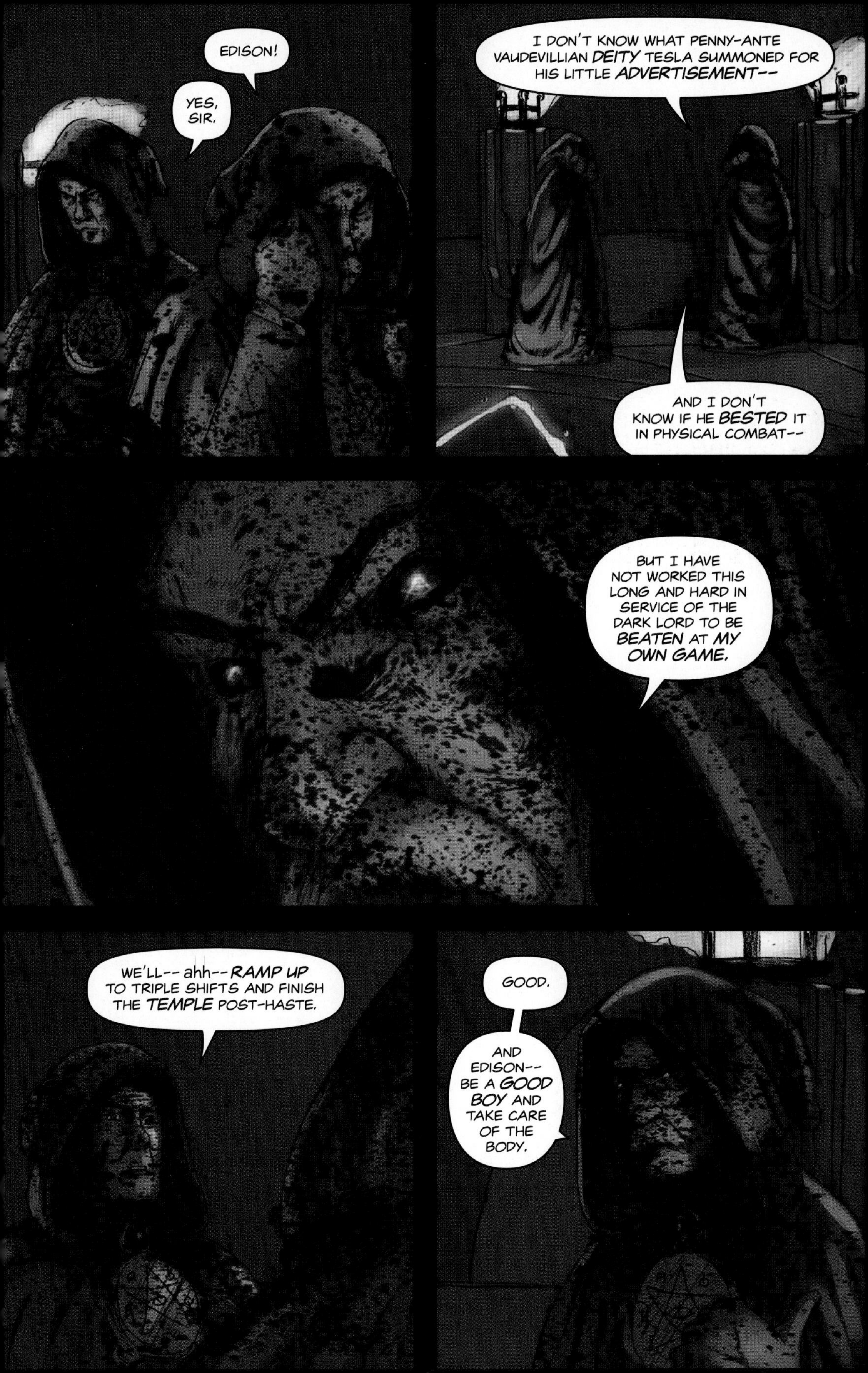
EDISON!
YES, SIR.
I DON'T KNOW WHAT PENNY-ANTE VAUDEVILLIAN DEITY TESLA SUMMONED FOR HIS LITTLE ADVERTISEMENT--
AND I DON'T KNOW IF HE BESTED IT IN PHYSICAL COMBAT--
BUT I HAVE NOT WORKED THIS LONG AND HARD IN SERVICE OF THE DARK LORD TO BE BEATEN AT MY OWN GAME.
WE'LL-- ahh-- RAMP UP TO TRIPLE SHIFTS AND FINISH THE TEMPLE POST-HASTE.
GOOD.
AND EDISON-- BE A GOOD BOY AND TAKE CARE OF THE BODY.

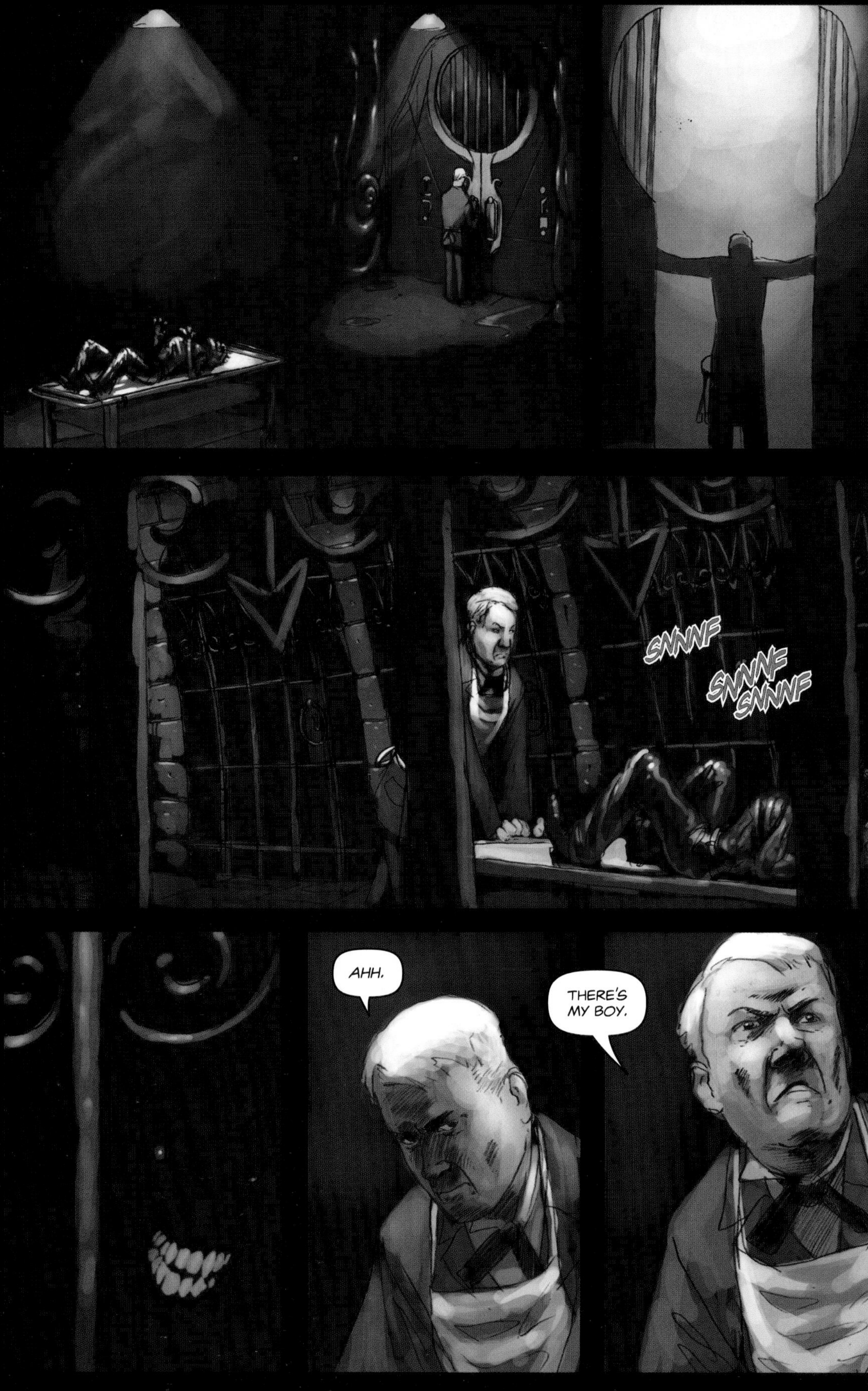
SNNNF
SNNNF
SNNNF
AHH.
THERE'S MY BOY.

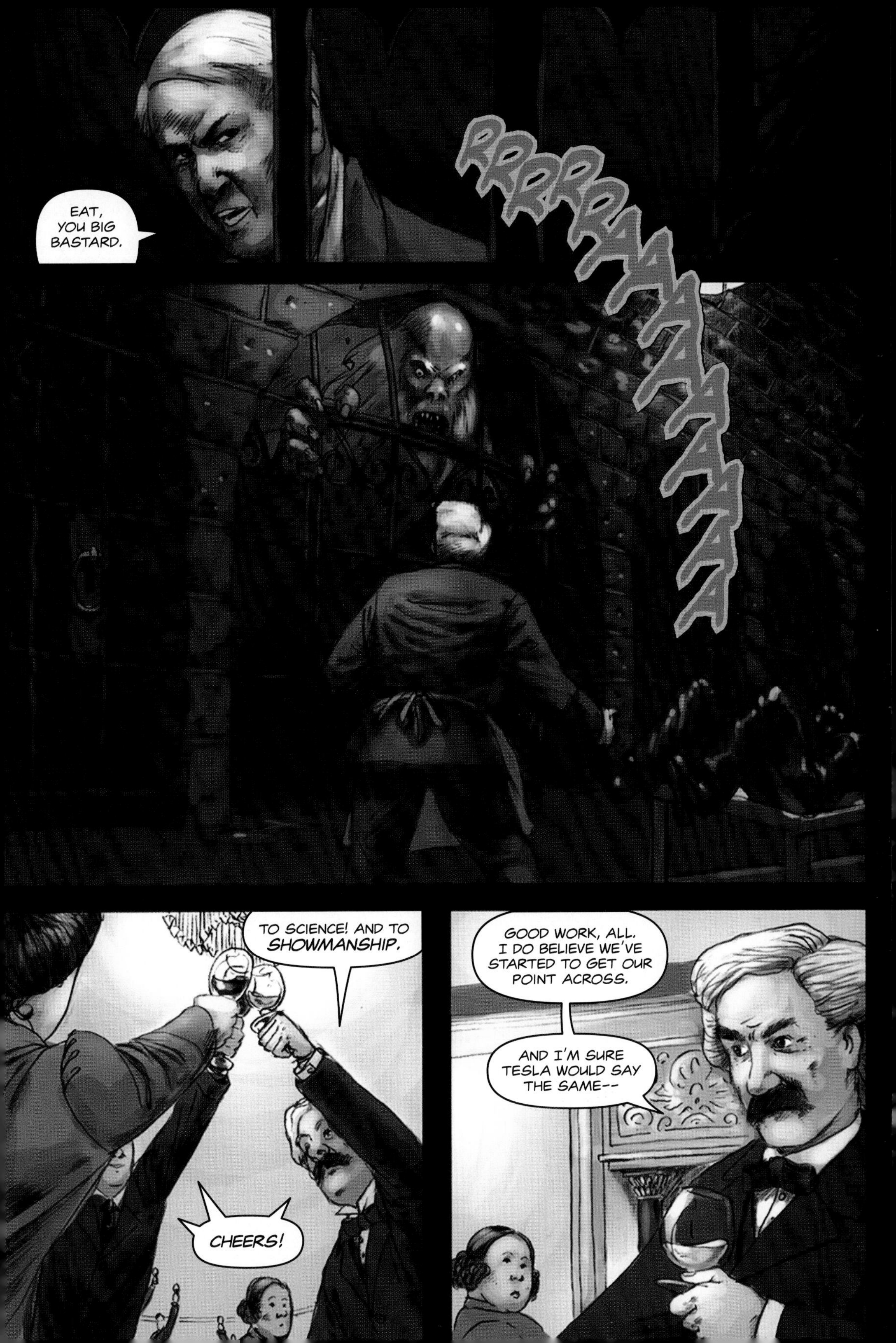
EAT, YOU BIG BASTARD.
RRRRRAAAAAAAAAAAAAA
TO SCIENCE! AND TO *SHOWMANSHIP.*
*CHEERS!*
GOOD WORK, ALL. I DO BELIEVE WE'VE STARTED TO GET OUR POINT ACROSS.
AND I'M SURE TESLA WOULD SAY THE SAME--

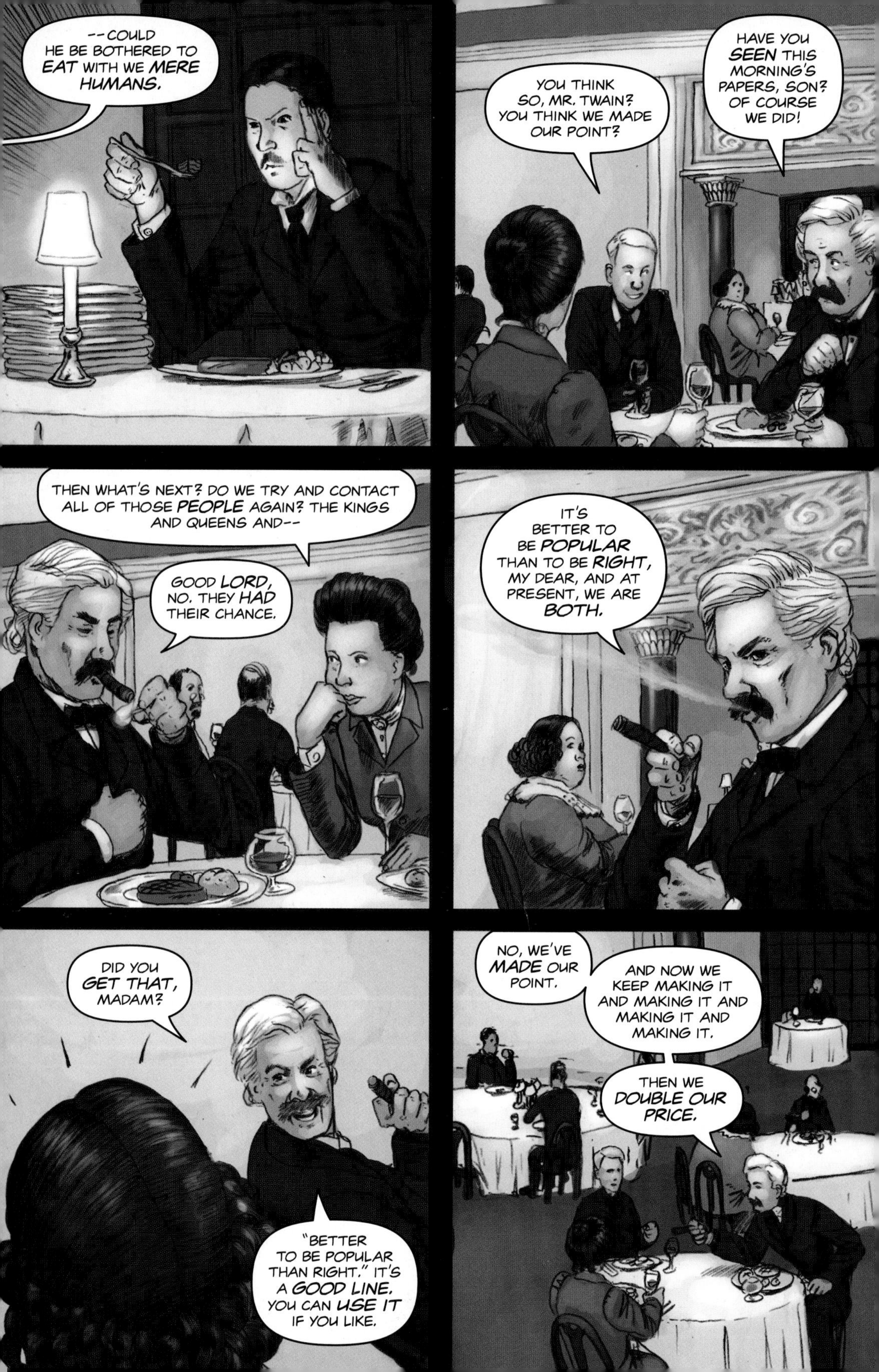
--COULD HE BE BOTHERED TO EAT WITH WE MERE HUMANS.
YOU THINK SO, MR. TWAIN? YOU THINK WE MADE OUR POINT?
HAVE YOU SEEN THIS MORNING'S PAPERS, SON? OF COURSE WE DID!
THEN WHAT'S NEXT? DO WE TRY AND CONTACT ALL OF THOSE PEOPLE AGAIN? THE KINGS AND QUEENS AND--
GOOD LORD, NO. THEY HAD THEIR CHANCE.
IT'S BETTER TO BE POPULAR THAN TO BE RIGHT, MY DEAR, AND AT PRESENT, WE ARE BOTH.
DID YOU GET THAT, MADAM?
"BETTER TO BE POPULAR THAN RIGHT." IT'S A GOOD LINE. YOU CAN USE IT IF YOU LIKE.
NO, WE'VE MADE OUR POINT.
AND NOW WE KEEP MAKING IT AND MAKING IT AND MAKING IT AND MAKING IT.
THEN WE DOUBLE OUR PRICE.

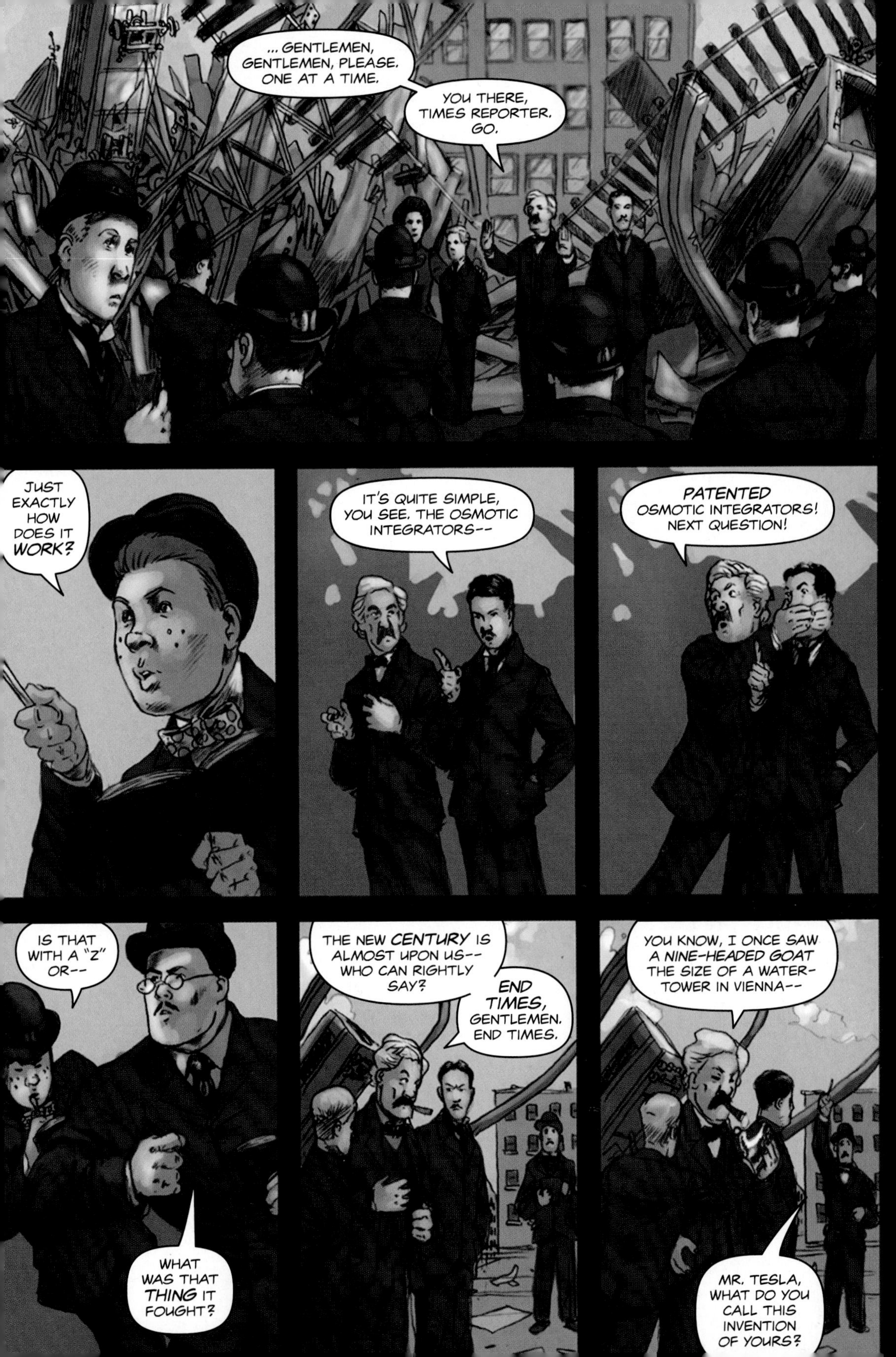
... GENTLEMEN, GENTLEMEN, PLEASE. ONE AT A TIME.
YOU THERE, TIMES REPORTER. GO.
JUST EXACTLY HOW DOES IT WORK?
IT'S QUITE SIMPLE, YOU SEE. THE OSMOTIC INTEGRATORS--
PATENTED OSMOTIC INTEGRATORS! NEXT QUESTION!
IS THAT WITH A "Z" OR--
WHAT WAS THAT THING IT FOUGHT?
THE NEW CENTURY IS ALMOST UPON US-- WHO CAN RIGHTLY SAY?
END TIMES, GENTLEMEN. END TIMES.
YOU KNOW, I ONCE SAW A NINE-HEADED GOAT THE SIZE OF A WATER-TOWER IN VIENNA--
MR. TESLA, WHAT DO YOU CALL THIS INVENTION OF YOURS?

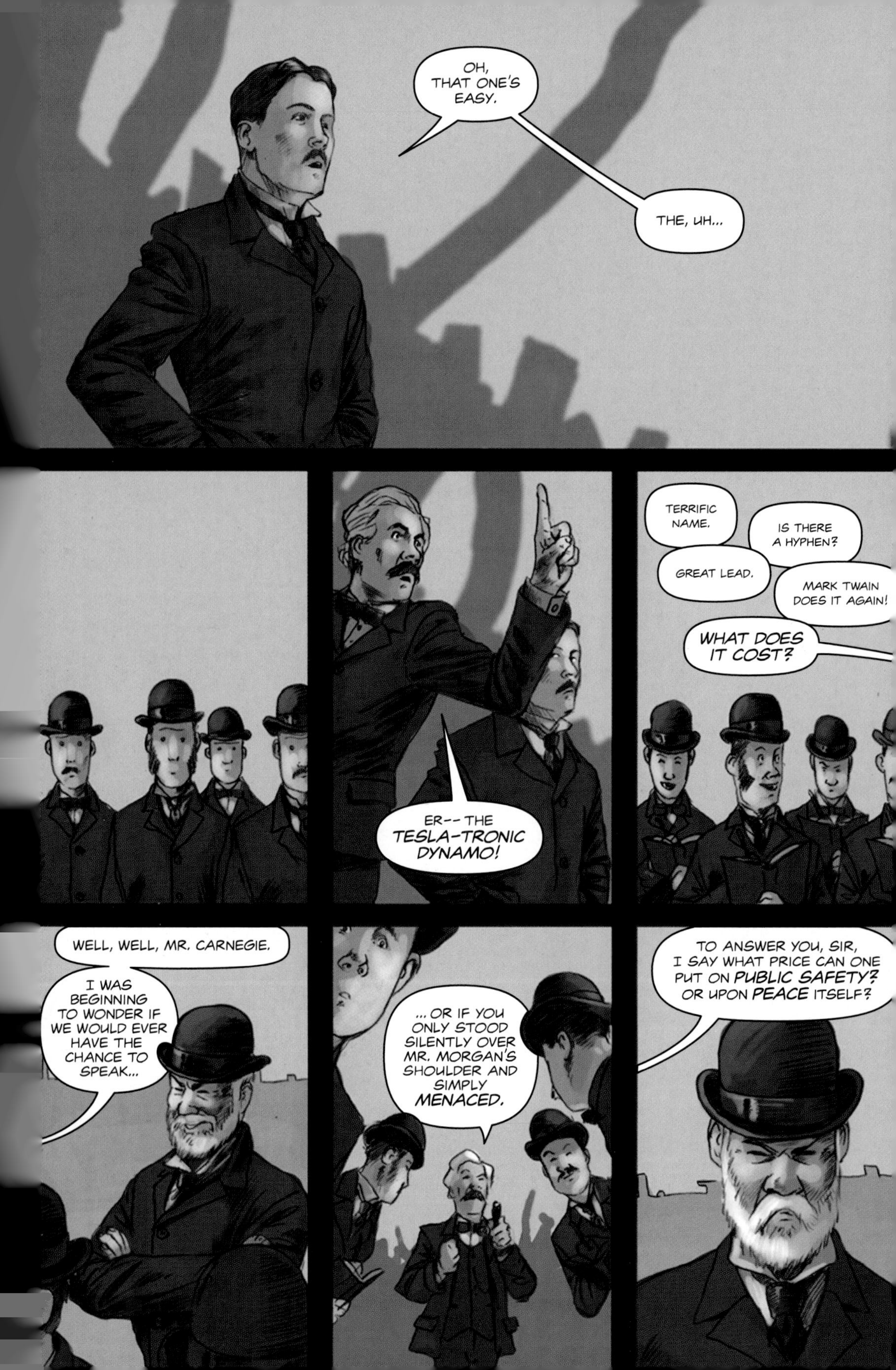
OH, THAT ONE'S EASY.
THE, UH...
ER-- THE TESLA-TRONIC DYNAMO!
TERRIFIC NAME.
IS THERE A HYPHEN?
GREAT LEAD.
MARK TWAIN DOES IT AGAIN!
WHAT DOES IT COST?
WELL, WELL, MR. CARNEGIE.
I WAS BEGINNING TO WONDER IF WE WOULD EVER HAVE THE CHANCE TO SPEAK...
...OR IF YOU ONLY STOOD SILENTLY OVER MR. MORGAN'S SHOULDER AND SIMPLY MENACED.
TO ANSWER YOU, SIR, I SAY WHAT PRICE CAN ONE PUT ON PUBLIC SAFETY? OR UPON PEACE ITSELF?

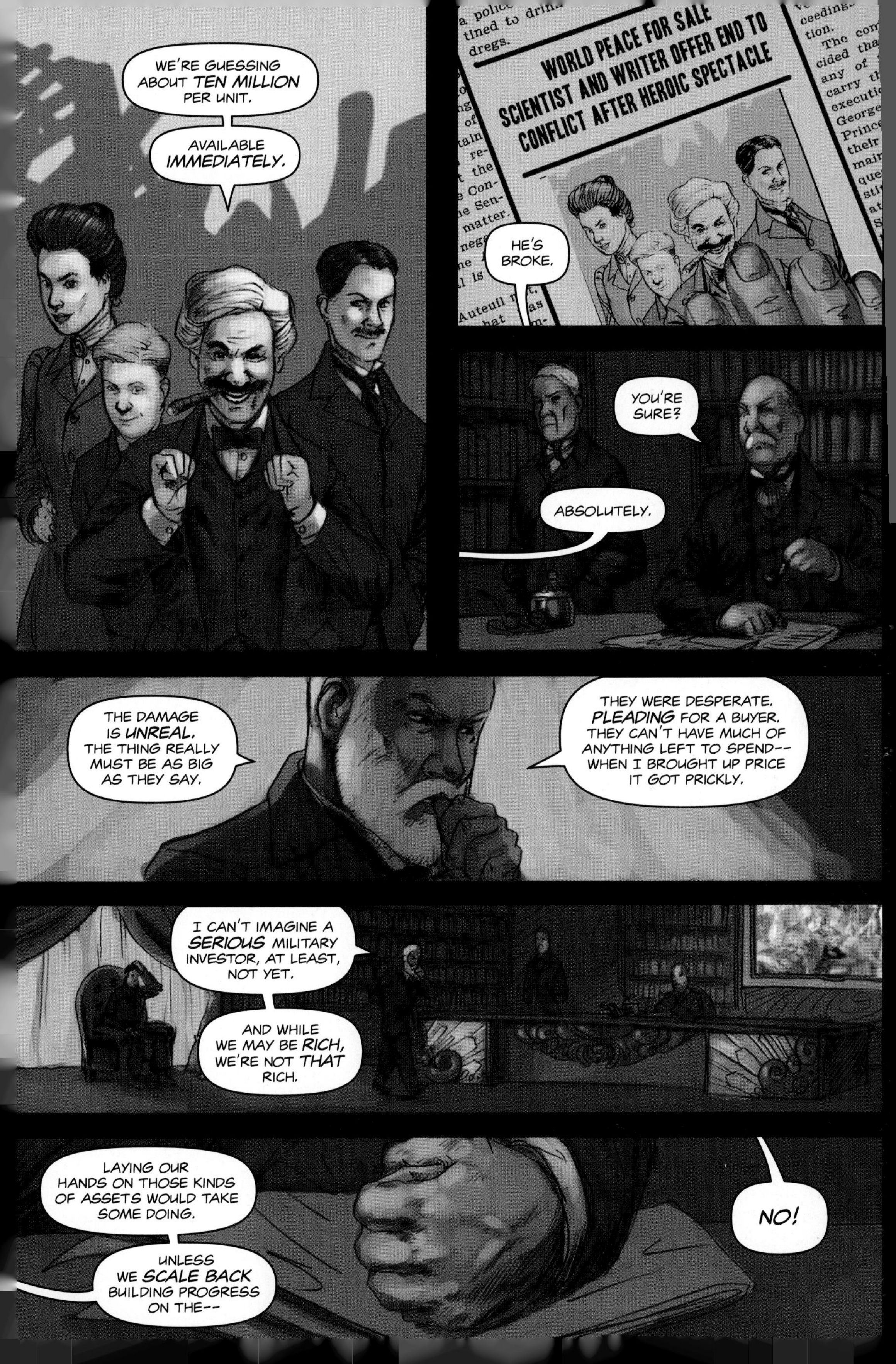
WE'RE GUESSING ABOUT TEN MILLION PER UNIT.
AVAILABLE IMMEDIATELY.
WORLD PEACE FOR SALE
SCIENTIST AND WRITER OFFER END TO CONFLICT AFTER HEROIC SPECTACLE
HE'S BROKE.
YOU'RE SURE?
ABSOLUTELY.
THE DAMAGE IS UNREAL. THE THING REALLY MUST BE AS BIG AS THEY SAY.
THEY WERE DESPERATE. PLEADING FOR A BUYER. THEY CAN'T HAVE MUCH OF ANYTHING LEFT TO SPEND-- WHEN I BROUGHT UP PRICE IT GOT PRICKLY.
I CAN'T IMAGINE A SERIOUS MILITARY INVESTOR, AT LEAST, NOT YET.
AND WHILE WE MAY BE RICH, WE'RE NOT THAT RICH.
LAYING OUR HANDS ON THOSE KINDS OF ASSETS WOULD TAKE SOME DOING.
UNLESS WE SCALE BACK BUILDING PROGRESS ON THE--
NO!

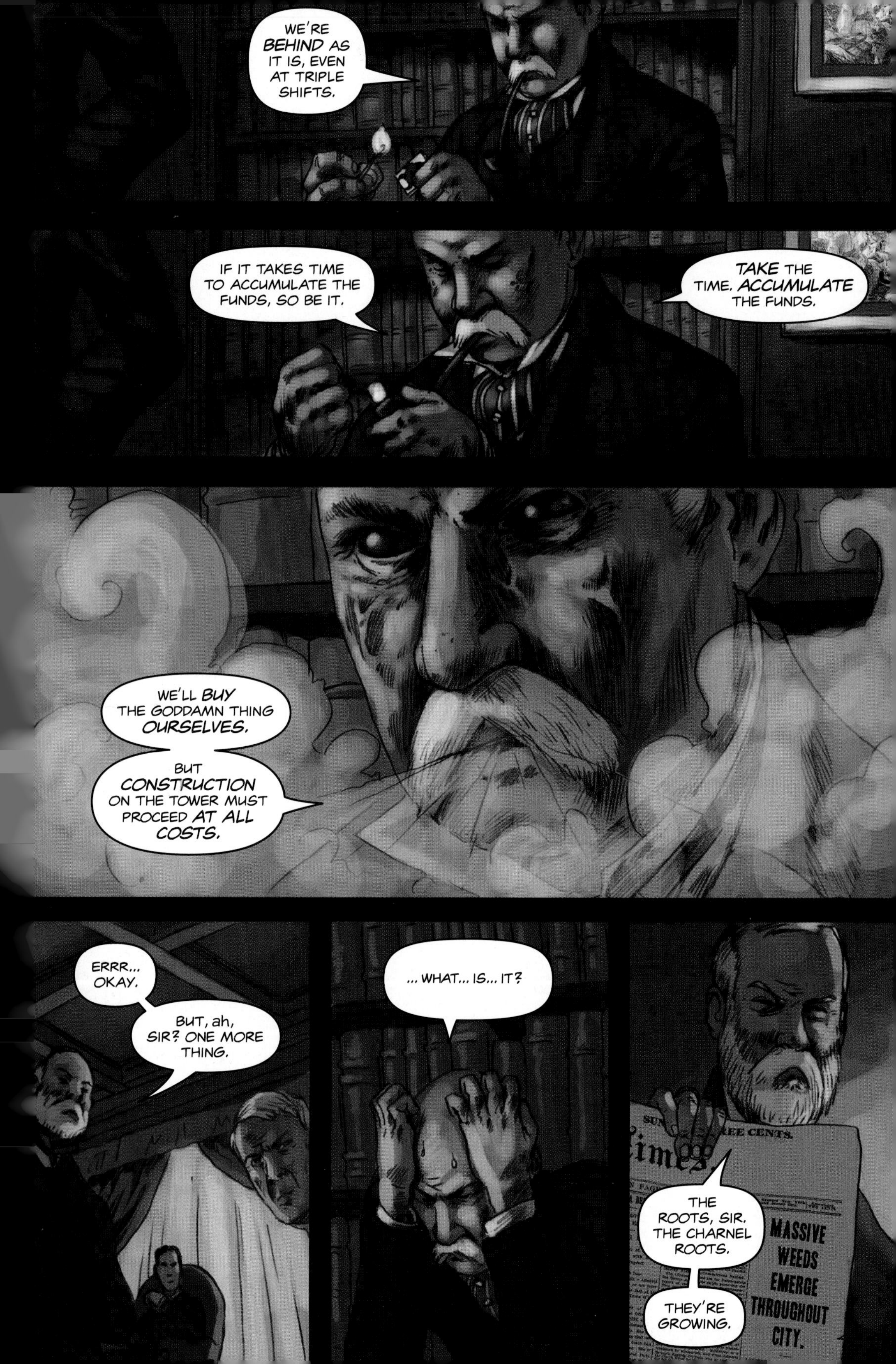
WE'RE BEHIND AS IT IS, EVEN AT TRIPLE SHIFTS.
IF IT TAKES TIME TO ACCUMULATE THE FUNDS, SO BE IT.
TAKE THE TIME. ACCUMULATE THE FUNDS.
WE'LL BUY THE GODDAMN THING OURSELVES.
BUT CONSTRUCTION ON THE TOWER MUST PROCEED AT ALL COSTS.
ERRR... OKAY.
BUT, ah, SIR? ONE MORE THING.
...WHAT... IS... IT?
THE ROOTS, SIR. THE CHARNEL ROOTS.
THEY'RE GROWING.
MASSIVE WEEDS EMERGE THROUGHOUT CITY.

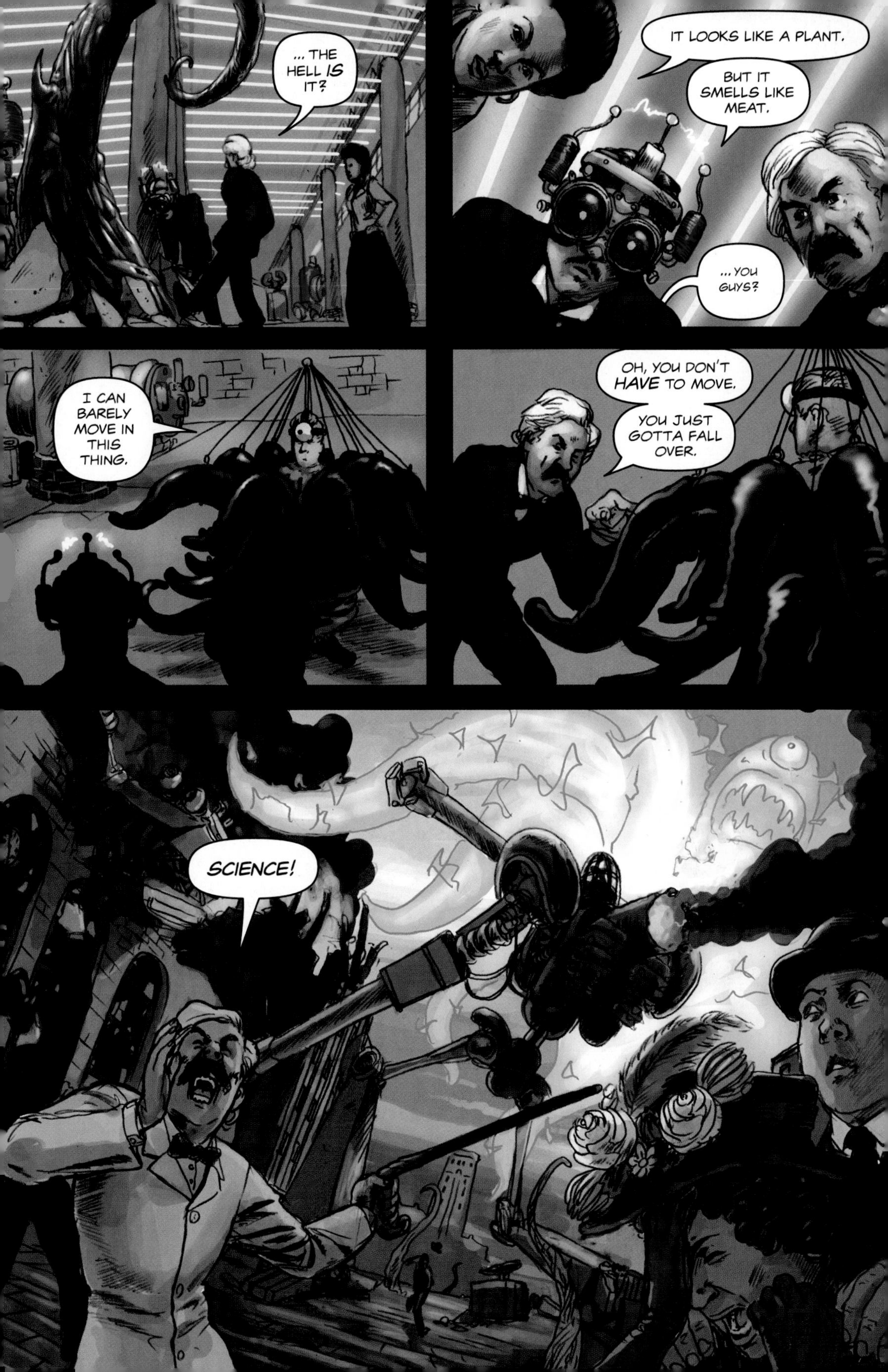
... THE HELL IS IT?
IT LOOKS LIKE A PLANT.
BUT IT SMELLS LIKE MEAT.
...YOU GUYS?
I CAN BARELY MOVE IN THIS THING.
OH, YOU DON'T HAVE TO MOVE.
YOU JUST GOTTA FALL OVER.
SCIENCE!

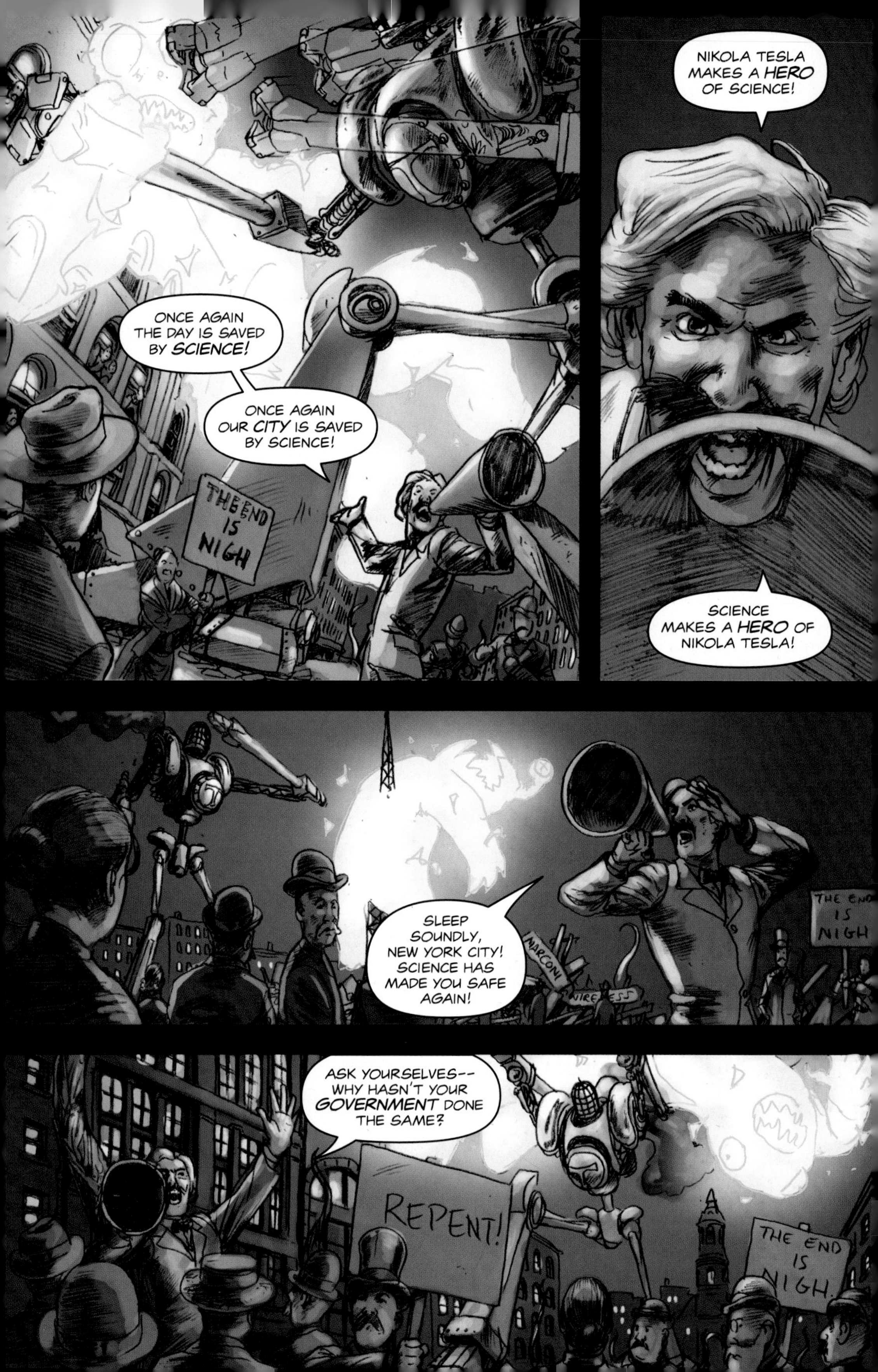
ONCE AGAIN THE DAY IS SAVED BY **SCIENCE!**
ONCE AGAIN OUR *CITY* IS SAVED BY SCIENCE!
THE END IS NIGH
NIKOLA TESLA MAKES A *HERO* OF SCIENCE!
SCIENCE MAKES A *HERO* OF NIKOLA TESLA!
SLEEP SOUNDLY, NEW YORK CITY! SCIENCE HAS MADE YOU SAFE AGAIN!
MARCONI
THE END IS NIGH
ASK YOURSELVES-- WHY HASN'T YOUR *GOVERNMENT* DONE THE SAME?
REPENT!
THE END IS NIGH.

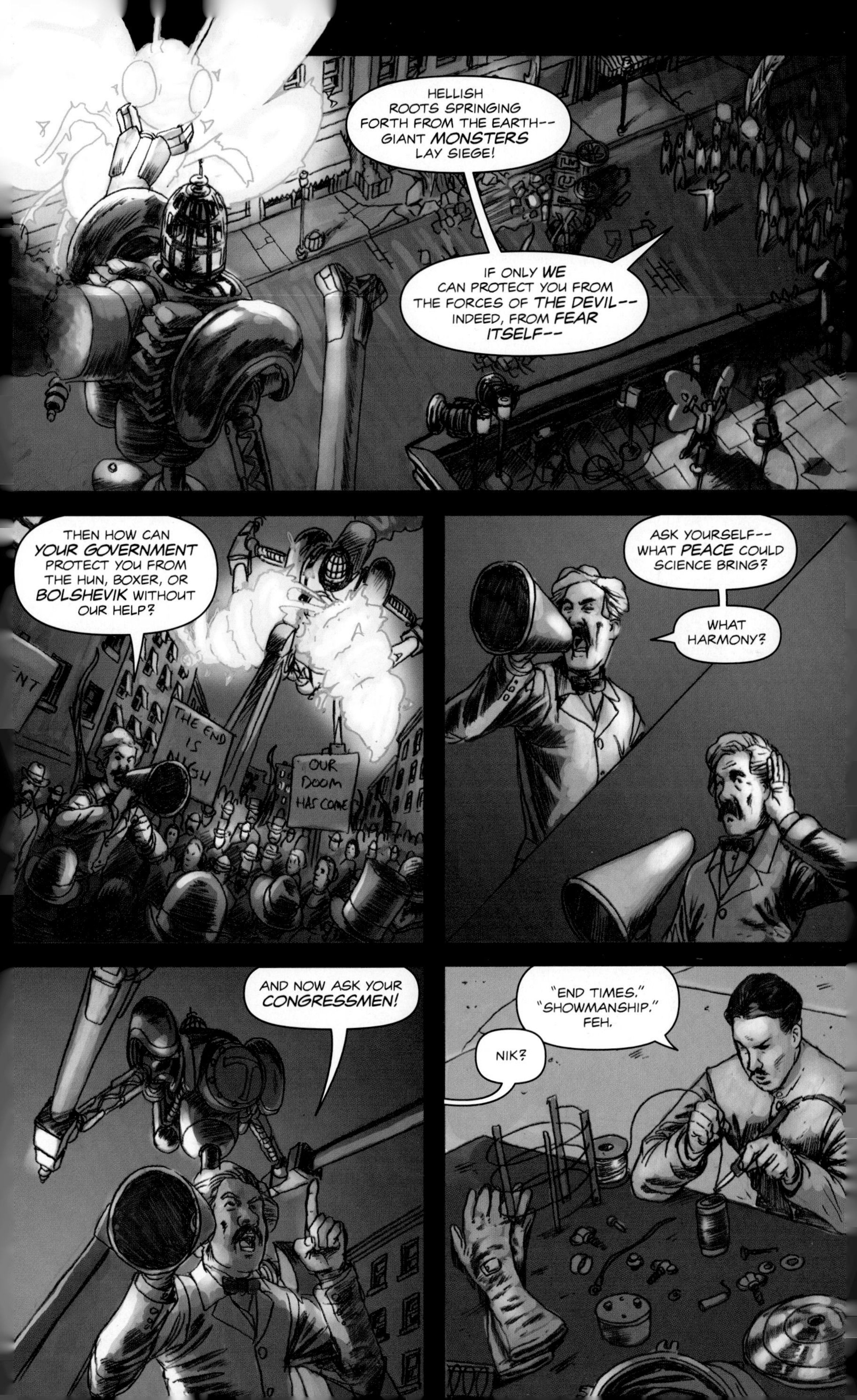
HELLISH ROOTS SPRINGING FORTH FROM THE EARTH-- GIANT MONSTERS LAY SIEGE!
IF ONLY WE CAN PROTECT YOU FROM THE FORCES OF THE DEVIL-- INDEED, FROM FEAR ITSELF--
THEN HOW CAN YOUR GOVERNMENT PROTECT YOU FROM THE HUN, BOXER, OR BOLSHEVIK WITHOUT OUR HELP?
THE END IS NIGH
OUR DOOM HAS COME
ASK YOURSELF-- WHAT PEACE COULD SCIENCE BRING?
WHAT HARMONY?
AND NOW ASK YOUR CONGRESSMEN!
"END TIMES." "SHOWMANSHIP." FEH.
NIK?

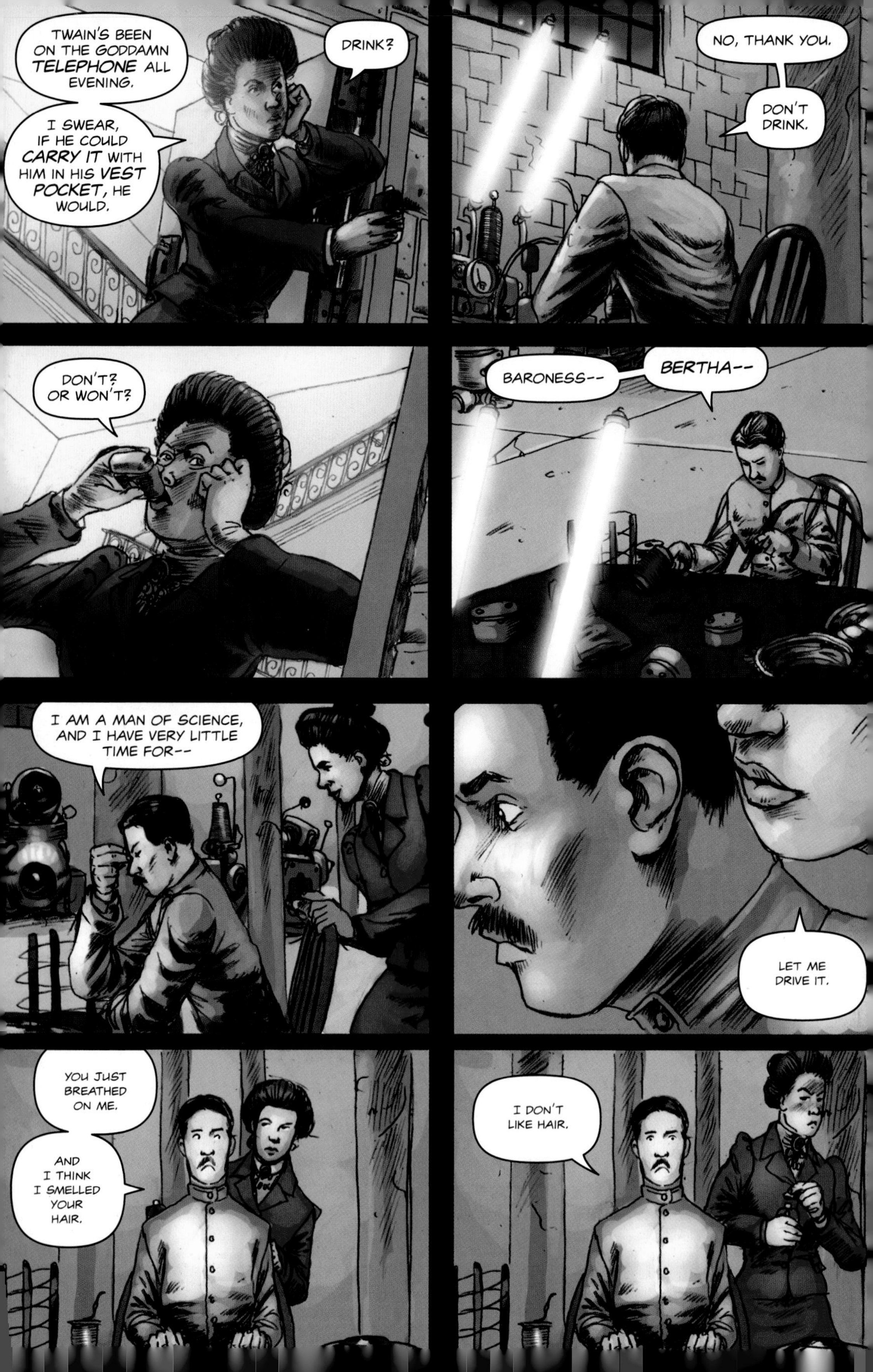
TWAIN'S BEEN ON THE GODDAMN TELEPHONE ALL EVENING.
I SWEAR, IF HE COULD CARRY IT WITH HIM IN HIS VEST POCKET, HE WOULD.
DRINK?
NO, THANK YOU.
DON'T DRINK.
DON'T? OR WON'T?
BARONESS--
BERTHA--
I AM A MAN OF SCIENCE, AND I HAVE VERY LITTLE TIME FOR--
LET ME DRIVE IT.
YOU JUST BREATHED ON ME.
AND I THINK I SMELLED YOUR HAIR.
I DON'T LIKE HAIR.

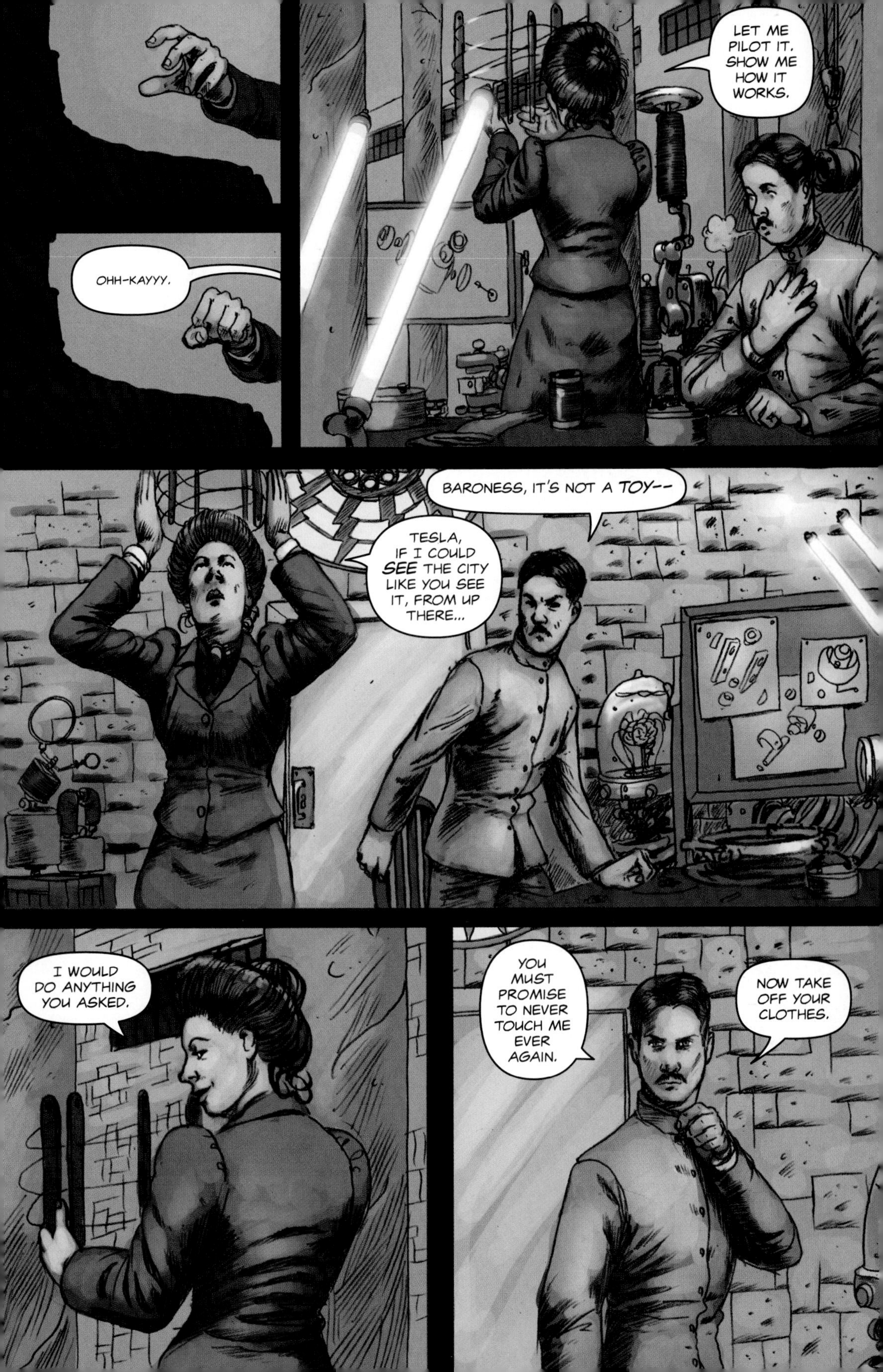
OHH-KAYYY.
LET ME PILOT IT. SHOW ME HOW IT WORKS.
BARONESS, IT'S NOT A TOY--
TESLA, IF I COULD SEE THE CITY LIKE YOU SEE IT, FROM UP THERE...
I WOULD DO ANYTHING YOU ASKED.
YOU MUST PROMISE TO NEVER TOUCH ME EVER AGAIN.
NOW TAKE OFF YOUR CLOTHES.

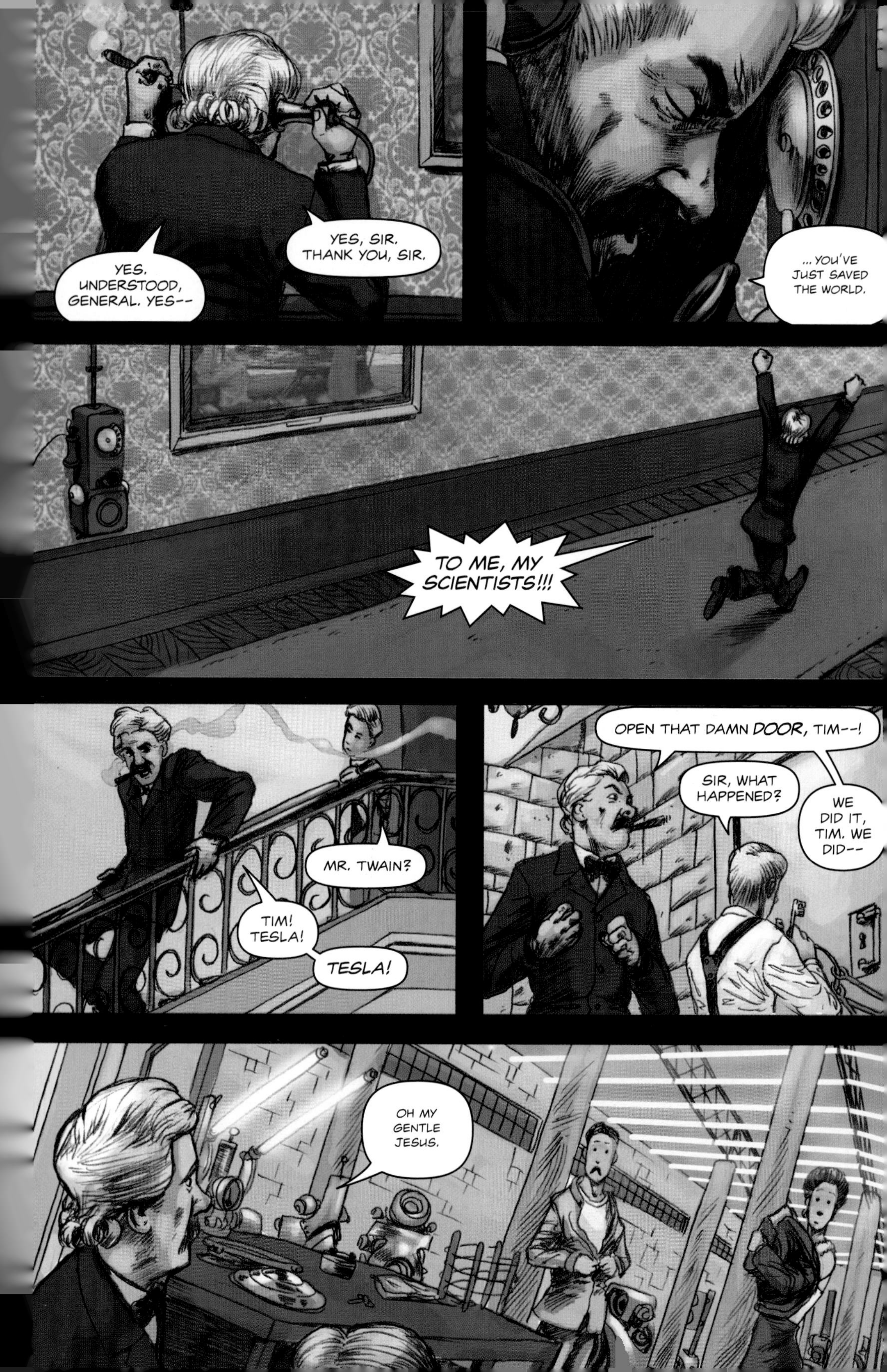
YES. UNDERSTOOD, GENERAL. YES--
YES, SIR. THANK YOU, SIR.
...YOU'VE JUST SAVED THE WORLD.
TO ME, MY SCIENTISTS!!!
MR. TWAIN?
TIM! TESLA!
TESLA!
OPEN THAT DAMN DOOR, TIM--!
SIR, WHAT HAPPENED?
WE DID IT, TIM. WE DID--
OH MY GENTLE JESUS.

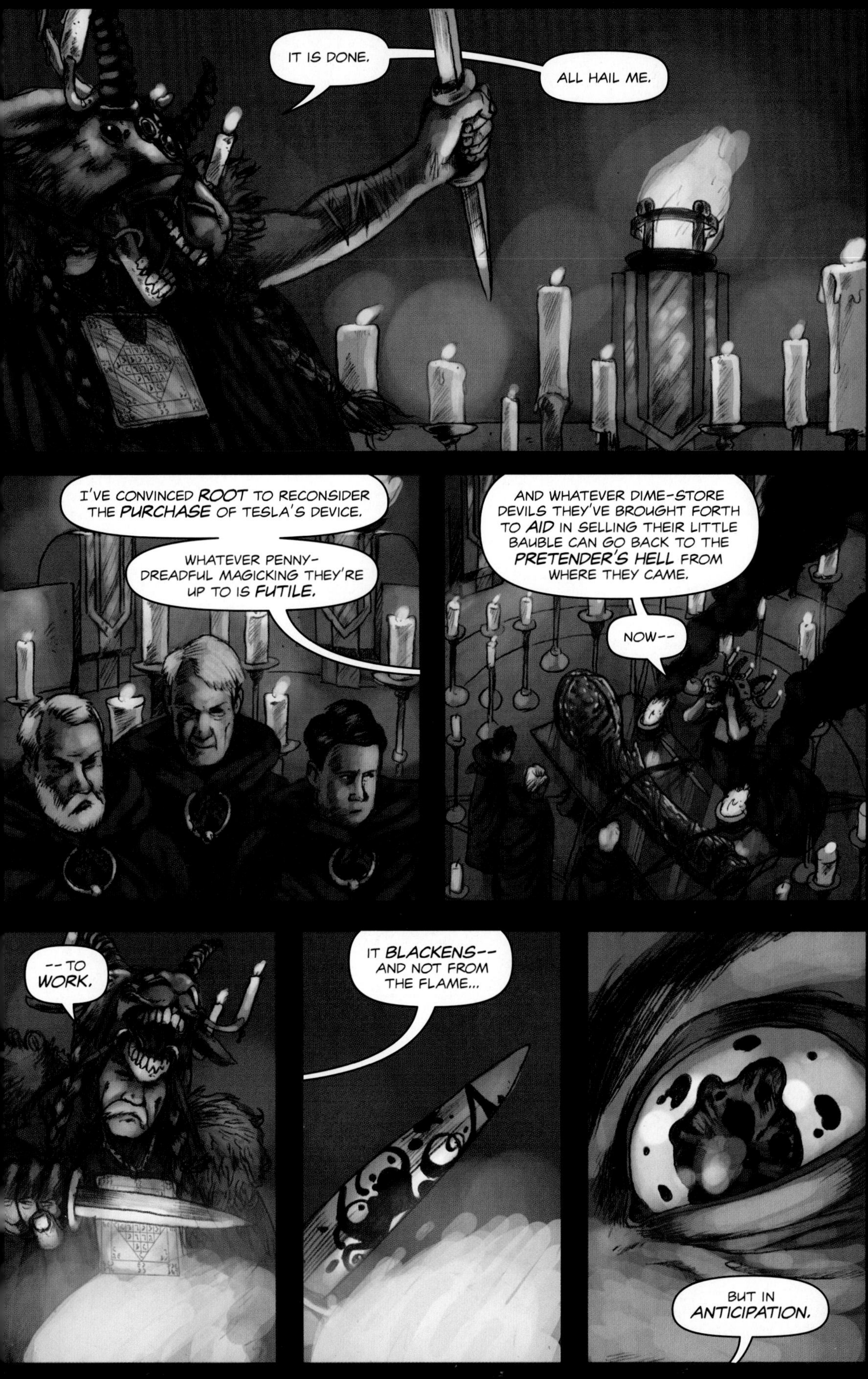
IT IS DONE.
ALL HAIL ME.
I'VE CONVINCED ROOT TO RECONSIDER THE PURCHASE OF TESLA'S DEVICE.
WHATEVER PENNY-DREADFUL MAGICKING THEY'RE UP TO IS FUTILE.
AND WHATEVER DIME-STORE DEVILS THEY'VE BROUGHT FORTH TO AID IN SELLING THEIR LITTLE BAUBLE CAN GO BACK TO THE PRETENDER'S HELL FROM WHERE THEY CAME.
NOW--
--TO WORK.
IT BLACKENS--AND NOT FROM THE FLAME...
BUT IN ANTICIPATION.

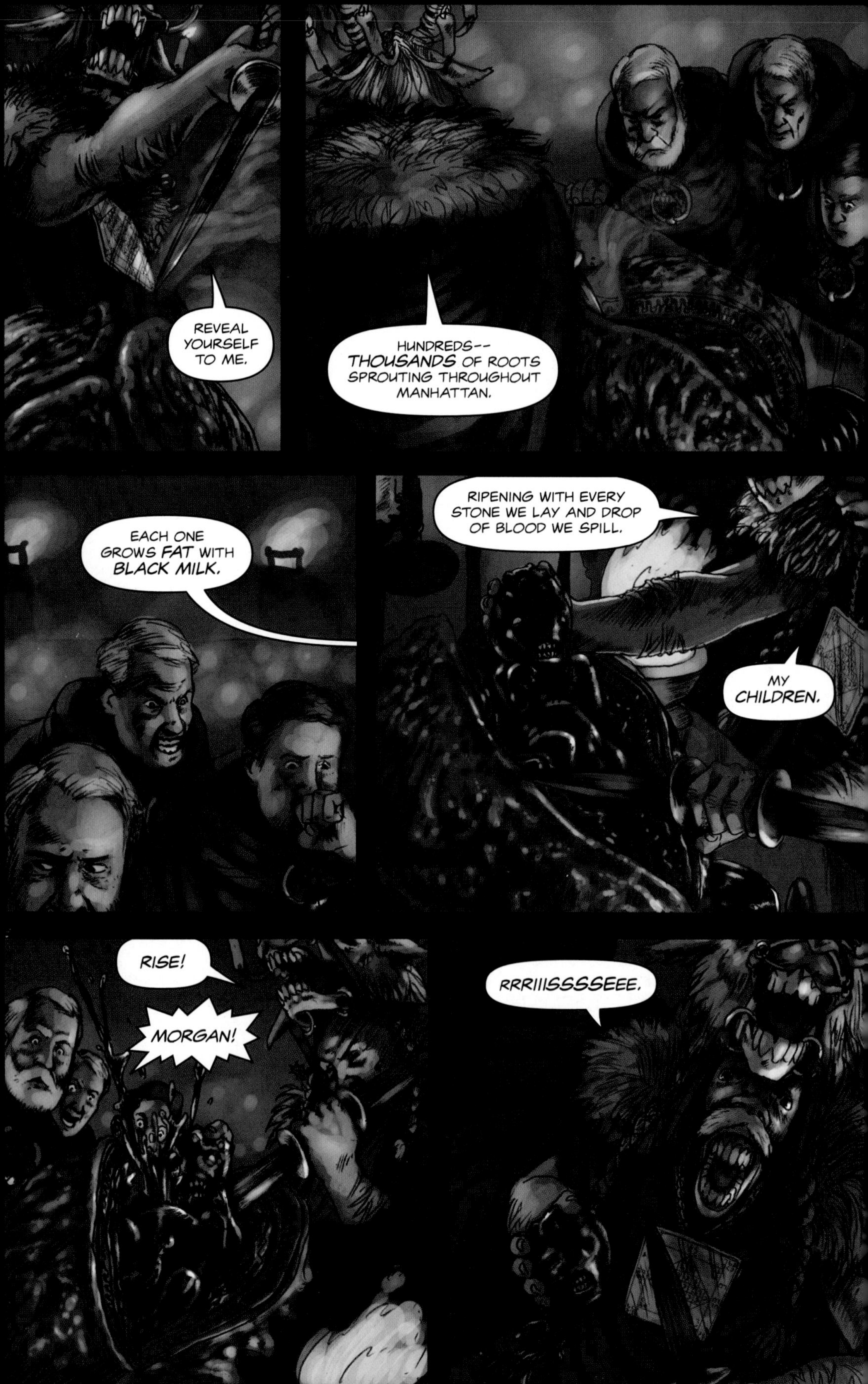
REVEAL YOURSELF TO ME.
HUNDREDS-- THOUSANDS OF ROOTS SPROUTING THROUGHOUT MANHATTAN.
EACH ONE GROWS FAT WITH BLACK MILK.
RIPENING WITH EVERY STONE WE LAY AND DROP OF BLOOD WE SPILL.
MY CHILDREN.
RISE!
MORGAN!
RRRIIISSSSEEE.

RRRRIIIIISSSSSSSSEEE!

GAH!

"ALL ACROSS THE CITY--"

"THE BLACK ROOTS RISE UP--"

"AND NOW POINT TO US."

AAAH!

WOMP!

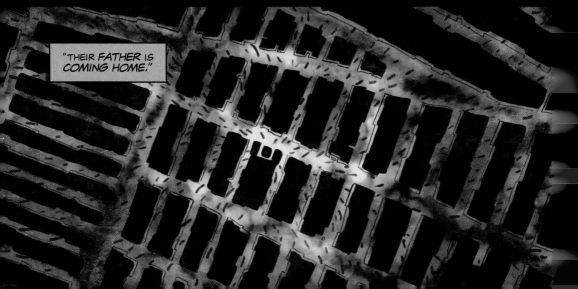

"THEIR FATHER IS COMING HOME."

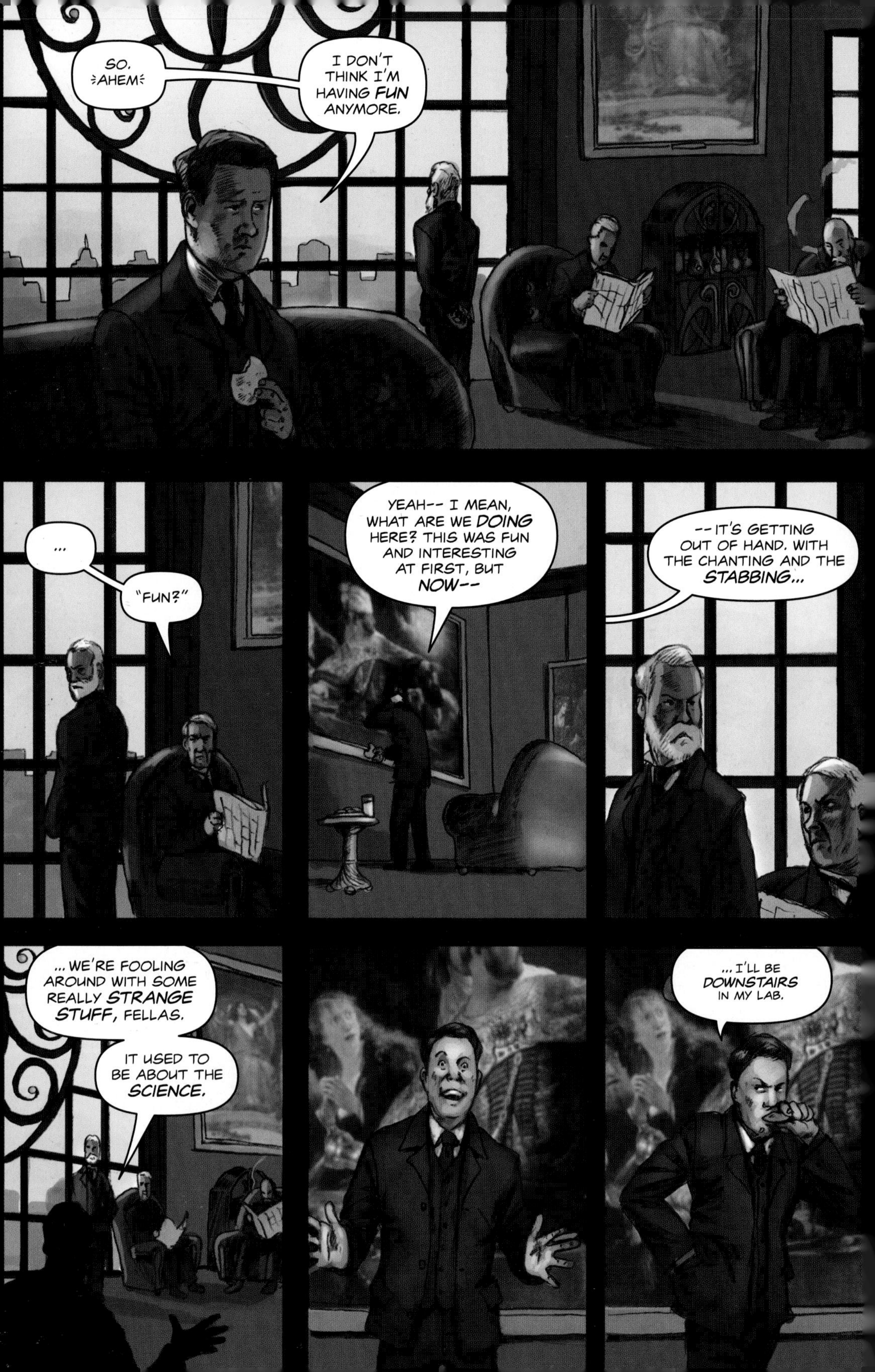
SO. ≈AHEM≈
I DON'T THINK I'M HAVING FUN ANYMORE.
...
"FUN?"
YEAH-- I MEAN, WHAT ARE WE DOING HERE? THIS WAS FUN AND INTERESTING AT FIRST, BUT NOW--
--IT'S GETTING OUT OF HAND. WITH THE CHANTING AND THE STABBING...
...WE'RE FOOLING AROUND WITH SOME REALLY STRANGE STUFF, FELLAS.
IT USED TO BE ABOUT THE SCIENCE.
...I'LL BE DOWNSTAIRS IN MY LAB.

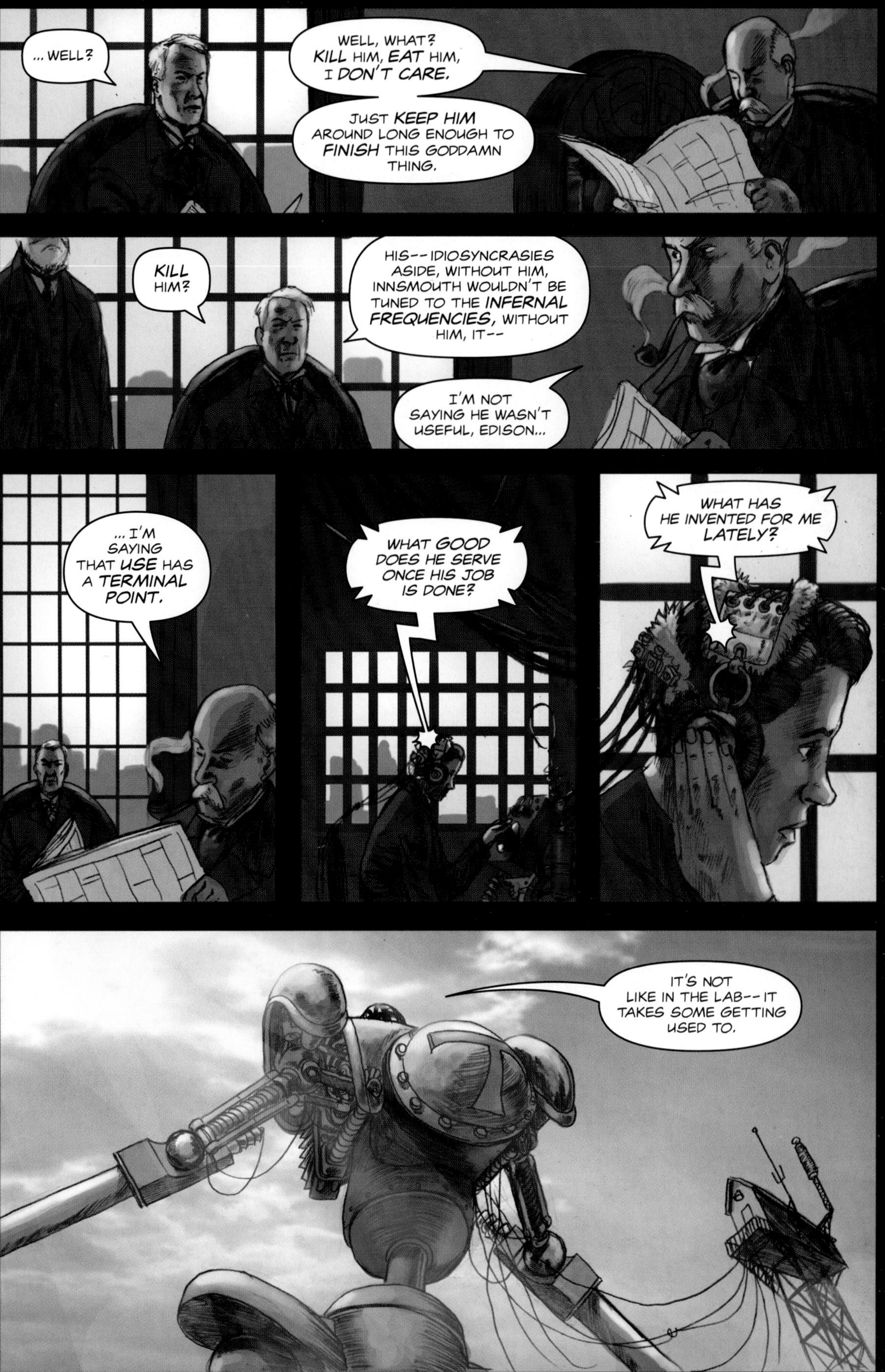

... WELL?
WELL, WHAT? KILL HIM, EAT HIM, I DON'T CARE.
JUST KEEP HIM AROUND LONG ENOUGH TO FINISH THIS GODDAMN THING.
KILL HIM?
HIS--IDIOSYNCRASIES ASIDE, WITHOUT HIM, INNSMOUTH WOULDN'T BE TUNED TO THE INFERNAL FREQUENCIES, WITHOUT HIM, IT--
I'M NOT SAYING HE WASN'T USEFUL, EDISON...
... I'M SAYING THAT USE HAS A TERMINAL POINT.
WHAT GOOD DOES HE SERVE ONCE HIS JOB IS DONE?
WHAT HAS HE INVENTED FOR ME LATELY?
IT'S NOT LIKE IN THE LAB-- IT TAKES SOME GETTING USED TO.

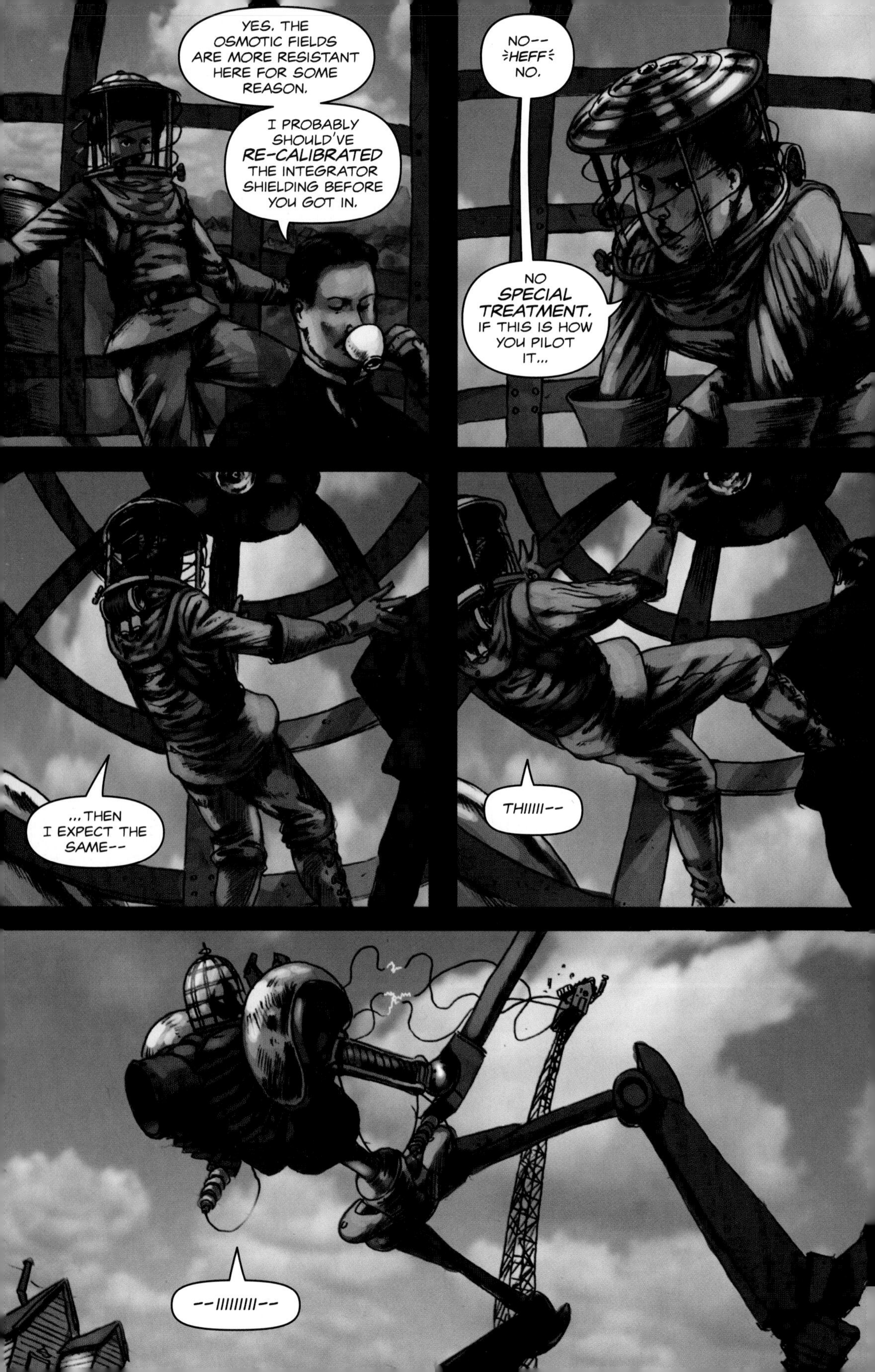
YES, THE OSMOTIC FIELDS ARE MORE RESISTANT HERE FOR SOME REASON.
I PROBABLY SHOULD'VE RE-CALIBRATED THE INTEGRATOR SHIELDING BEFORE YOU GOT IN.
NO-- HEFF NO.
NO SPECIAL TREATMENT. IF THIS IS HOW YOU PILOT IT...
...THEN I EXPECT THE SAME--
THIIIII--
--IIIIIIII--

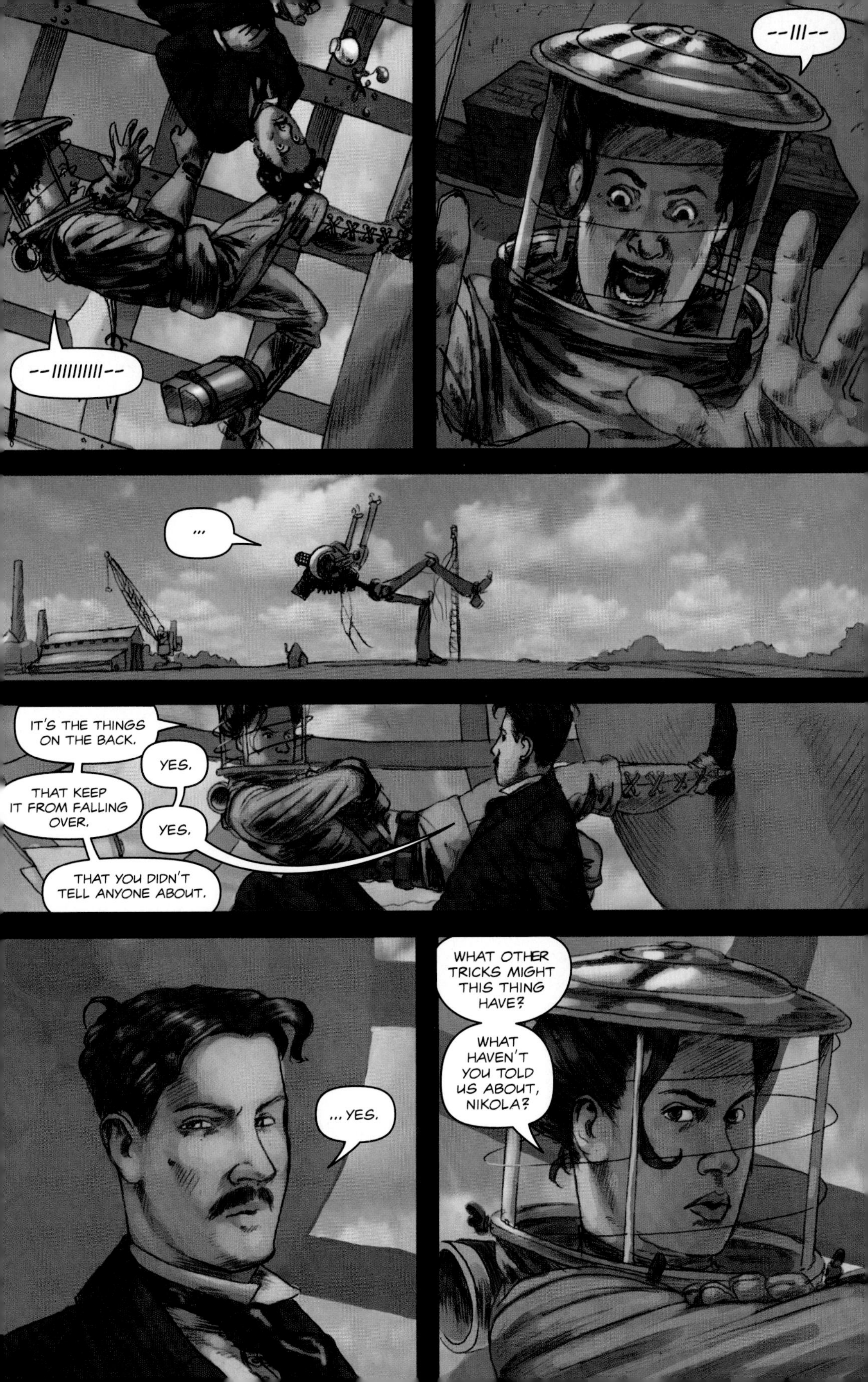
--IIIIIIIII--
--III--
...
IT'S THE THINGS ON THE BACK.
YES.
THAT KEEP IT FROM FALLING OVER.
YES.
THAT YOU DIDN'T TELL ANYONE ABOUT.
...YES.
WHAT OTHER TRICKS MIGHT THIS THING HAVE?
WHAT HAVEN'T YOU TOLD US ABOUT, NIKOLA?

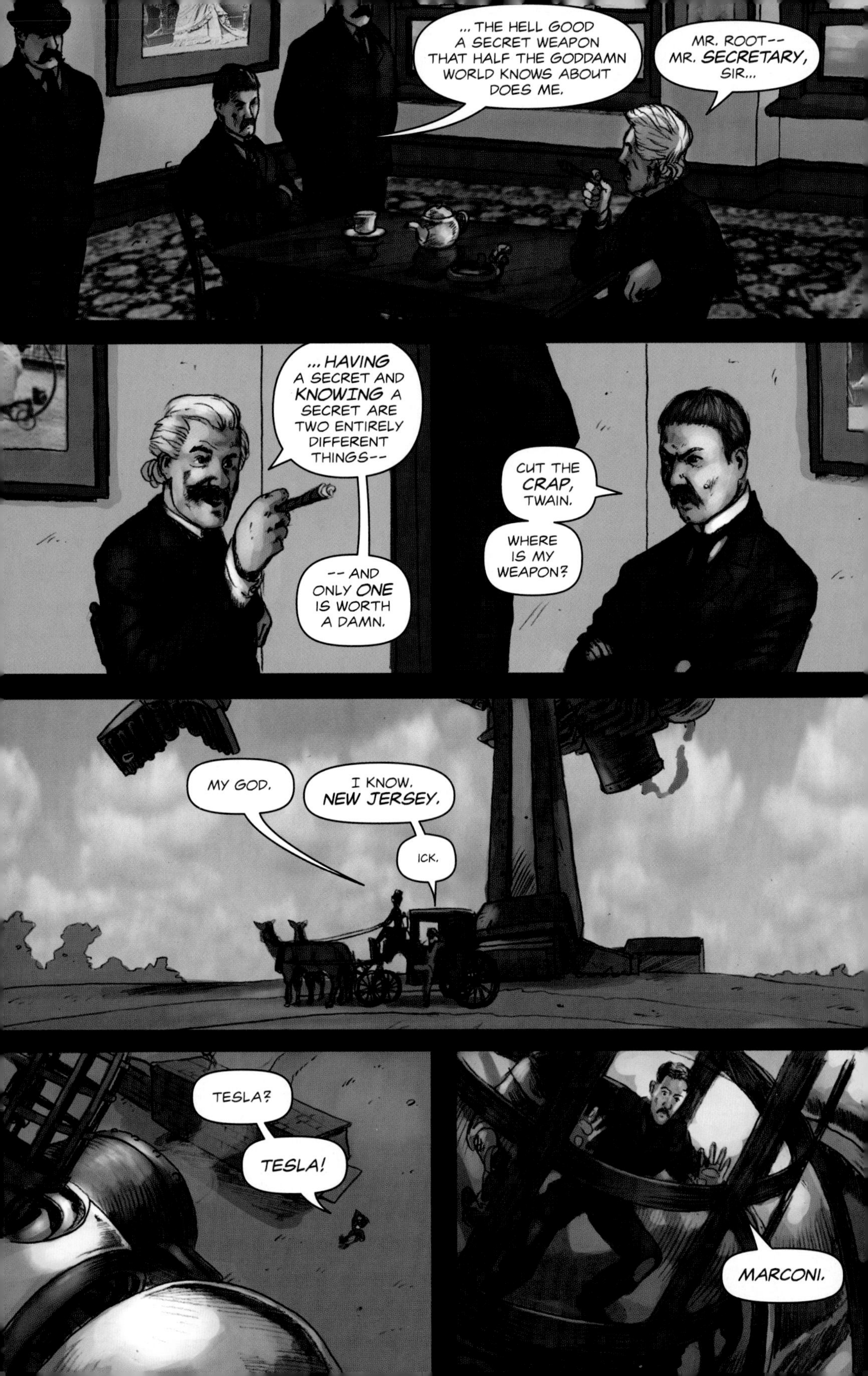
... THE HELL GOOD A SECRET WEAPON THAT HALF THE GODDAMN WORLD KNOWS ABOUT DOES ME.
MR. ROOT-- MR. SECRETARY, SIR...
... HAVING A SECRET AND KNOWING A SECRET ARE TWO ENTIRELY DIFFERENT THINGS--
-- AND ONLY ONE IS WORTH A DAMN.
CUT THE CRAP, TWAIN.
WHERE IS MY WEAPON?
MY GOD.
I KNOW. NEW JERSEY.
ICK.
TESLA?
TESLA!
MARCONI.

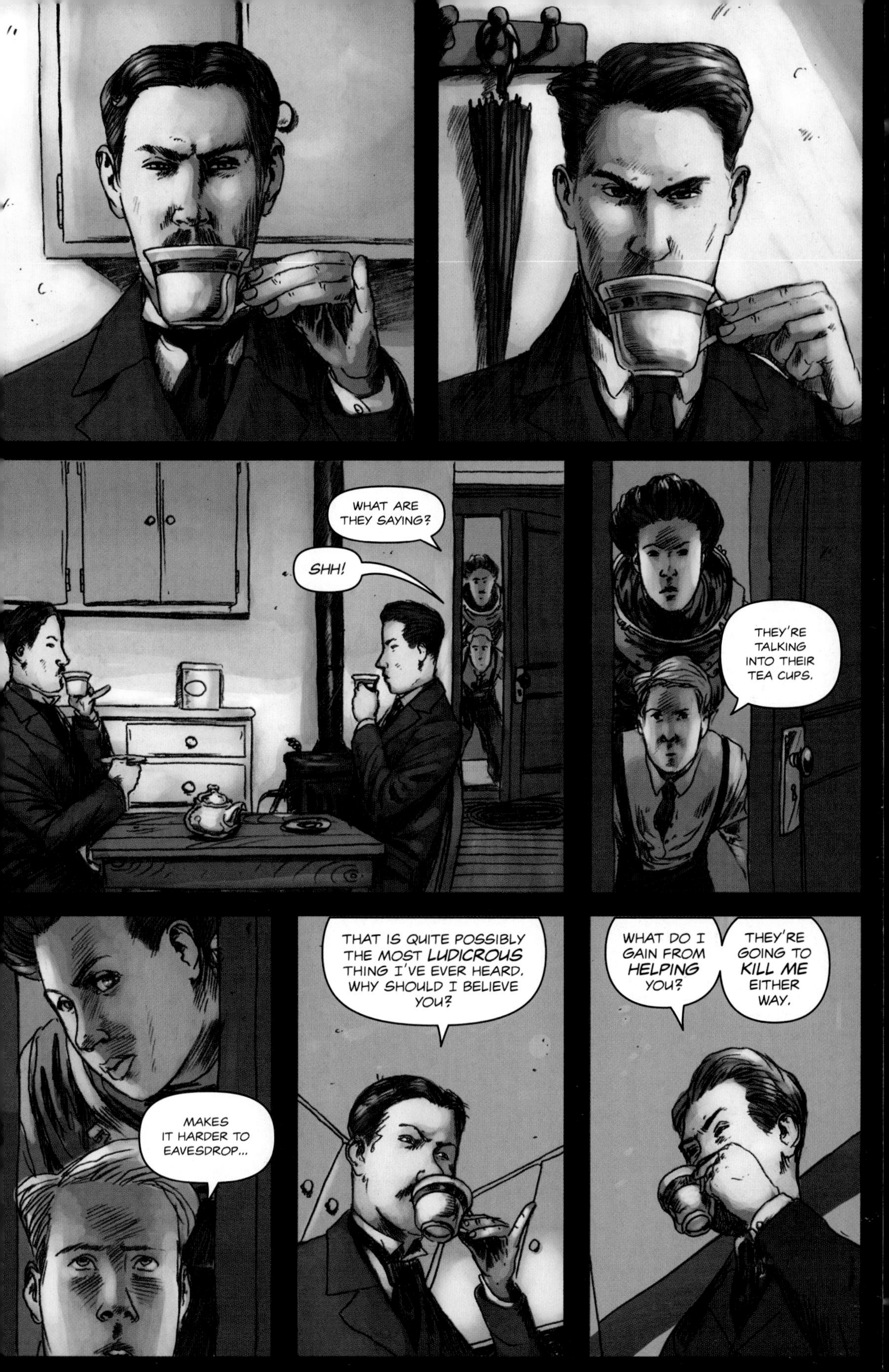
WHAT ARE THEY SAYING?
SHH!
THEY'RE TALKING INTO THEIR TEA CUPS.
MAKES IT HARDER TO EAVESDROP...
THAT IS QUITE POSSIBLY THE MOST LUDICROUS THING I'VE EVER HEARD. WHY SHOULD I BELIEVE YOU?
WHAT DO I GAIN FROM HELPING YOU?
THEY'RE GOING TO KILL ME EITHER WAY.

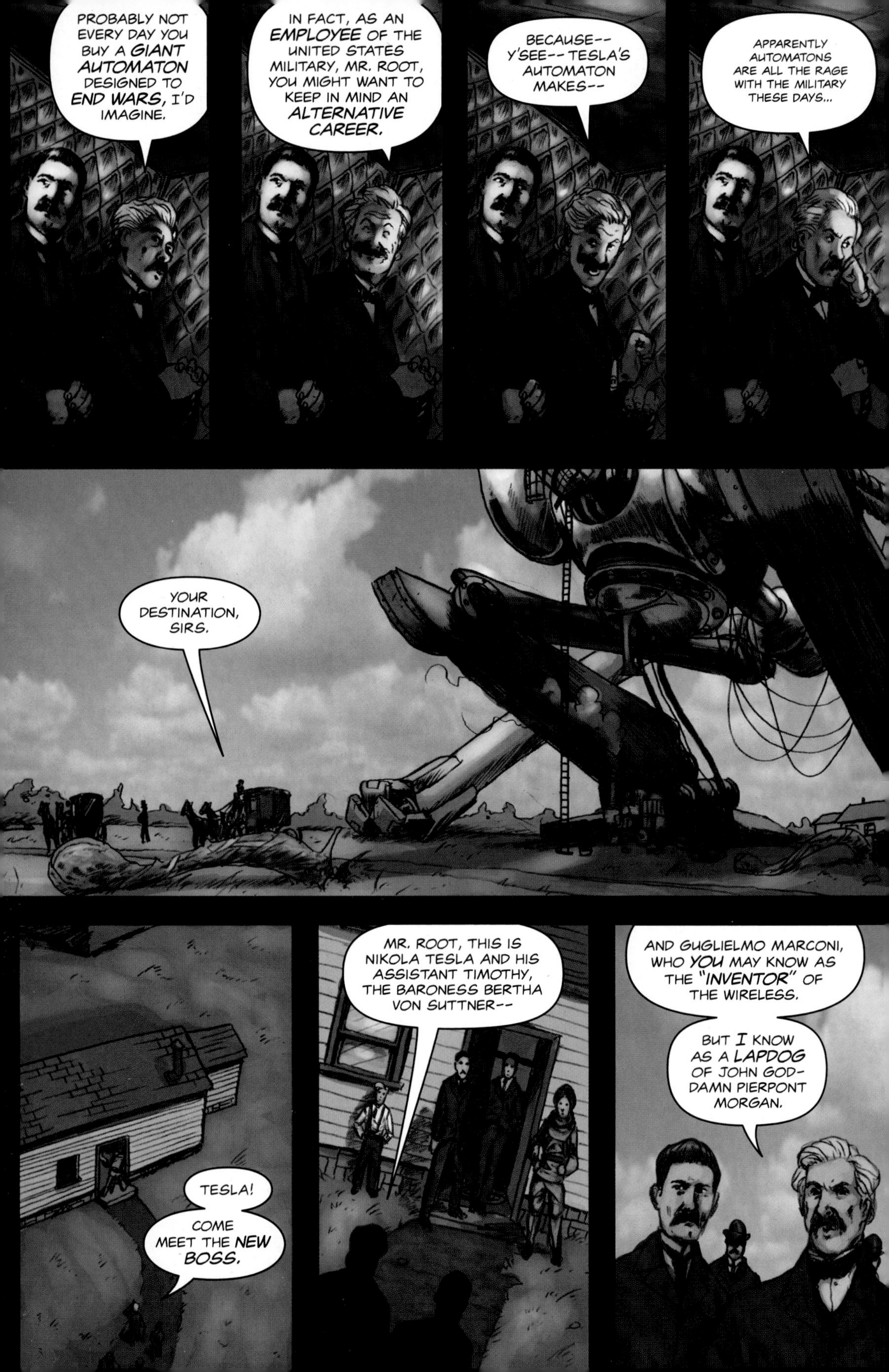
PROBABLY NOT EVERY DAY YOU BUY A GIANT AUTOMATON DESIGNED TO END WARS, I'D IMAGINE.
IN FACT, AS AN EMPLOYEE OF THE UNITED STATES MILITARY, MR. ROOT, YOU MIGHT WANT TO KEEP IN MIND AN ALTERNATIVE CAREER.
BECAUSE-- Y'SEE-- TESLA'S AUTOMATON MAKES--
APPARENTLY AUTOMATONS ARE ALL THE RAGE WITH THE MILITARY THESE DAYS...
YOUR DESTINATION, SIRS.
TESLA!
COME MEET THE NEW BOSS.
MR. ROOT, THIS IS NIKOLA TESLA AND HIS ASSISTANT TIMOTHY, THE BARONESS BERTHA VON SUTTNER--
AND GUGLIELMO MARCONI, WHO YOU MAY KNOW AS THE "INVENTOR" OF THE WIRELESS.
BUT I KNOW AS A LAPDOG OF JOHN GOD-DAMN PIERPONT MORGAN.

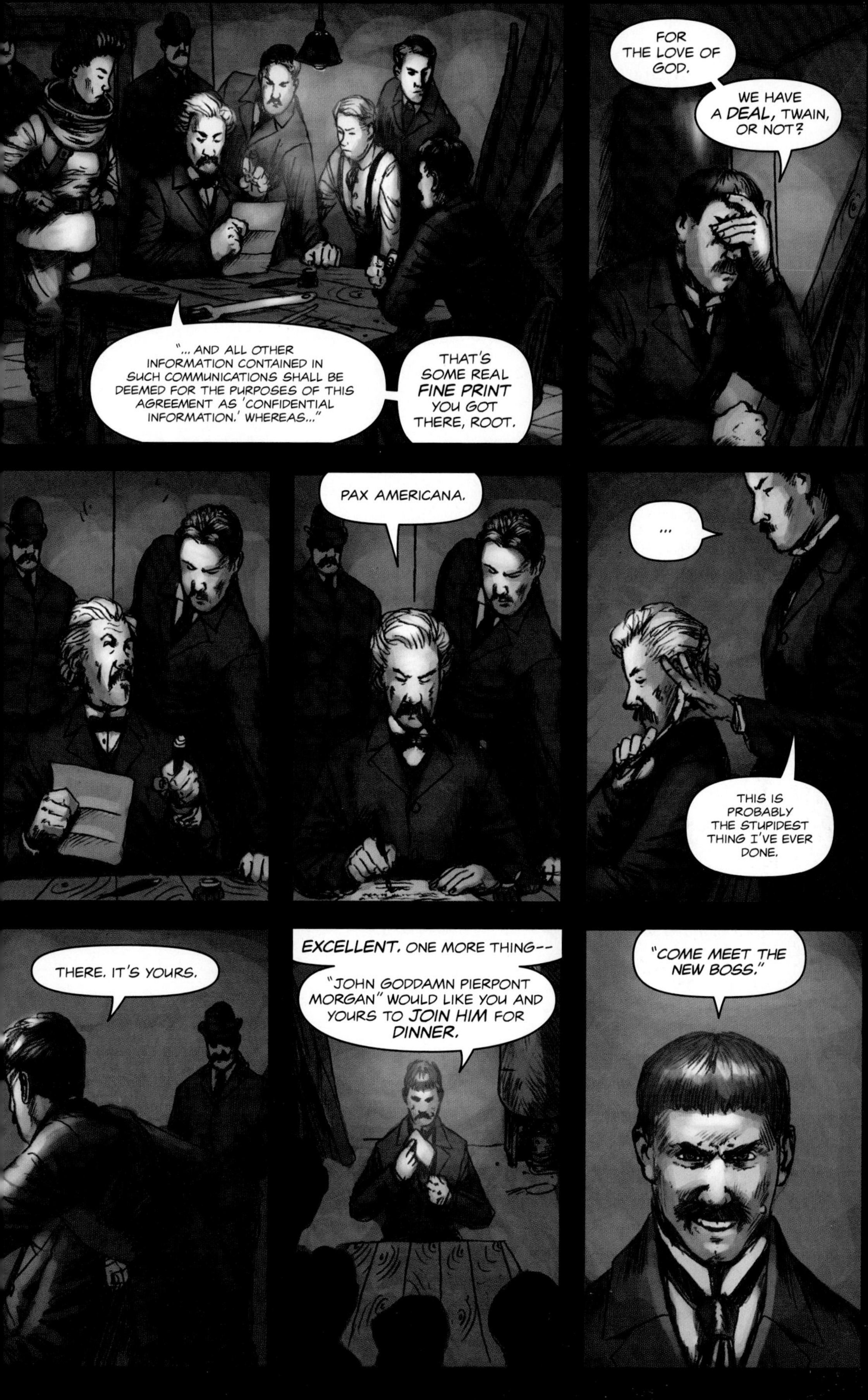
"... AND ALL OTHER INFORMATION CONTAINED IN SUCH COMMUNICATIONS SHALL BE DEEMED FOR THE PURPOSES OF THIS AGREEMENT AS 'CONFIDENTIAL INFORMATION.' WHEREAS..."
THAT'S SOME REAL FINE PRINT YOU GOT THERE, ROOT.
FOR THE LOVE OF GOD.
WE HAVE A DEAL, TWAIN, OR NOT?
PAX AMERICANA.
...
THIS IS PROBABLY THE STUPIDEST THING I'VE EVER DONE.
THERE. IT'S YOURS.
EXCELLENT. ONE MORE THING--
"JOHN GODDAMN PIERPONT MORGAN" WOULD LIKE YOU AND YOURS TO JOIN HIM FOR DINNER.
"COME MEET THE NEW BOSS."

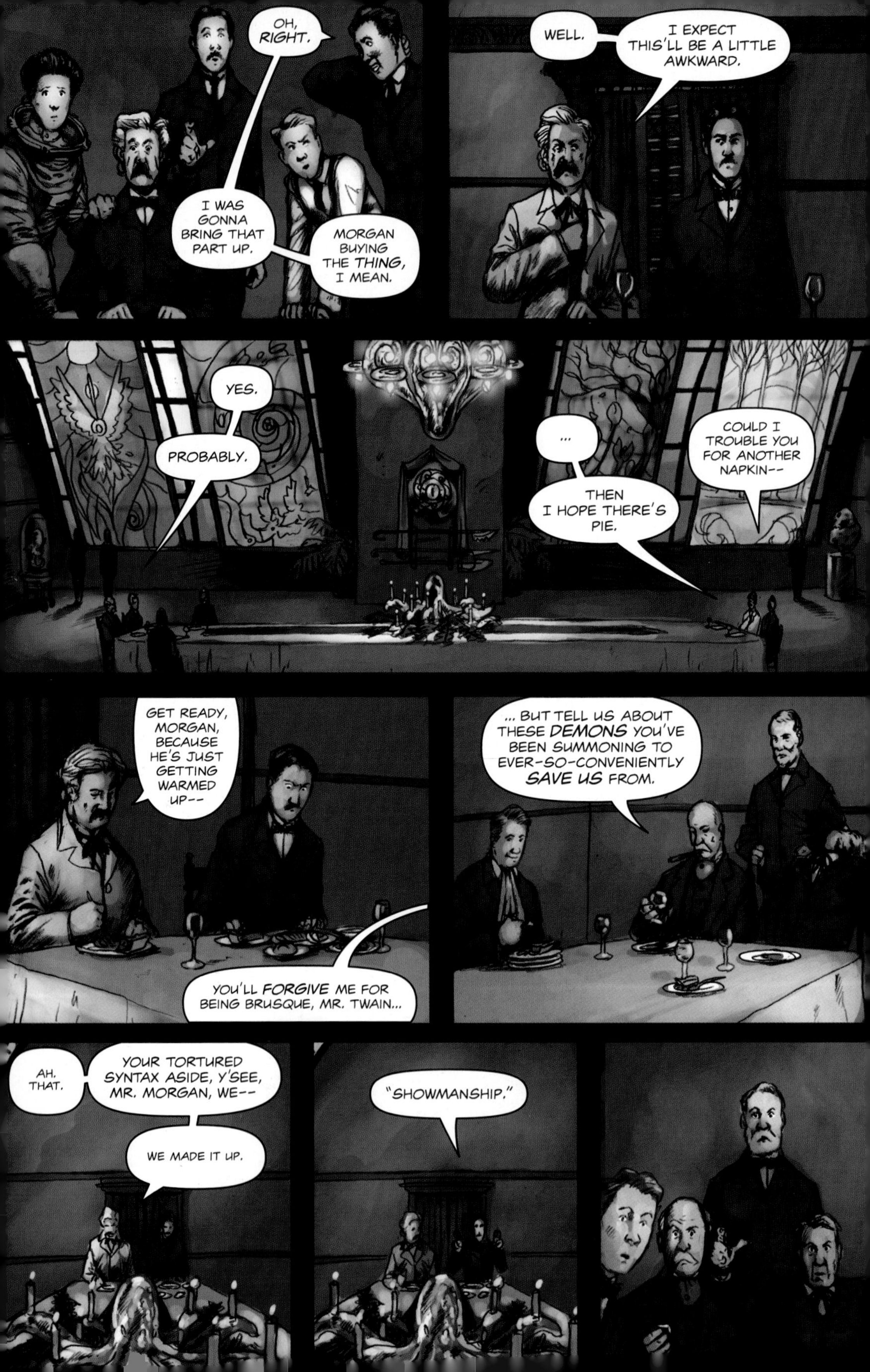
OH, RIGHT.
I WAS GONNA BRING THAT PART UP.
MORGAN BUYING THE THING, I MEAN.
WELL.
I EXPECT THIS'LL BE A LITTLE AWKWARD.
YES.
PROBABLY.
...
THEN I HOPE THERE'S PIE.
COULD I TROUBLE YOU FOR ANOTHER NAPKIN--
GET READY, MORGAN, BECAUSE HE'S JUST GETTING WARMED UP--
YOU'LL FORGIVE ME FOR BEING BRUSQUE, MR. TWAIN...
... BUT TELL US ABOUT THESE DEMONS YOU'VE BEEN SUMMONING TO EVER-SO-CONVENIENTLY SAVE US FROM.
AH. THAT.
YOUR TORTURED SYNTAX ASIDE, Y'SEE, MR. MORGAN, WE--
WE MADE IT UP.
"SHOWMANSHIP."

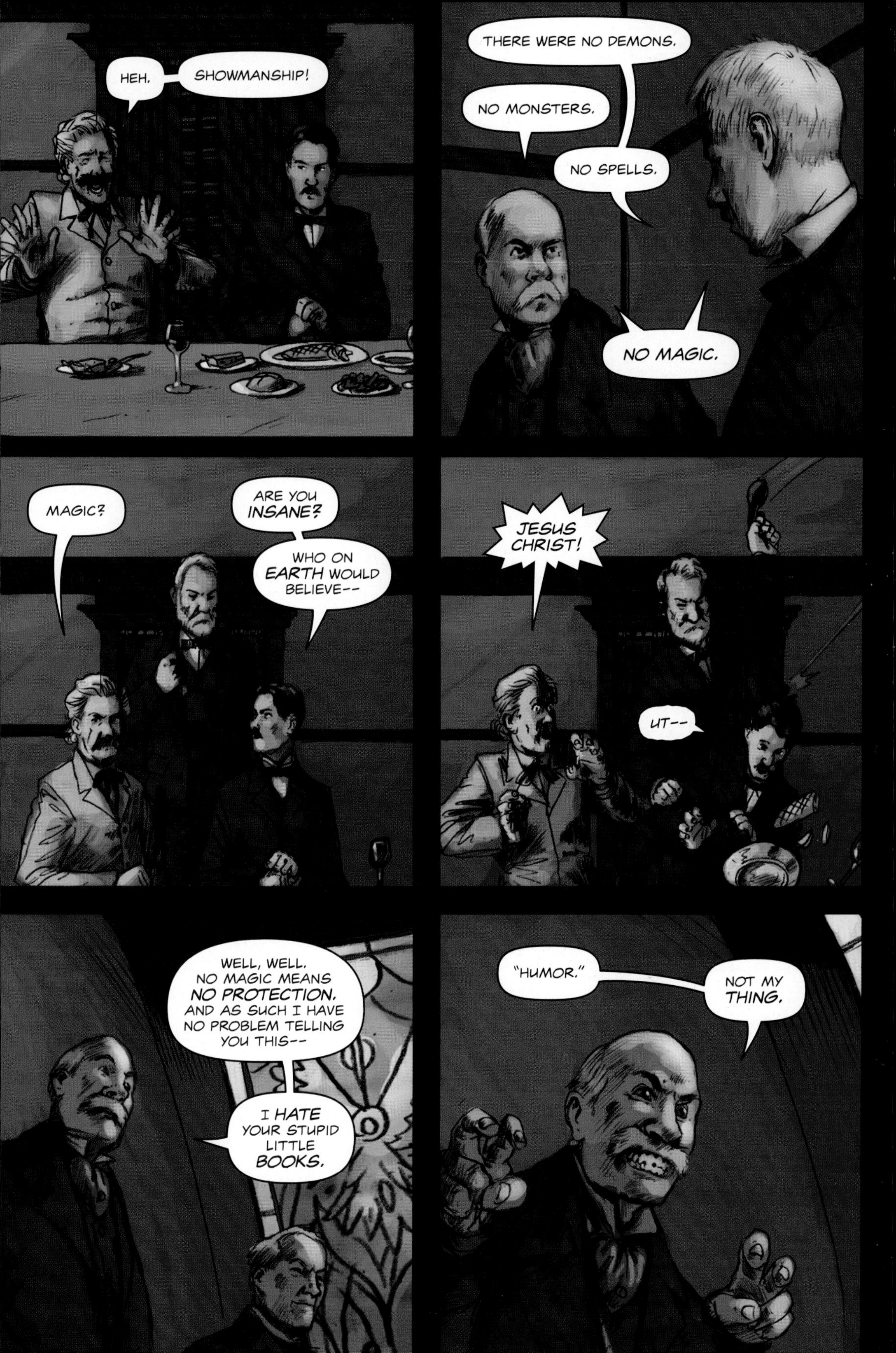
HEH.
SHOWMANSHIP!
THERE WERE NO DEMONS.
NO MONSTERS.
NO SPELLS.
NO MAGIC.
MAGIC?
ARE YOU INSANE?
WHO ON EARTH WOULD BELIEVE--
JESUS CHRIST!
UT--
WELL, WELL. NO MAGIC MEANS NO PROTECTION. AND AS SUCH I HAVE NO PROBLEM TELLING YOU THIS--
I HATE YOUR STUPID LITTLE BOOKS.
"HUMOR."
NOT MY THING.

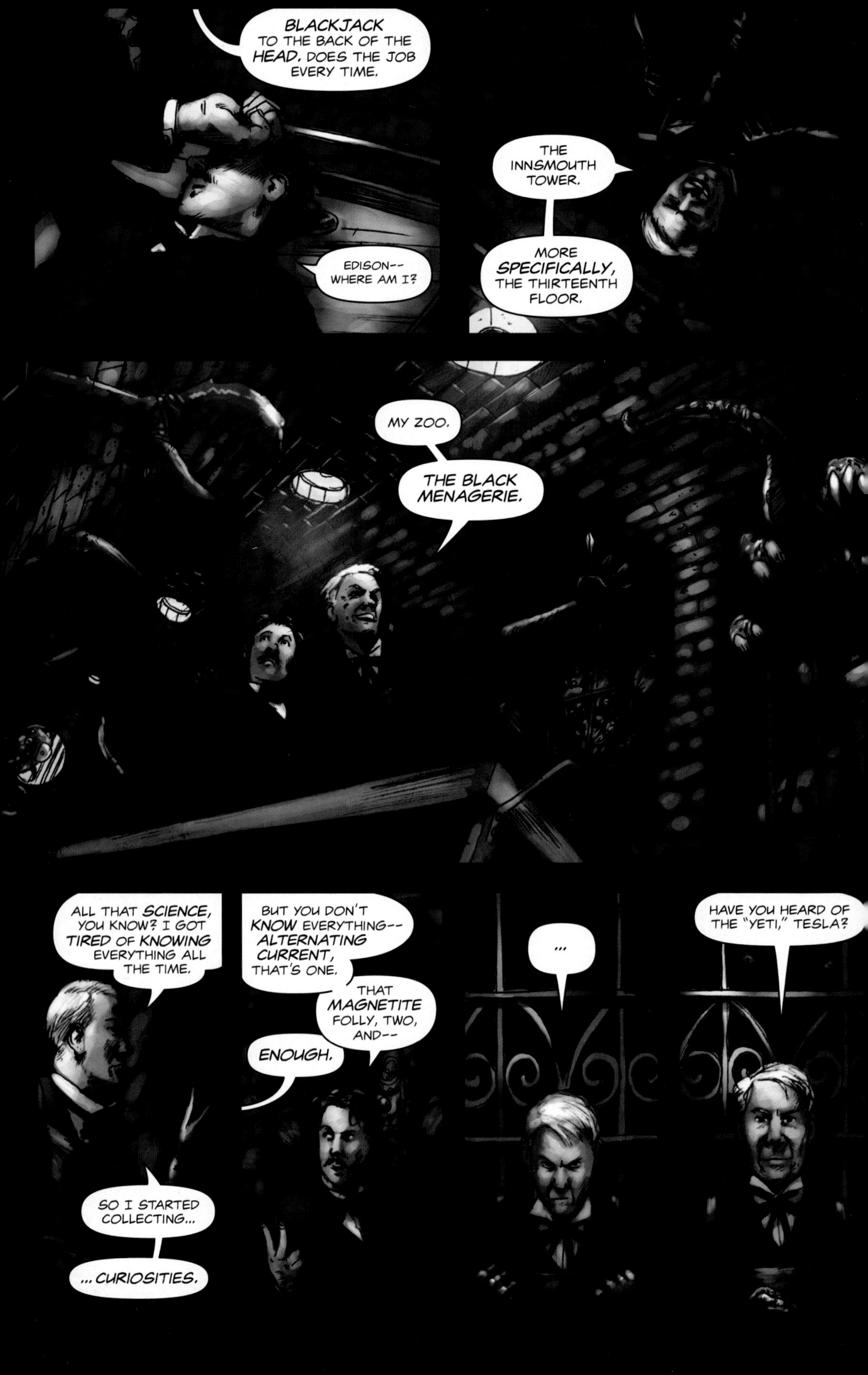
BLACKJACK TO THE BACK OF THE HEAD. DOES THE JOB EVERY TIME.
EDISON-- WHERE AM I?
THE INNSMOUTH TOWER.
MORE SPECIFICALLY, THE THIRTEENTH FLOOR.
MY ZOO.
THE BLACK MENAGERIE.
ALL THAT SCIENCE, YOU KNOW? I GOT TIRED OF KNOWING EVERYTHING ALL THE TIME.
SO I STARTED COLLECTING...
...CURIOSITIES.
BUT YOU DON'T KNOW EVERYTHING-- ALTERNATING CURRENT, THAT'S ONE.
THAT MAGNETITE FOLLY, TWO, AND--
ENOUGH.
...
HAVE YOU HEARD OF THE "YETI," TESLA?

"I JUST THINK YOU SHOULD ALWAYS LISTEN TO YOUR *GUT*, BARONESS."

"AND YOUR GUT SAYS *WHAT*, TIM? THAT WE SHOULDN'T SELL IT?"

IT'S NOT EVEN THAT. THESE GUYS ARE--

SOMETHING'S *GOING ON* AND THEY'RE NOT TELLING US WHAT.

IF THE CHECK CASHES, I DON'T CARE.

I DON'T MEAN IT LIKE THAT. I MEAN, THEY--

...WHAT? THEY WHAT?

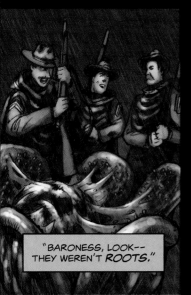

"BARONESS, LOOK-- THEY WEREN'T *ROOTS*."

"THEY WERE BLOODY *PODS!*"

EEE

YOU KNOW HOW MANY PEOPLE HAVE DIED IN THE CONSTRUCTION OF THIS BUILDING TO DATE?

SIXTY-FIVE.

THE PRESS ONLY KNOWS ABOUT A *DOZEN*.

FASCINATING, MR. MORGAN, I'M SURE.

AND AM I MEANT TO BE *SIXTY-SIX*, THEN?

THAT'D BE A LITTLE ON THE NOSE, DON'T YOU THINK?

NO...

... I'D THINK BUILDING A SKYSCRAPER AS SOME KIND OF INSANE MONUMENT TO--

OH, MY--

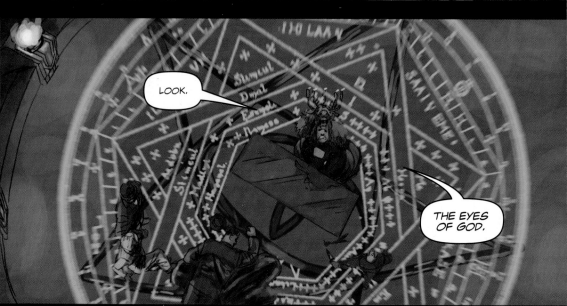

LOOK.

THE EYES OF GOD.

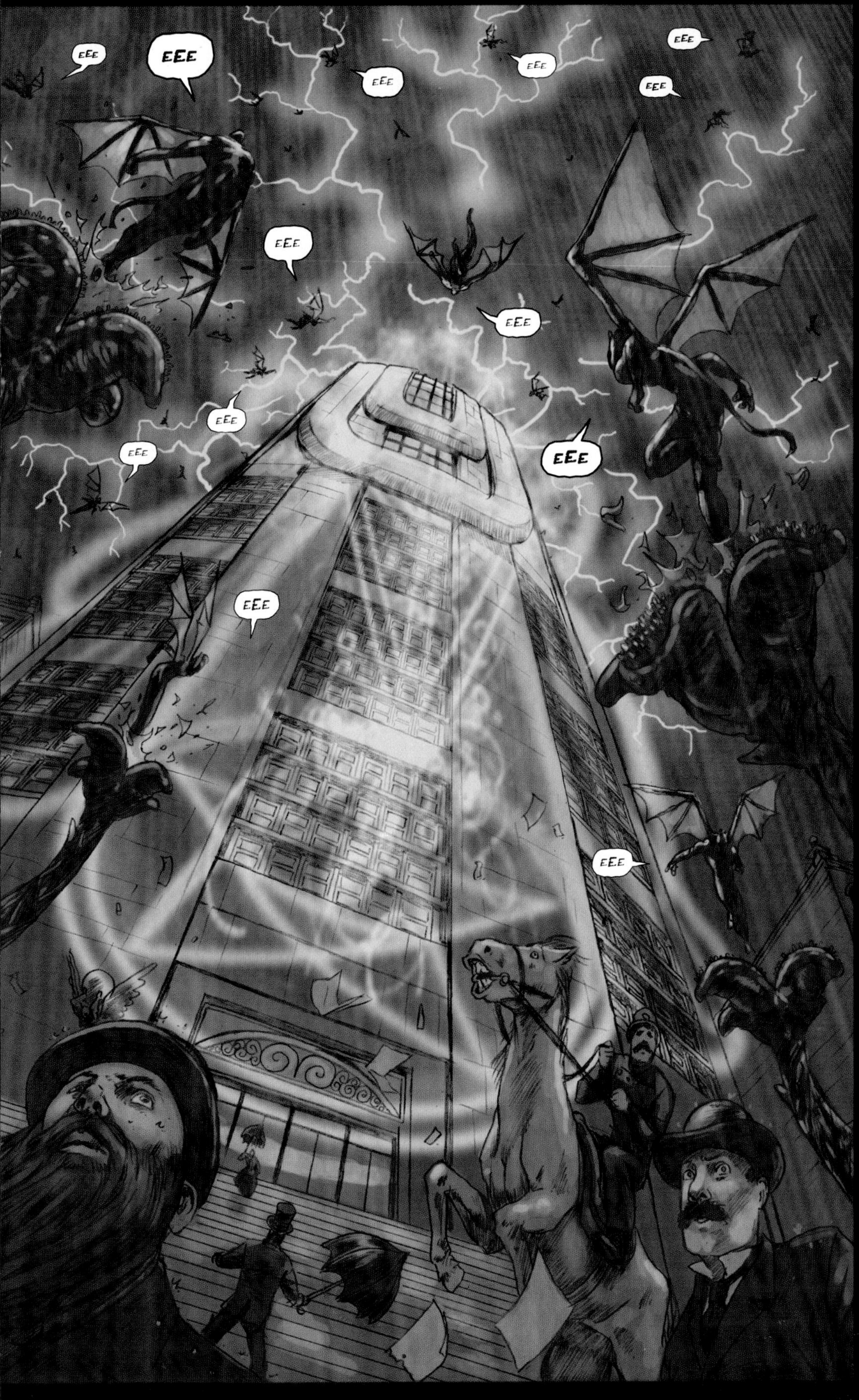
EEE
EEE
EEE
EEE
EEE
EEE
EEE
EEE
EEE
EEE
EEE
EEE
EEE

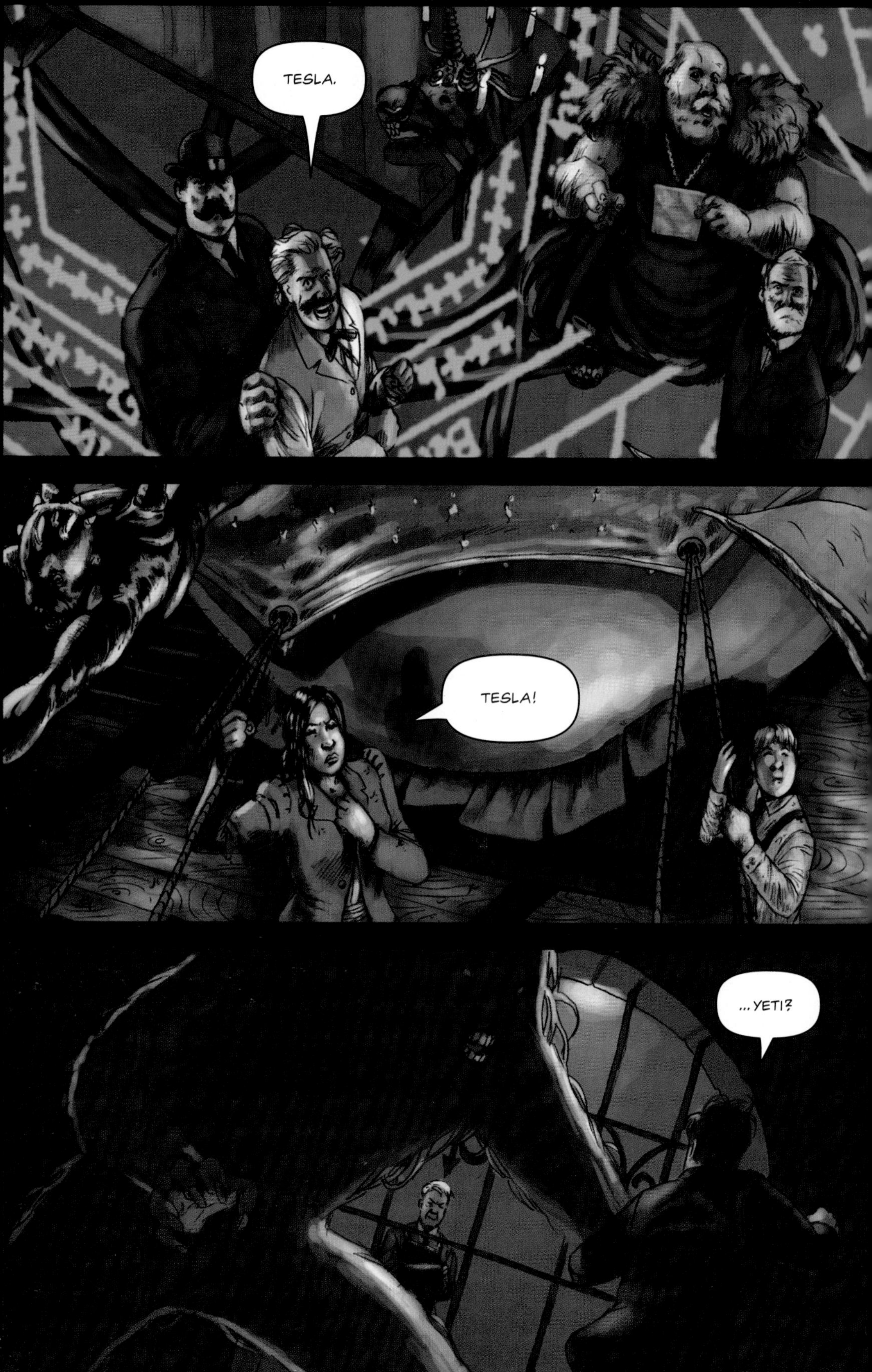
TESLA.
TESLA!
...YETI?

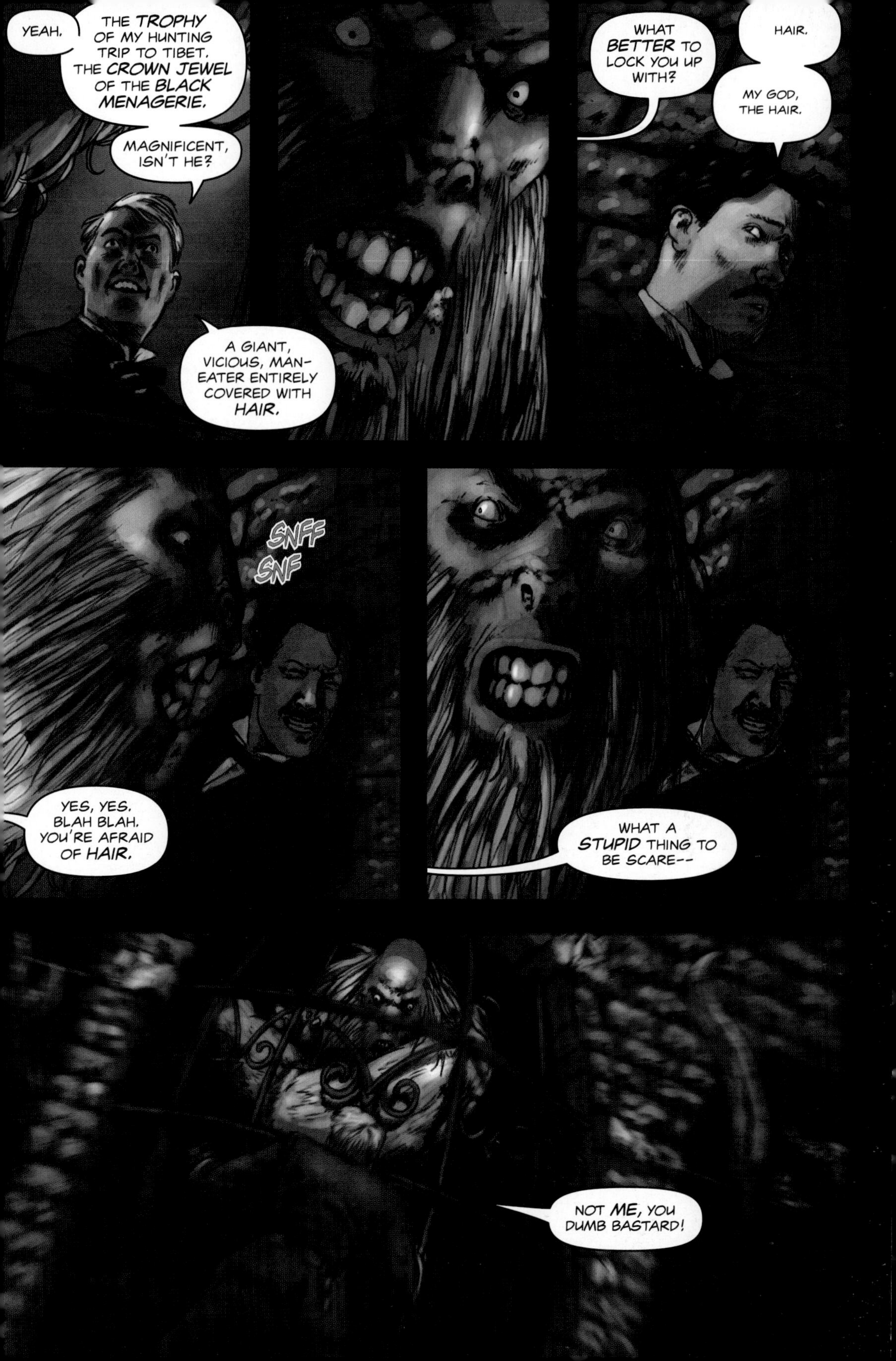
YEAH.
THE TROPHY OF MY HUNTING TRIP TO TIBET. THE CROWN JEWEL OF THE BLACK MENAGERIE.
MAGNIFICENT, ISN'T HE?
A GIANT, VICIOUS, MAN-EATER ENTIRELY COVERED WITH HAIR.
WHAT BETTER TO LOCK YOU UP WITH?
HAIR.
MY GOD, THE HAIR.
SNFF
SNF
YES, YES. BLAH BLAH. YOU'RE AFRAID OF HAIR.
WHAT A STUPID THING TO BE SCARE--
NOT ME, YOU DUMB BASTARD!

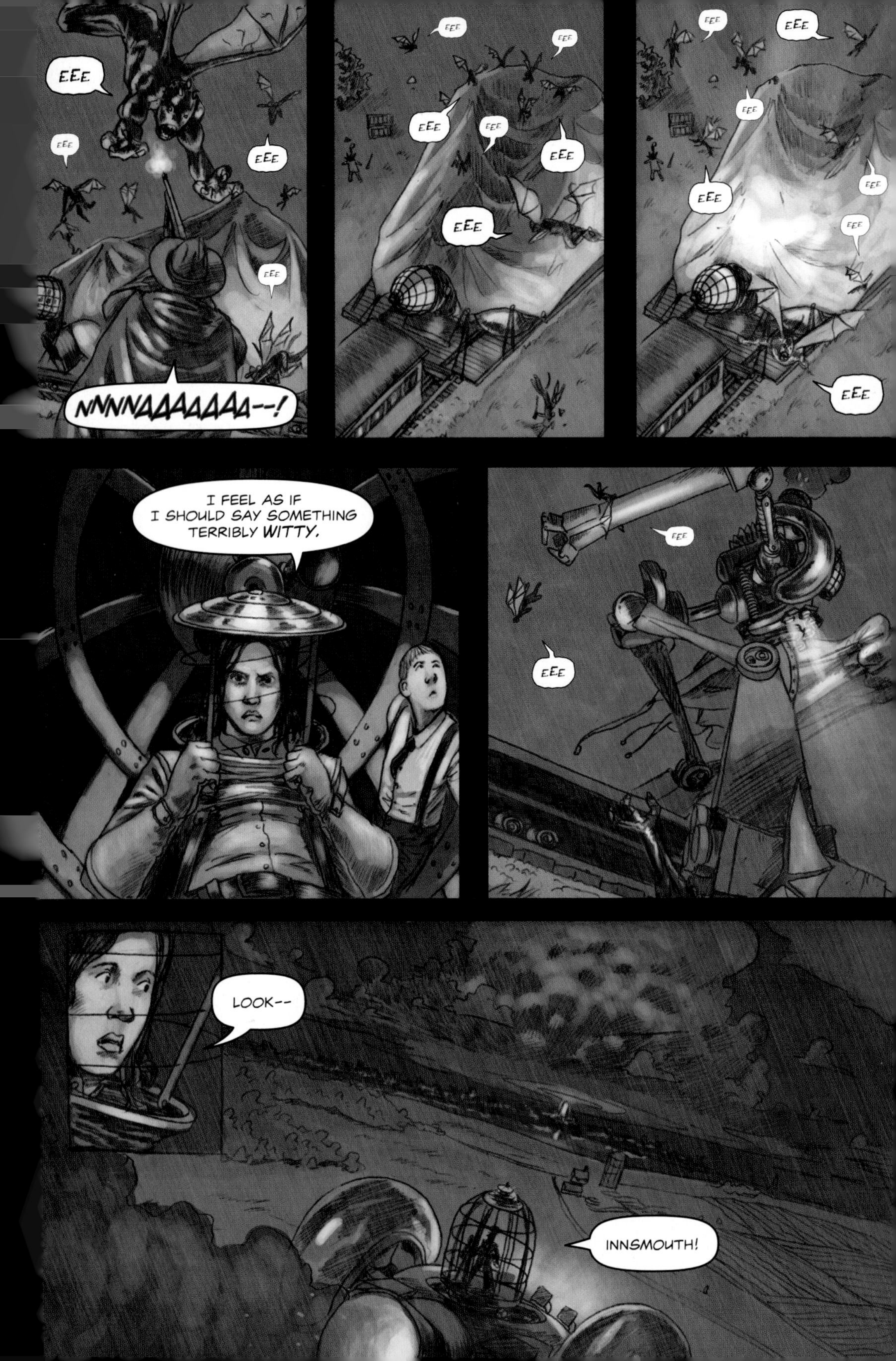

EEE
EEE
EEE
EEE
NNNNAAAAAAA--!
EEE
EEE
EEE
EEE
EEE
EEE
EEE
EEE
EEE
EEE
EEE
EEE
EEE
I FEEL AS IF I SHOULD SAY SOMETHING TERRIBLY WITTY.
EEE
EEE
LOOK--
INNSMOUTH!

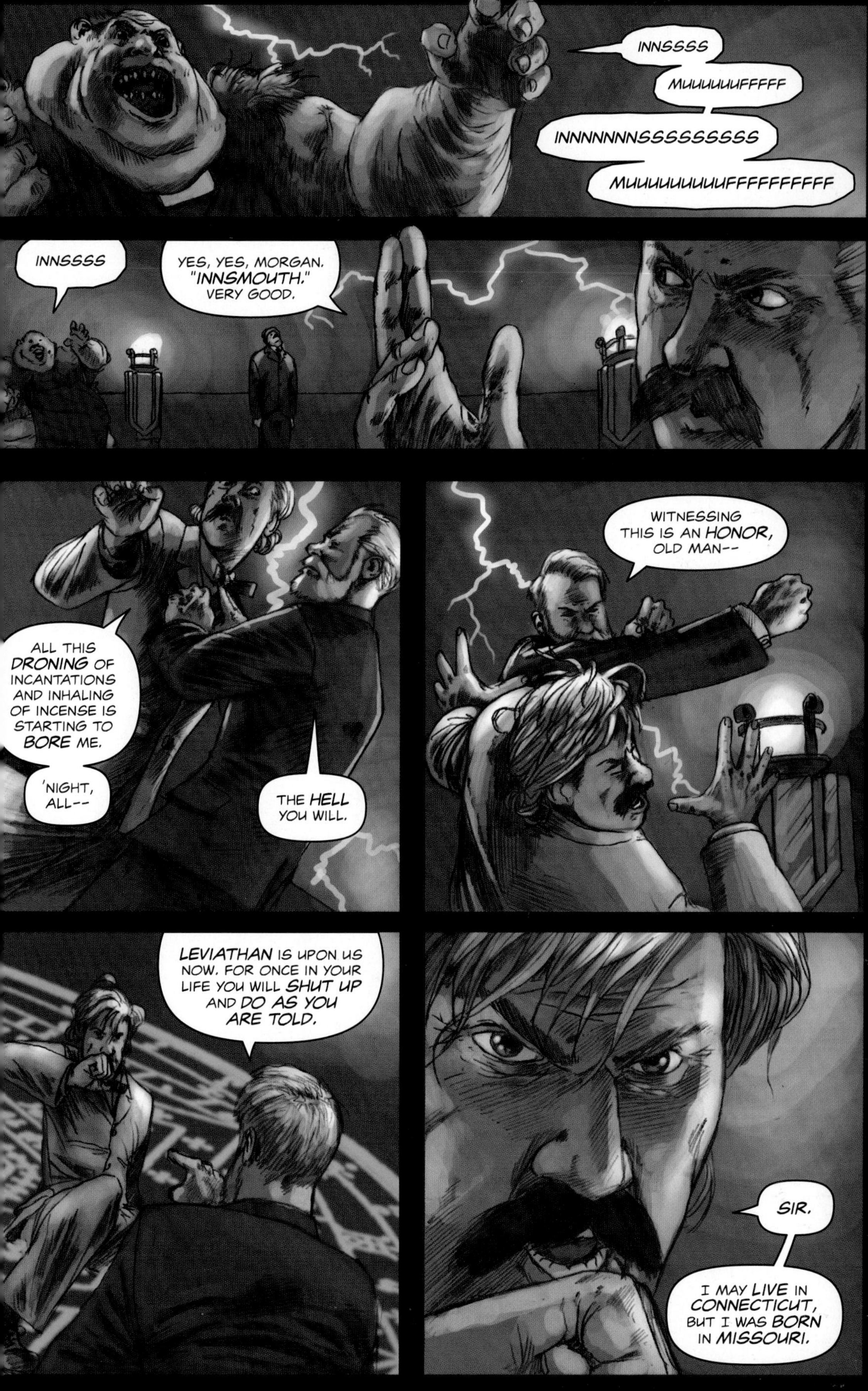
INNSSSS
MUUUUUUFFFFF
INNNNNNNSSSSSSSSS
MUUUUUUUUFFFFFFFFFF
INNSSSS
YES, YES, MORGAN. "INNSMOUTH." VERY GOOD.
ALL THIS DRONING OF INCANTATIONS AND INHALING OF INCENSE IS STARTING TO BORE ME.
'NIGHT, ALL--
THE HELL YOU WILL.
WITNESSING THIS IS AN HONOR, OLD MAN--
LEVIATHAN IS UPON US NOW. FOR ONCE IN YOUR LIFE YOU WILL SHUT UP AND DO AS YOU ARE TOLD.
SIR.
I MAY LIVE IN CONNECTICUT, BUT I WAS BORN IN MISSOURI.

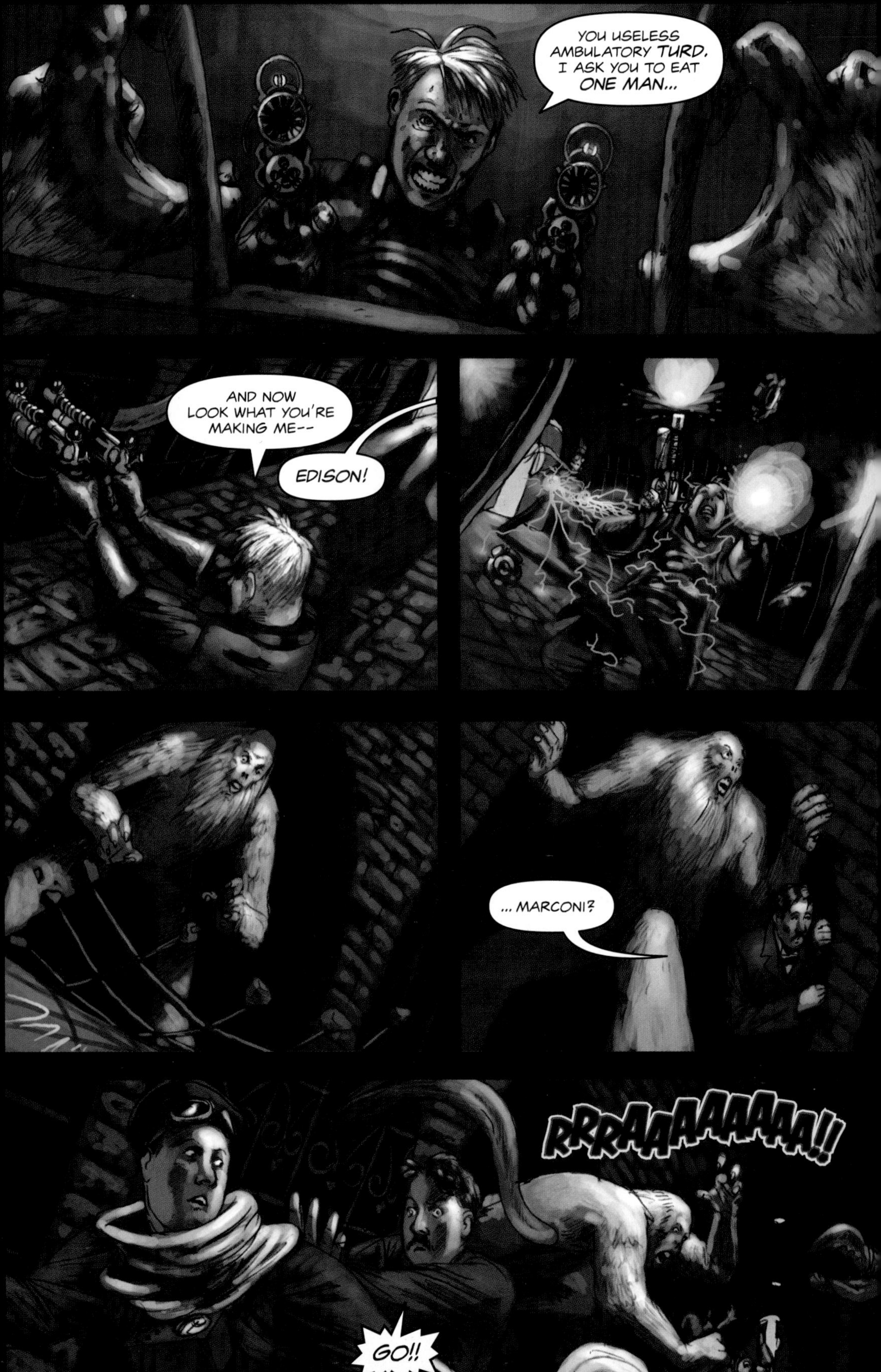
YOU USELESS AMBULATORY TURD. I ASK YOU TO EAT ONE MAN...
AND NOW LOOK WHAT YOU'RE MAKING ME--
EDISON!
... MARCONI?
RRRAAAAAAAA!!
GO!!

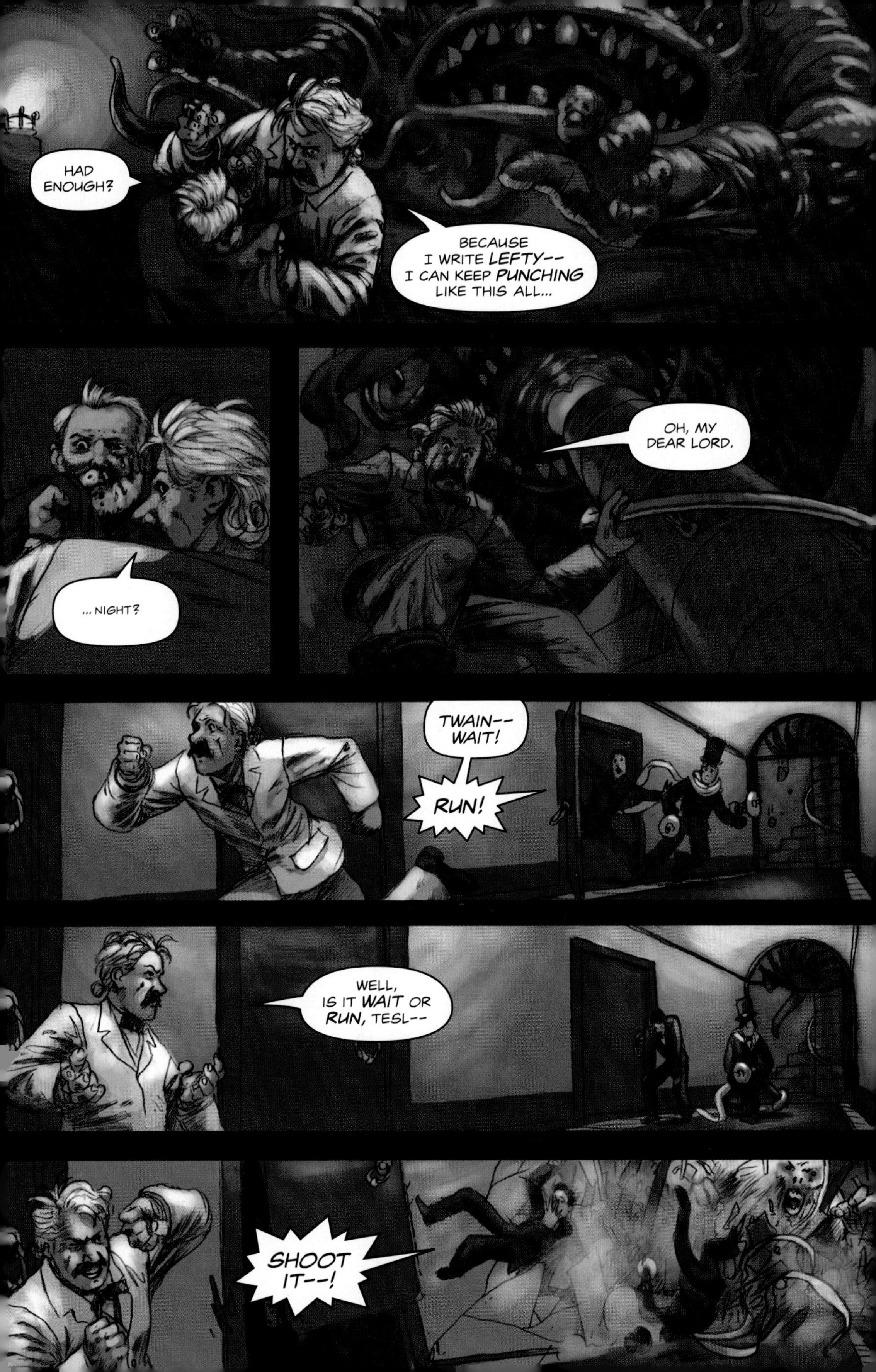
HAD ENOUGH?
BECAUSE I WRITE LEFTY-- I CAN KEEP PUNCHING LIKE THIS ALL...
...NIGHT?
OH, MY DEAR LORD.
TWAIN-- WAIT!
RUN!
WELL, IS IT WAIT OR RUN, TESL--
SHOOT IT--!

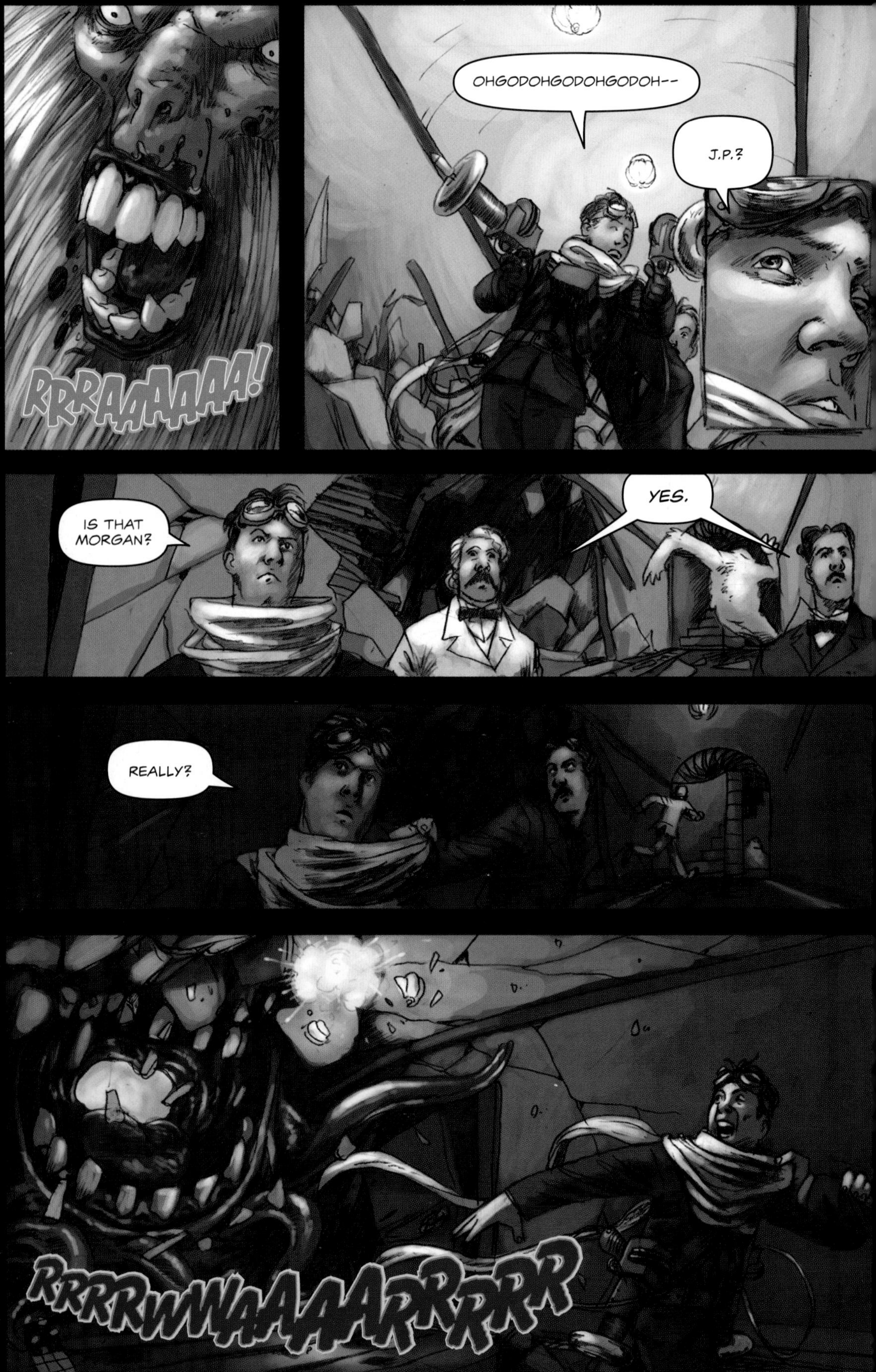
RRRAAAAAAA!
OHGODOHGODOHGODOH--
J.P.?
IS THAT MORGAN?
YES.
REALLY?
RRRRWAAAAARRRRR

IT COULD BE WORSE.

WE COULD HAVE TO FACE THAT THING AND NOT BE IN A GIANT STEEL WAR AUTOMATON.

TESLA'S STILL IN THERE.

HOLD ON.

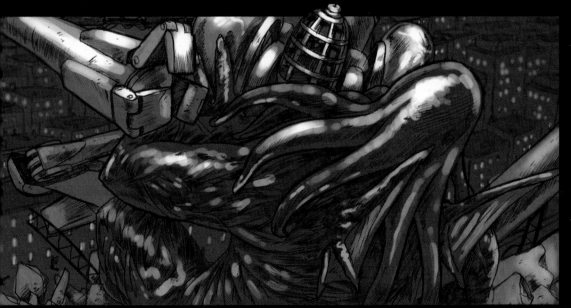

WOW.

UH-- LISTEN, FELLAS...

"...WE NEED TO TALK ABOUT THE ROOT BABIES."

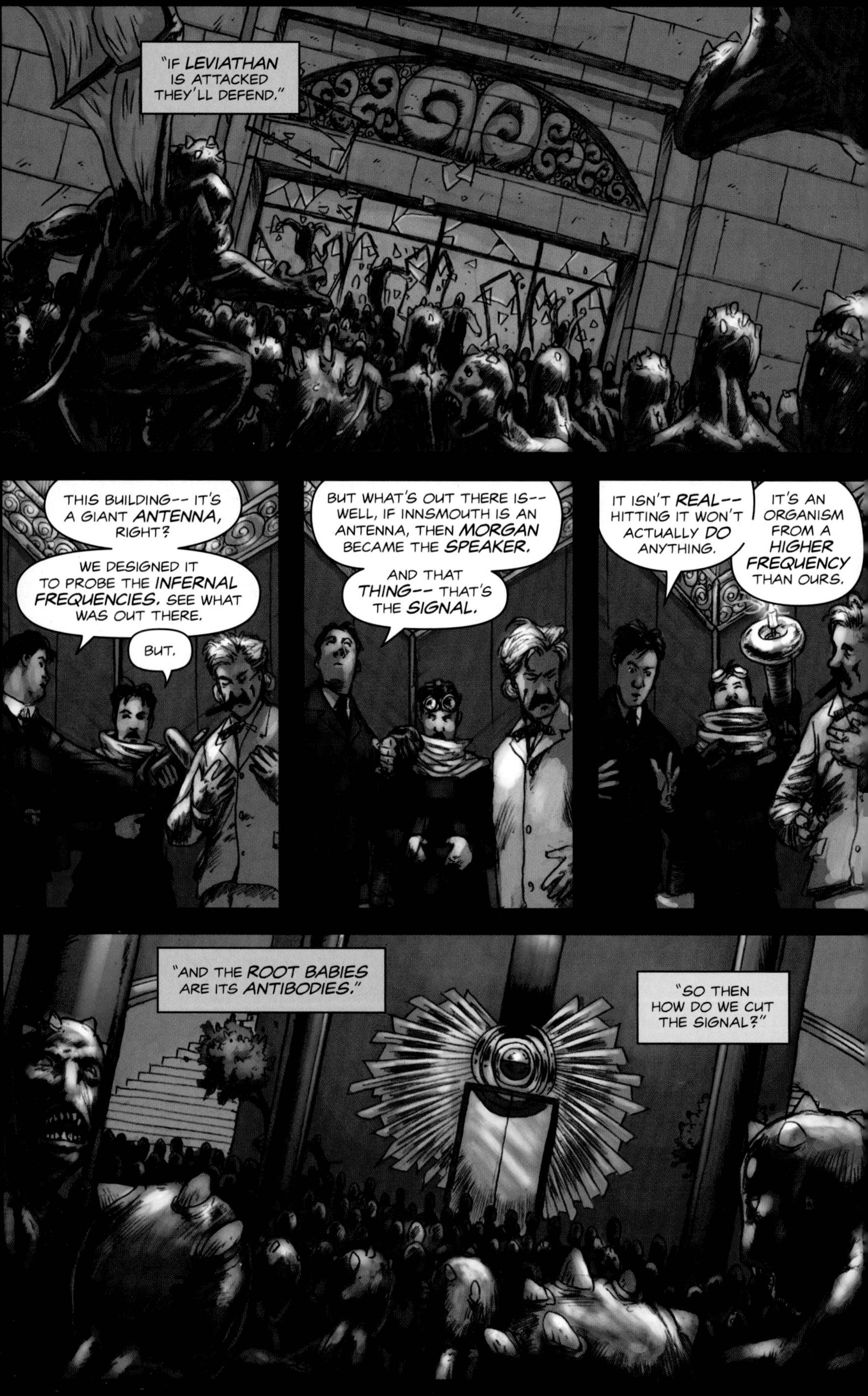
"IF LEVIATHAN IS ATTACKED THEY'LL DEFEND."
THIS BUILDING-- IT'S A GIANT ANTENNA, RIGHT?
WE DESIGNED IT TO PROBE THE INFERNAL FREQUENCIES. SEE WHAT WAS OUT THERE.
BUT.
BUT WHAT'S OUT THERE IS-- WELL, IF INNSMOUTH IS AN ANTENNA, THEN MORGAN BECAME THE SPEAKER.
AND THAT THING-- THAT'S THE SIGNAL.
IT ISN'T REAL-- HITTING IT WON'T ACTUALLY DO ANYTHING.
IT'S AN ORGANISM FROM A HIGHER FREQUENCY THAN OURS.
"AND THE ROOT BABIES ARE ITS ANTIBODIES."
"SO THEN HOW DO WE CUT THE SIGNAL?"

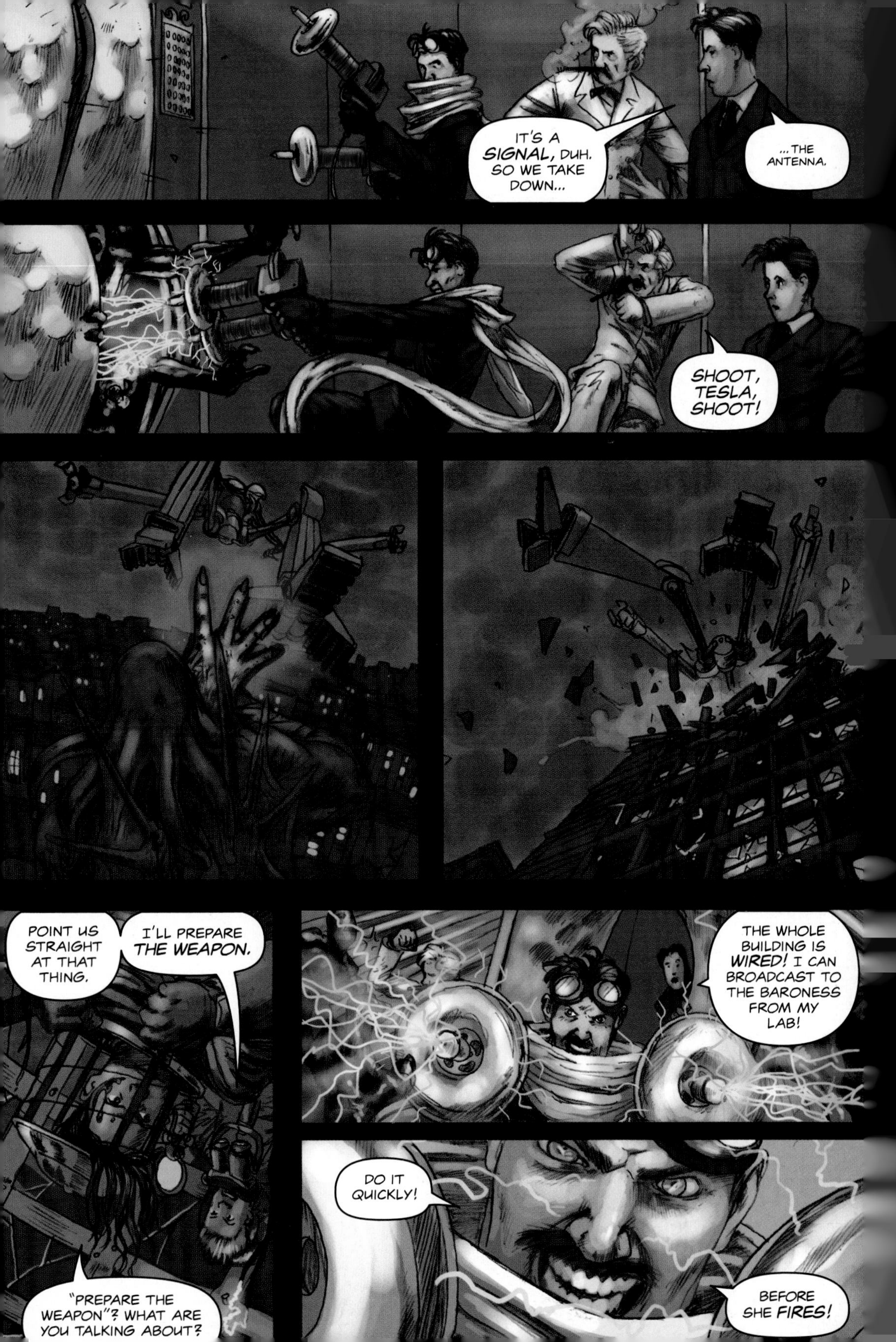
IT'S A SIGNAL, DUH. SO WE TAKE DOWN...
...THE ANTENNA.
SHOOT, TESLA, SHOOT!
POINT US STRAIGHT AT THAT THING.
I'LL PREPARE THE WEAPON.
"PREPARE THE WEAPON"? WHAT ARE YOU TALKING ABOUT?
THE WHOLE BUILDING IS WIRED! I CAN BROADCAST TO THE BARONESS FROM MY LAB!
DO IT QUICKLY!
BEFORE SHE FIRES!

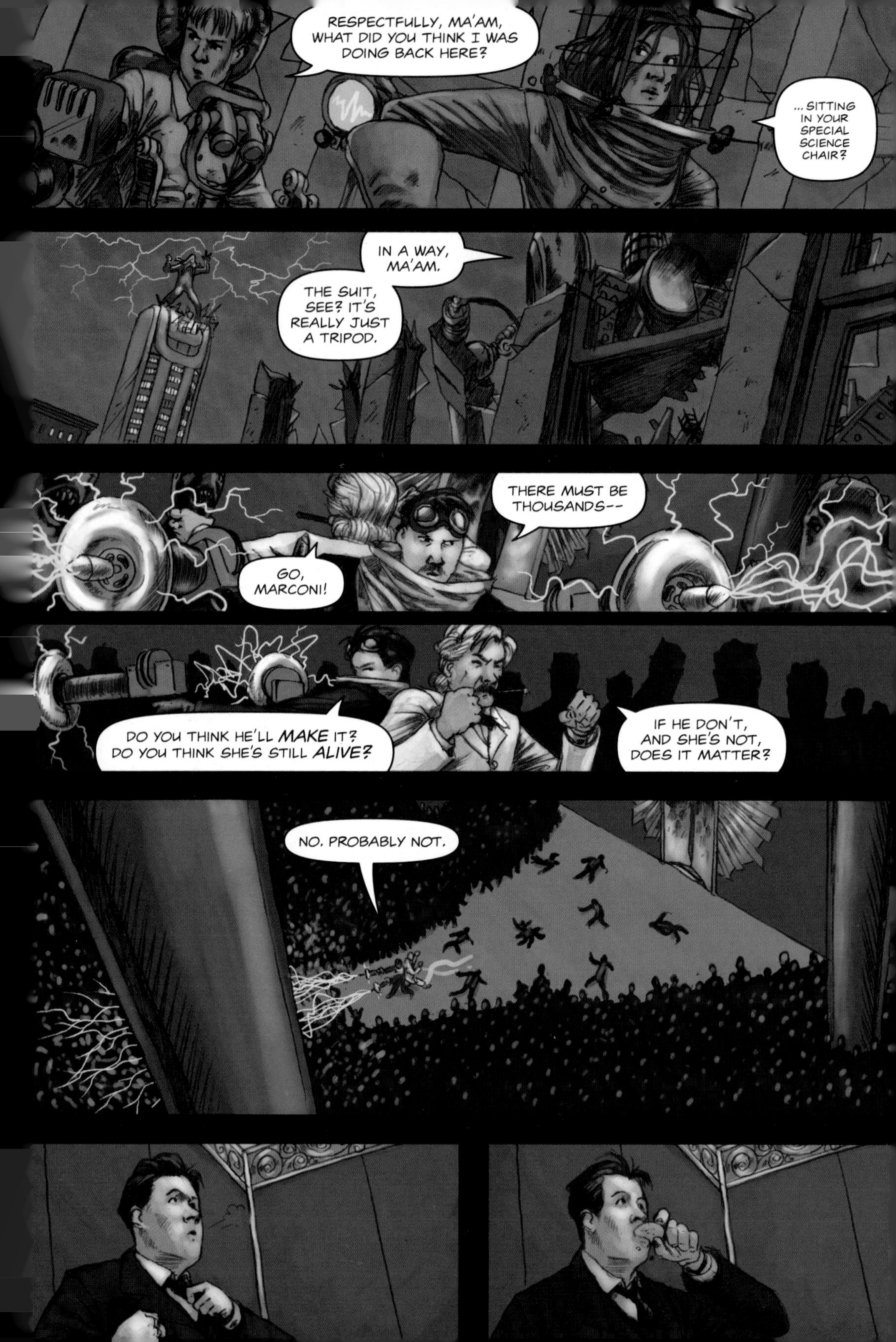
RESPECTFULLY, MA'AM, WHAT DID YOU THINK I WAS DOING BACK HERE?
...SITTING IN YOUR SPECIAL SCIENCE CHAIR?
IN A WAY, MA'AM.
THE SUIT, SEE? IT'S REALLY JUST A TRIPOD.
THERE MUST BE THOUSANDS--
GO, MARCONI!
DO YOU THINK HE'LL MAKE IT? DO YOU THINK SHE'S STILL ALIVE?
IF HE DON'T, AND SHE'S NOT, DOES IT MATTER?
NO. PROBABLY NOT.

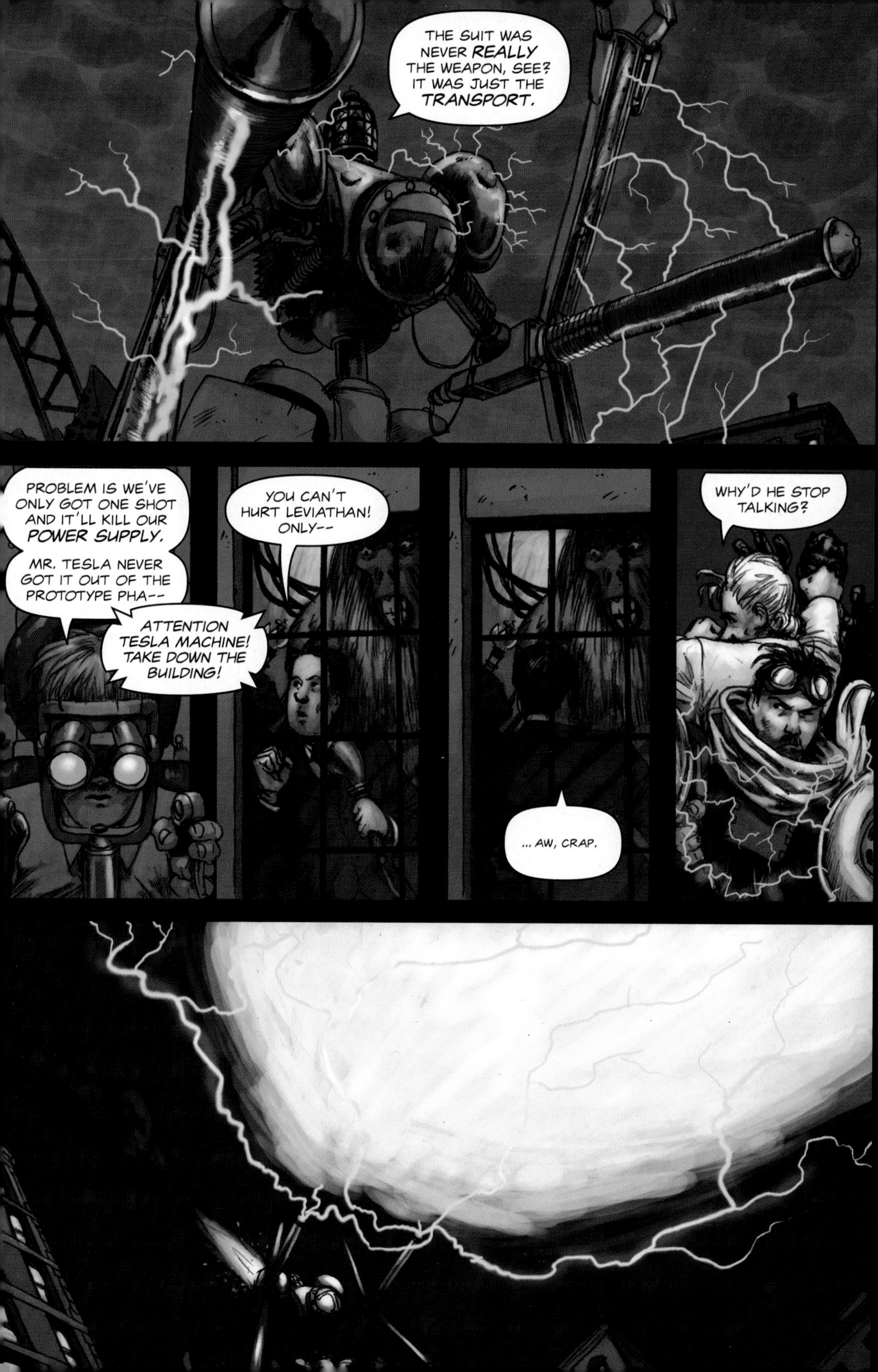
THE SUIT WAS NEVER REALLY THE WEAPON, SEE? IT WAS JUST THE TRANSPORT.
PROBLEM IS WE'VE ONLY GOT ONE SHOT AND IT'LL KILL OUR POWER SUPPLY.
MR. TESLA NEVER GOT IT OUT OF THE PROTOTYPE PHA--
ATTENTION TESLA MACHINE! TAKE DOWN THE BUILDING!
YOU CAN'T HURT LEVIATHAN! ONLY--
... AW, CRAP.
WHY'D HE STOP TALKING?

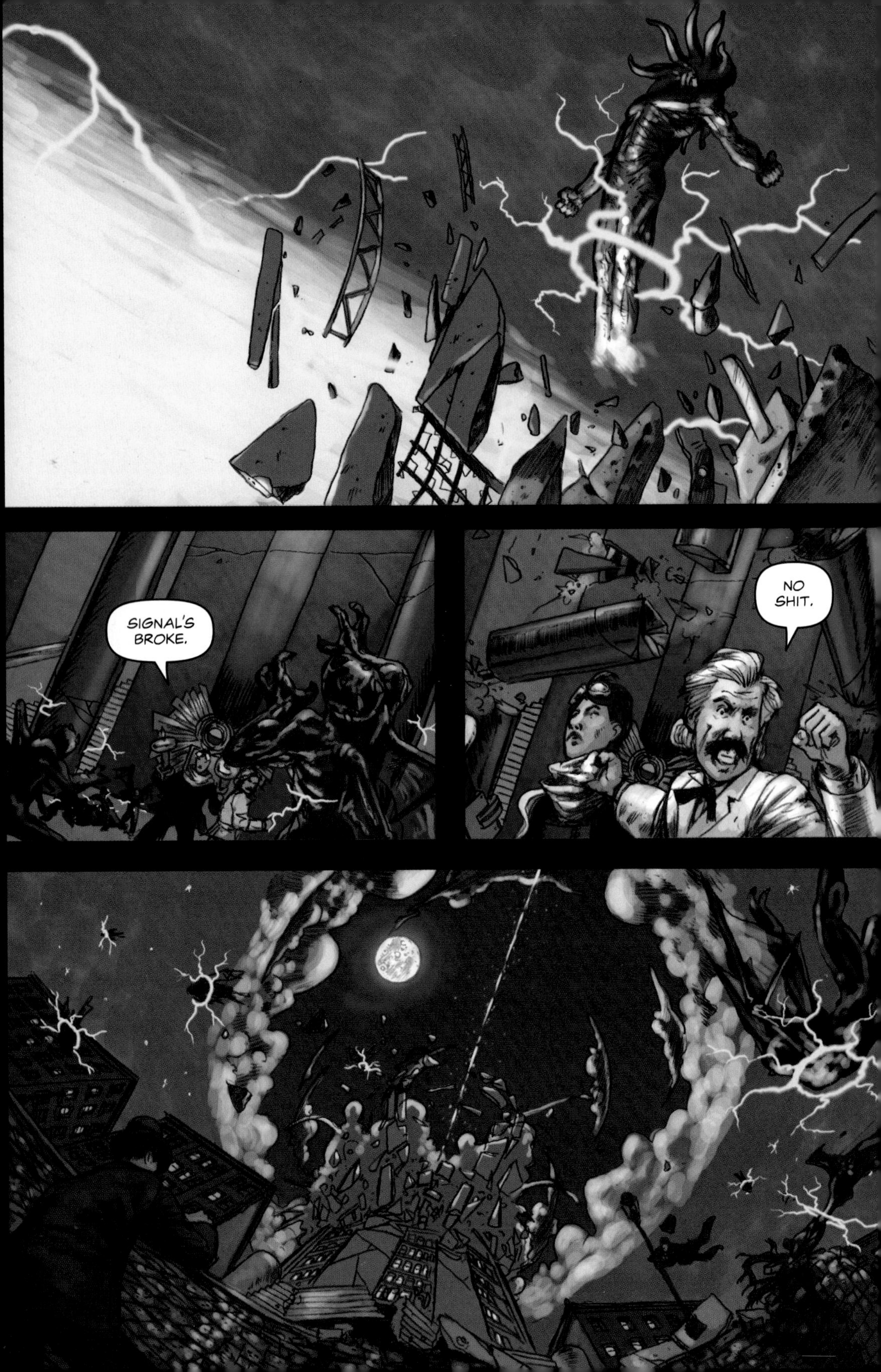
SIGNAL'S BROKE.
NO SHIT.

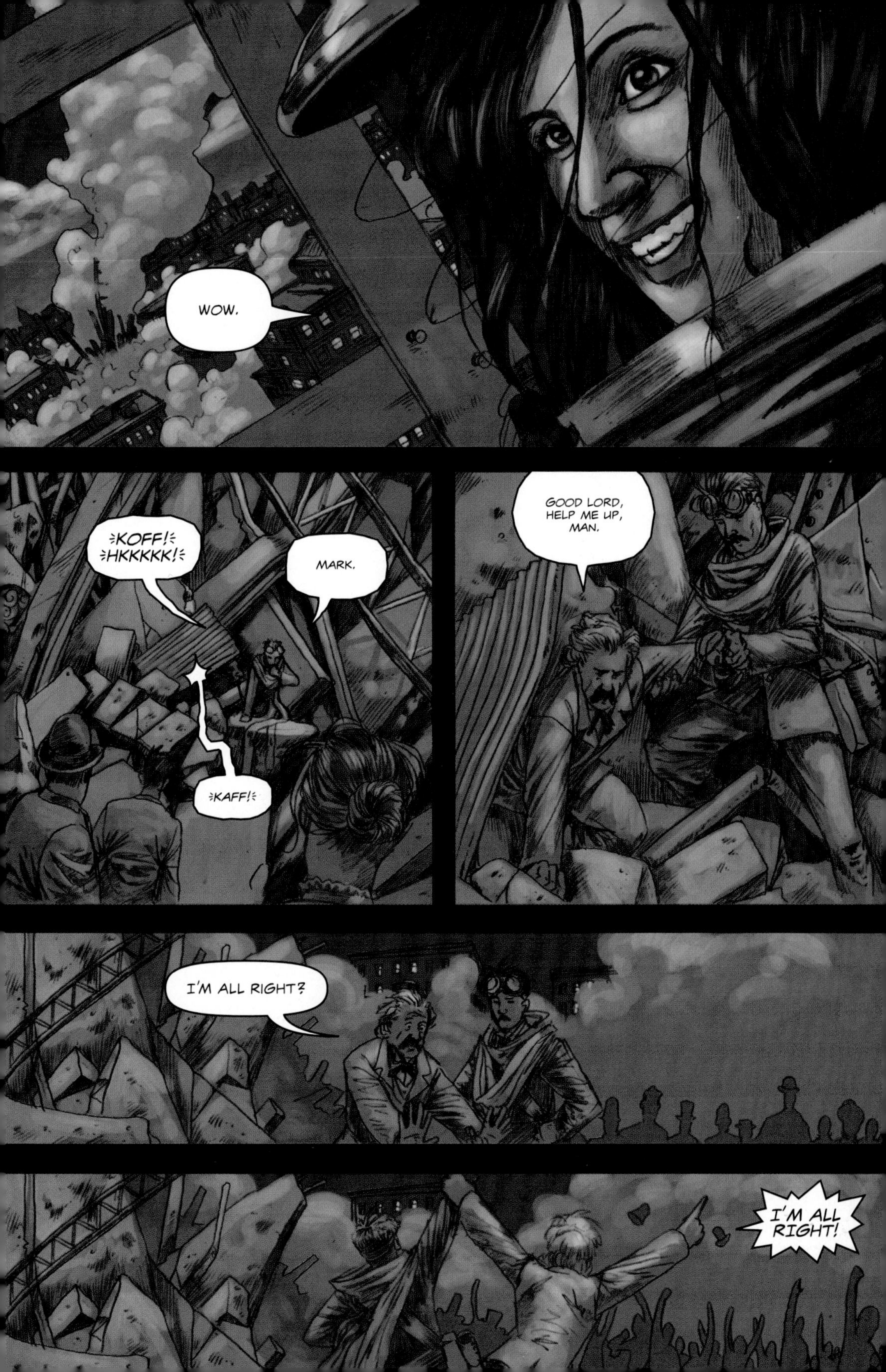
WOW.
KOFF! HKKKKK!
MARK.
KAFF!
GOOD LORD, HELP ME UP, MAN.
I'M ALL RIGHT?
I'M ALL RIGHT!

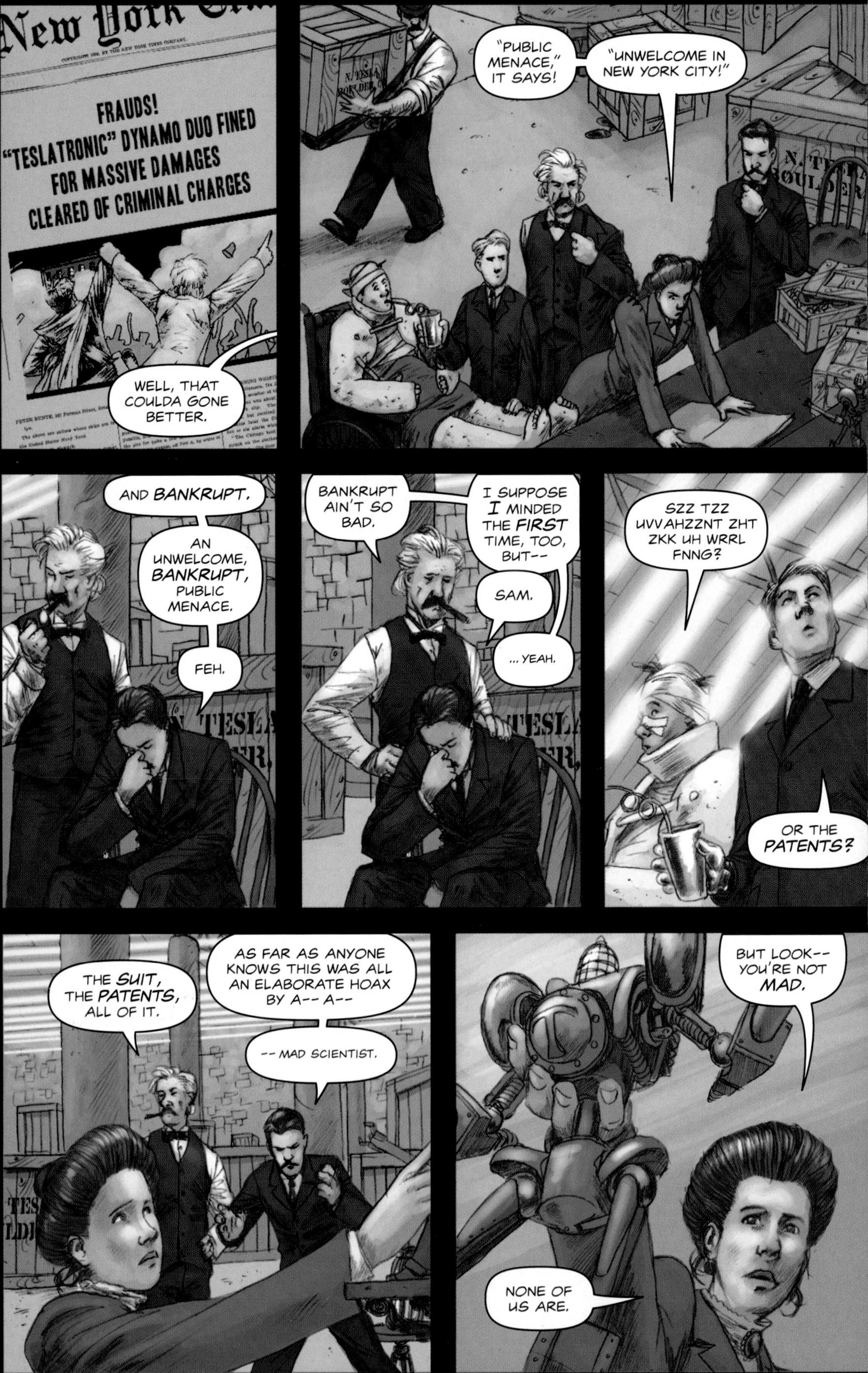
New York Times
FRAUDS!
"TESLATRONIC" DYNAMO DUO FINED
FOR MASSIVE DAMAGES
CLEARED OF CRIMINAL CHARGES
WELL, THAT COULDA GONE BETTER.
"PUBLIC MENACE," IT SAYS!
"UNWELCOME IN NEW YORK CITY!"
AND BANKRUPT.
AN UNWELCOME, BANKRUPT, PUBLIC MENACE.
FEH.
BANKRUPT AIN'T SO BAD.
I SUPPOSE I MINDED THE FIRST TIME, TOO, BUT--
SAM.
...YEAH.
SZZ TZZ UVVAHZZNT ZHT ZKK UH WRRL FNNG?
OR THE PATENTS?
THE SUIT, THE PATENTS, ALL OF IT.
AS FAR AS ANYONE KNOWS THIS WAS ALL AN ELABORATE HOAX BY A-- A--
-- MAD SCIENTIST.
BUT LOOK-- YOU'RE NOT MAD.
NONE OF US ARE.

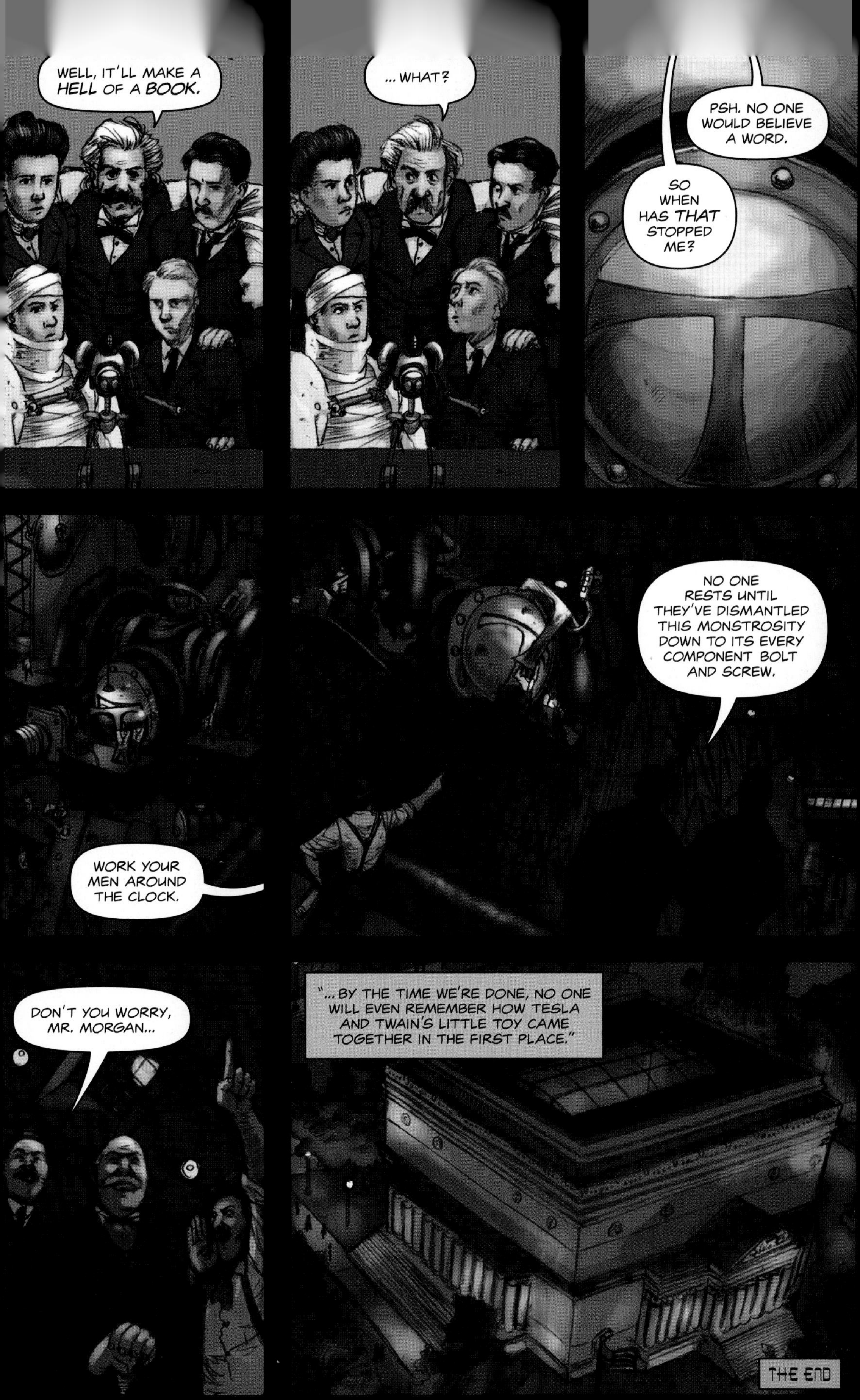
WELL, IT'LL MAKE A HELL OF A BOOK.
... WHAT?
PSH. NO ONE WOULD BELIEVE A WORD.
SO WHEN HAS THAT STOPPED ME?
WORK YOUR MEN AROUND THE CLOCK.
NO ONE RESTS UNTIL THEY'VE DISMANTLED THIS MONSTROSITY DOWN TO ITS EVERY COMPONENT BOLT AND SCREW.
DON'T YOU WORRY, MR. MORGAN...
"... BY THE TIME WE'RE DONE, NO ONE WILL EVEN REMEMBER HOW TESLA AND TWAIN'S LITTLE TOY CAME TOGETHER IN THE FIRST PLACE."
THE END

# INQUIRIES

CONCERNING

# CONCEPT ART

OF

# SUNDRY ITEMS

**EIGHTEENTH EDITION.**

LONDON:

JOHN MURRAY, ALBEMARLE STREET.

1899.

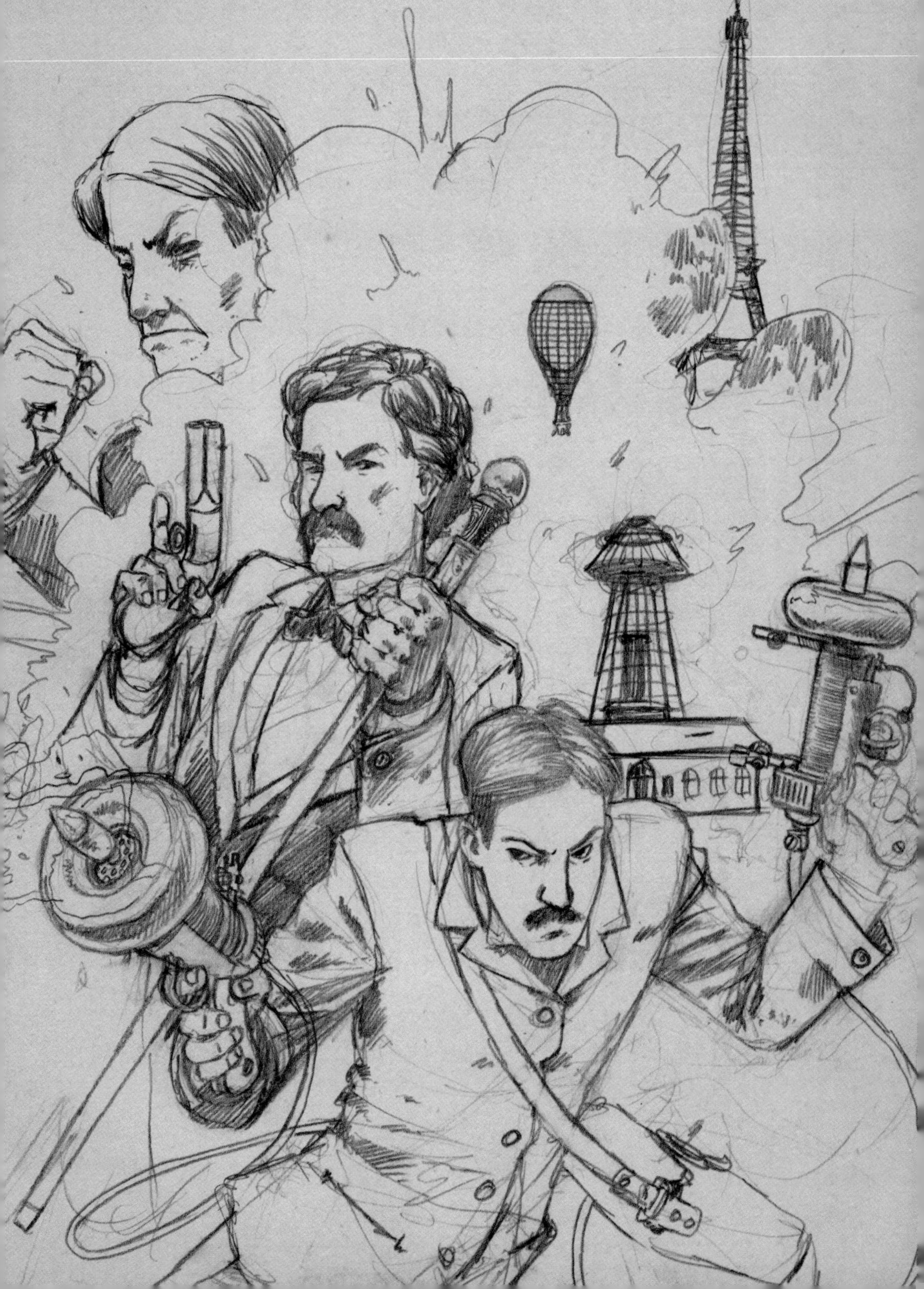

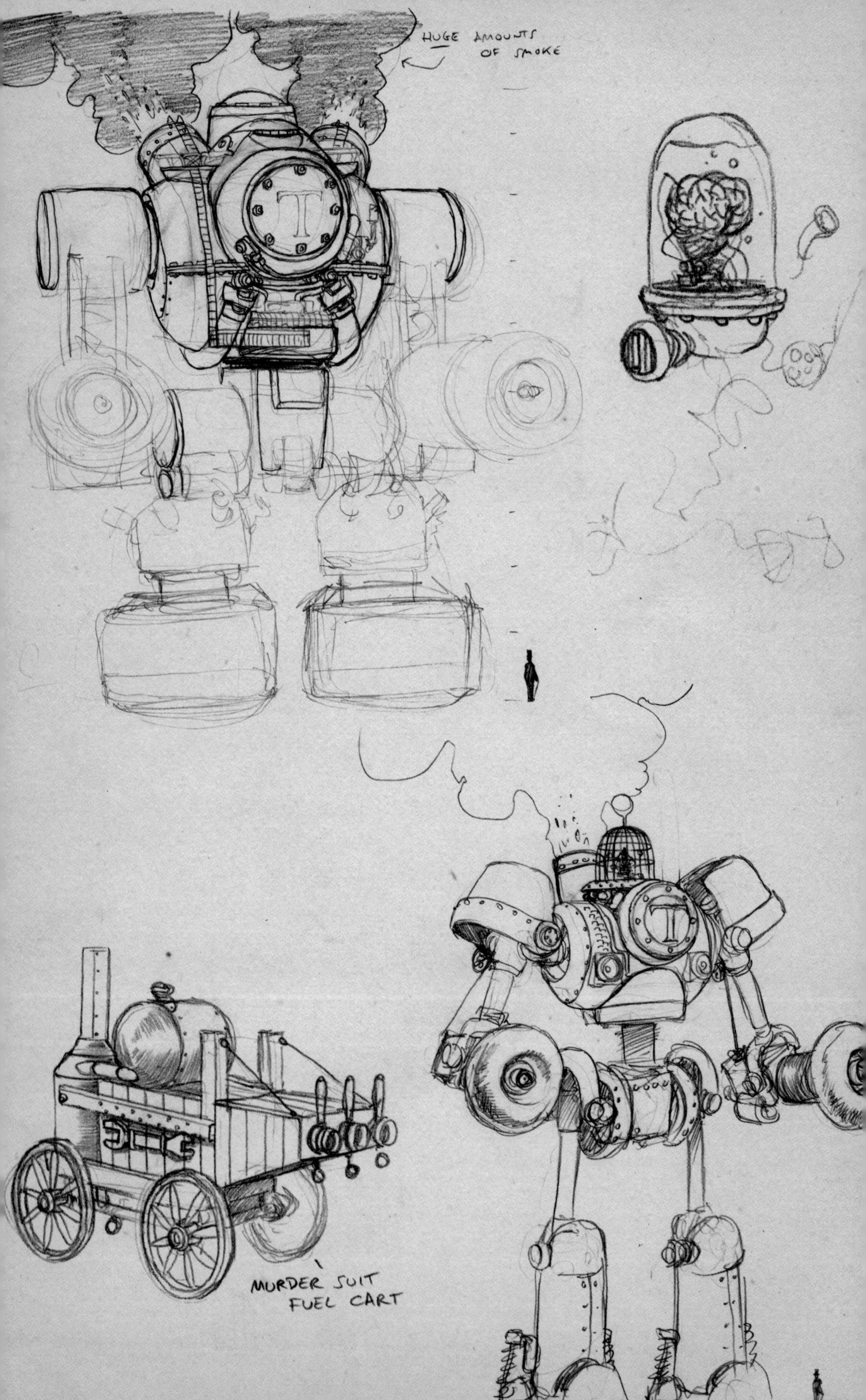
HUGE AMOUNTS OF SMOKE
MURDER SUIT FUEL CART

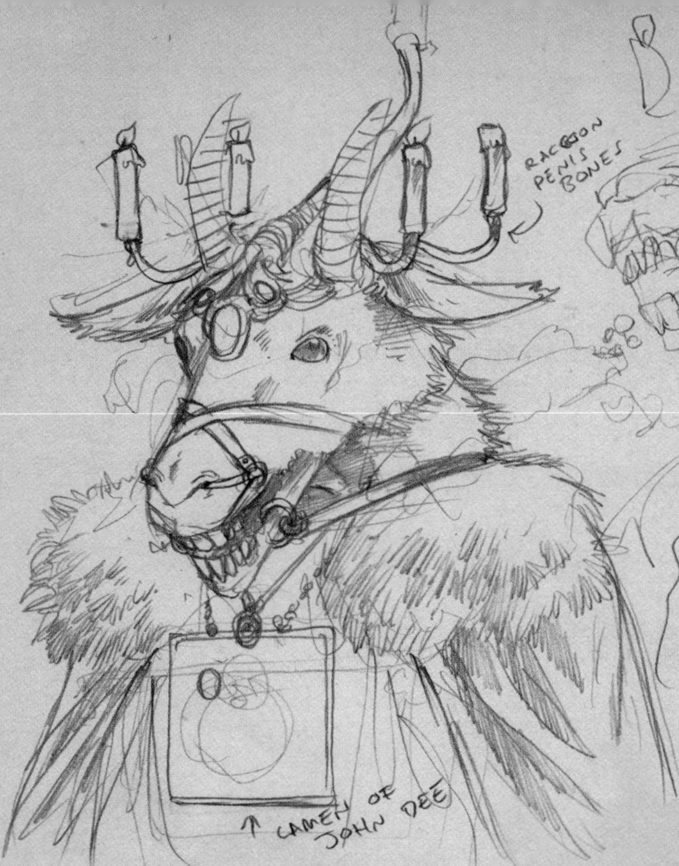
RACCOON PENIS BONES
LAMEN OF JOHN DEE

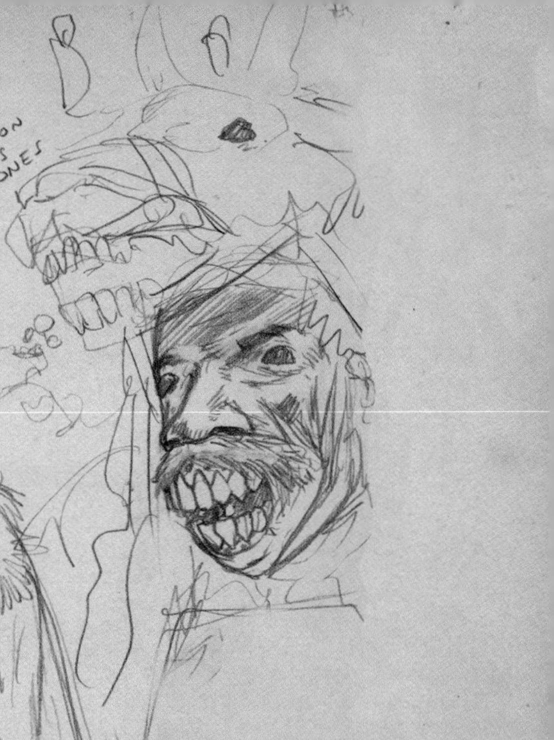

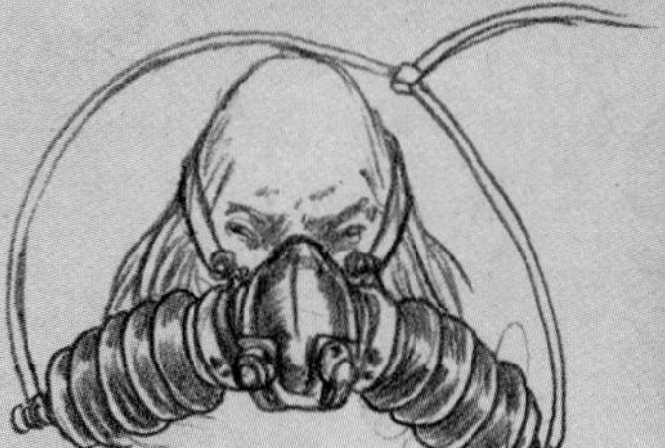

CURARE-FILLED DARTS PARALYZE AND PREVENT BREATHING. YETI NEEDS ARTIFICIAL RESPIRATION TO SURVIV[E] POISON.

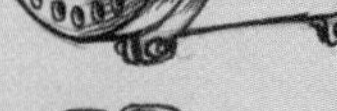

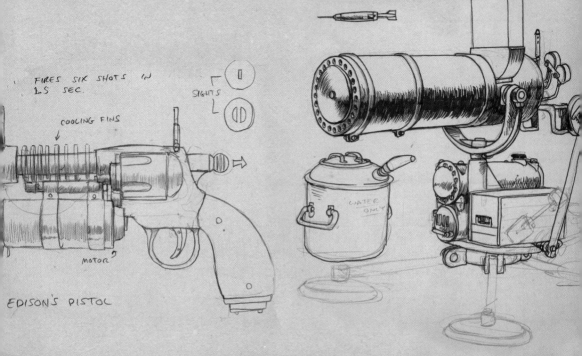

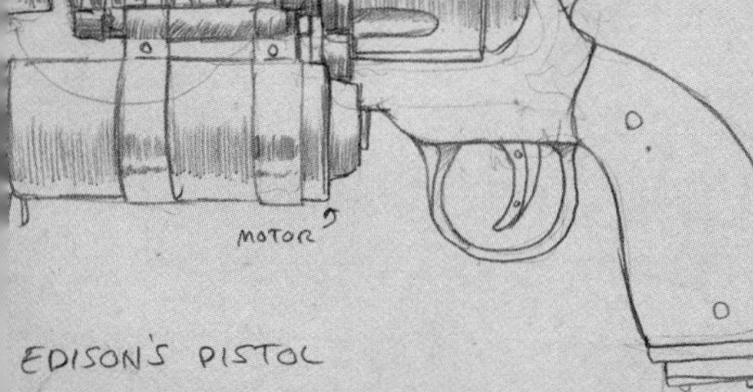
FIRES SIX SHOTS IN 1.5 SEC.
SIGHTS
COOLING FINS
MOTOR
EDISON'S PISTOL

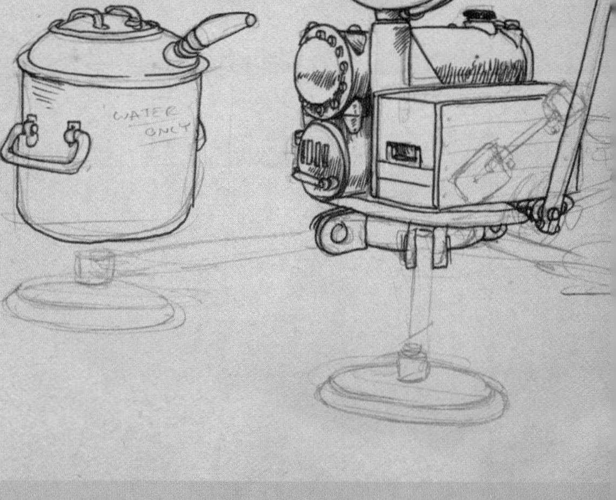
WATER ONLY

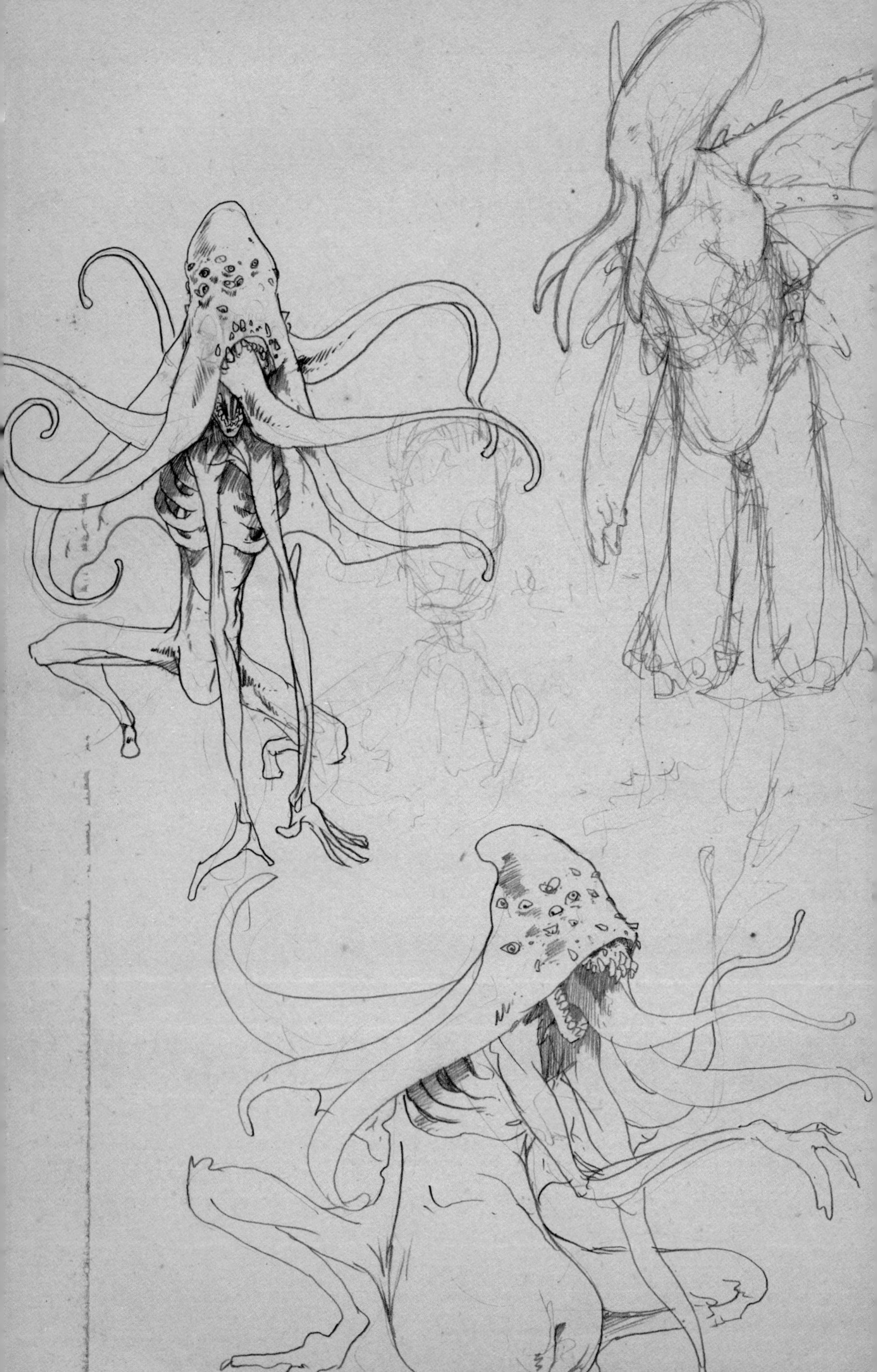